What's a Wine Lover to Do?

What's a Wine Lover to Do?

WES MARSHALL

ARTISAN

For Emily, always

Published by Artisan
A Division of Workman Publishing Company, Inc.
225 Varick Street
New York, NY 10014-4381
www.artisanbooks.com

Library of Congress Cataloging-in-Publication Data

Marshall, Wes, 1953–
What's a wine lover to do? / Wes Marshall.
    p. cm.
Includes index.
ISBN-13: 978-1-57965-370-5
1. Wine and wine making—Popular works. I. Title.
TP548.M375 2010
641.2'2—dc22   2009038947

Principal photography by John Anderson
Maps by Otto Steininger

Printed in China
First printing, April 2010

10 9 8 7 6 5 4 3 2 1

Contents

Introduction

Wine is food. It can be an integral part of a meal, enhancing food's flavors, aiding digestion, and acting as a social lubricant. While selecting a wine can be endlessly fascinating and as complicated as brain surgery, it needn't be any more difficult than picking a good porterhouse at the butcher's counter or choosing a ripe avocado from the grocer's bin.

My goal with *What's a Wine Lover to Do?* is to offer advice for readers with an interest in wine. The information is designed to help people who are just starting to drink wine, continuing to offer useful knowledge even after you gain enough confidence to be comfortable trekking through a wine list at a high-end restaurant.

One thing I've learned in the seminars and workshops I've led is that most folks come because they feel curious about wine, but many of them feel intimidated by the trappings. And while I can assure all of you that nothing about wine is scary, I also understand that for the uninitiated, some of the accessories and routines can be puzzling. So there are a good many sections in this book on how to navigate through the more mystifying parts of the world of wine, from how to read a label, to which wine openers uncork a bottle with the least amount of hassle, to what types of glasses work best.

A few notes on how to use this book: You will notice a large number of cross-references. These are for folks who are just starting to learn about wine and may not know what terms like "Old World style" or "terroir" mean. If you know the meaning of the terms, you will be able to just read past the cross-references, otherwise, the help is conveniently there without having to refer to the index. There are also cross-references that provide helpful jumping off points (kind of like a hyperlink) to see other sections in the book that relate to the current section.

The best way to learn about wine is to taste a lot of them and then visit as many wineries as possible (I know, tough work). In order to help, I've provided organized tastings along with recommended brands and forms to keep records. The more wines you taste, the more you will appreciate having some sort of record-keeping procedure, so I've recommended a system.

Visiting wineries is one of life's great pleasures. They are almost always in lovely agricultural areas, and the people who inhabit the tasting rooms are invariably entertaining and full of helpful information. You'll find a list of great wineries to visit in each of the main winemaking areas of the world.

Carefully placed throughout the book are recommendations from other wine experts, with a few celebrities sprinkled here and there for fun. I asked their opinions on the best values in wines under $20, but since all of us aspire to the occasional fancy bottle of wine, I asked for high-end recommendations as well. And for those of you hoping for specific advice on which wines to buy, you'll find my ideas about the best of the best all through the book.

My hope is that by six months from this date, this book will have numerous wine stains, your handwriting will be on half the pages, and it will look well used. Feel free to dip in here and there. There is no need to read it straight through, though the intrepid souls who approach it that way will learn a lot. Enjoy the trip.

Old World versus New World

Before you head off to the store or sit down to peruse a wine list, it's important to figure out what style most appeals to you.

In the context of wine, Old World means European. For centuries, Old World winemakers have had to deal with tough weather that forced early harvests. Pulling the grapes from the vines early means less sugar in the grapes, and that leads to the perception that the wine has higher acidity. It also makes for less alcohol in the wine.

New World wine lovers thought the Old World wines were too lean, acidic, and austere. Conversely, Europeans thought the New World wines were overstated, sweet, and too rich. Europeans thought nothing of laying a wine down for ten years before it would even be drinkable. New World drinkers generally open the bottle the same day they buy it. Over the past two thousand years, Old World cuisine has evolved to suit the local wines. Oddly, some people in the New World have recently developed a taste for Old World styles, just as a small coterie of European drinkers have switched allegiances to New World wines. The dichotomy is likely to last a long time yet.

HINT *The distinction between Old World and New World is one of the easiest and most precise in the world of wine. No other idiom elicits a helpful suggestion as quickly, in either a restaurant or a store. More important, using the term can be like giving the secret handshake that allows you into the club: it means you've spent some time doing serious tasting, which will usually get you some serious attention. Those two-word phrases are shorthand for flavor profile, alcohol level, and food friendliness. Stipulating a style means you will always end up with a better recommendation from whoever is helping you.*

What is New World style?

In wine, the New World is everyplace where wine is made other than Europe. In most places, New World wines are blessed with weather that is much more dependable than in the Old World. This allows them to harvest extremely ripe grapes that yield dense, fruity wines with intense flavors and high alcohol. Those big flavors let the winemakers use powerful new oak barrels with the wine, and that gives New World wines caramel, toast, and vanilla aromas. The wines are drinkable on the day of release or shortly thereafter, an important trait, because New World wine drinkers generally want to pop the cork the same day they buy their wine. The bad news is that most New World–style wines are not worthy of aging, so consumers who choose them exclusively have little notion of the charms of older wines. Finally, New World chefs are working hard to develop cuisines that match New World wines (which can be more difficult to pair with food because of their generally softer acid and tannin structure, and their more vibrant fruit flavors), but the Old World has a head start of a couple of thousand years.

Ultimately, neither style is innately superior to the other. Much of the American wine-drinking public prefers the more comfortable New World style because it can do dual duty as an aperitif or with a meal. Old World proponents tend to see wine strictly as a part of a meal. Consequently, they want wine to combine forces and collaborate with food, not dominate it. The important thing is to have enough knowledge to know what you prefer at a specific moment. Having a casual party for friends? Pick an Old World Champagne or a New World Chardonnay. Hamburgers for dinner? New World food goes with New World wine. Finally got reservations at the French Laundry? Tell the sommelier you want an Old World–style wine that will create some synergy with the delicate shadings of Chef Keller's food.

Old World = elegance, restraint, subtlety, profundity
New World = generosity, intensity, friendliness, power

What's a Wine Lover to Do?

Buying Wine

The good news is there are so many different wines available that you could drink a bottle a day for the rest of your life and not come near to trying them all. But while that creates a lot of opportunity for serendipity, it also offers its own set of challenges. So here, we offer some tips of the trade, ways to navigate store racks and restaurant wine lists, and assure yourself the highest likelihood of finding a wine that is a bargain at the price and a joy to drink.

1 Are there different types of wine shops?

Yes. If you are shopping for the best price possible on a specific wine, look for a wine or liquor megastore. Major urban areas will have at least a few huge stores competing over price, helping to push prices down. Costco sells more premium wine than any other mercantile operation on earth, plus they have very smart buyers who are always on the lookout for undiscovered wines at value prices.

If you want to discover fascinating new wines, nothing beats building a relationship with one or two smart sellers at a good, dedicated wine shop (that is, one that sells only wine and spirits). Over time, they'll understand what you like, and they will think of you as a regular customer. At that point, you will start getting access to discounts, as well as first shot at their most exciting wines.

In some states, all alcohol sales are made only through state-run stores, and in other states, supermarkets, drugstores, and convenience stores can legally sell wine (but see entry 2). There are also many online wine stores (see entry 3).

2 Wine shops to avoid

In general, drugstores and convenience marts aren't very good places for buying wine, and while grocers have gotten better over the years, some still just hunt for what's popular. A dead giveaway for where not to shop is a store that displays the bottles standing up, which allows the cork to dry out and the wine to oxidize over time. (A few very popular stores violate this rule, but they sell the wines so quickly that it doesn't matter.) The worst places not only stand the wines up but also keep the bottles sitting there long enough to get dusty. Also, stores where wine is a convenience for customers and merely a profit center for the store can't be expected to care very much about their wines. If the brands are mostly big names, such as Gallo, Kendall-Jackson, or Woodbridge, then the buyer isn't getting very creative with the selection. (All three companies make great wines, but they are also big enough to be present in almost any retail establishment.) The best indicator that you are in a place to avoid is if you can't find any employees hovering around the wine area looking like they want to talk about wine.

3 Buying wine online

For people who live a long way from a good wine shop, the Internet is a blessing. The following sites offer excellent service, but do be aware of both shipping costs and the impact on the wine of either hot or cold weather during shipping (see entry 4). Also note that certain states do not allow alcohol to be shipped across state lines. Check the small print on the wine site you want to use to confirm that they can ship to your state.

NINE DEPENDABLE ONLINE MERCHANTS

1. **Bountyhunterwine.com**: A gold mine for the cult-wine addict.
2. **Chambersstwines.com:** The type of store that makes us wish we lived in New York City. A great slate of inexpensive wines, a fabulous collection of Loire rarities, and a staff that prefers drinking wine to collecting wine.
3. **Finestwine.com:** As you might guess from the name, this is the place to track down that magnum of 1945 Domaine de la Romanée-Conti "Romanée-Conti." (How you ship a $50,000 bottle of wine is obviously a question you will want to research—very carefully.)
4. **KermitLynch.com**: Probably the least user-friendly merchant on the web, but manna for fans of Old World wines.
5. **KLwines.com**: A great collection overall, but heaven for the California wine lover, plus excellent shipping costs.
6. **PJwine.com**: Lots of very expensive wines with big scores, but a good selection of inexpensive finds, mostly Old World (European). Very fair shipping prices.
7. **Sherry-Lehmann.com**: The other reason to live in Manhattan. Does any store in France have as good a collection of French wines? And the shipping is in the $3-per-bottle range.
8. **2020wines.com**: For the person who sees wine buying as a contact sport. If you like to show your hundred-point trophy wines to your friends, this is the place to find them.
9. **Wines.com**: Easy to use, good information, lots of wine, and state-of-the-art shipping.

4 Should I buy from a winery?

If you live close to any great wineries, the answer is yes. Making friends at the winery means you will have the opportunity to get first choice when new vintages come out. Small wineries often give regular customers discounts because the winery gets about three times more of the selling price selling directly to you rather than through a distributor at wholesale. Larger wineries may not offer as much of a bargain, but if you really love the wine, take comfort in the fact that all your money is going to the winery instead of being split among winery, wholesaler, and retailer.

For those who don't live close to a winery, the answer is more complicated. The cost of shipping a case of wine runs from $2 to $10 per bottle. If the wine costs more than $25 a bottle, the cheapest form of shipping might pay for itself by saving you the sales tax. Otherwise, you'll lose money over ordering the wine from your local wine shop. Wine should only be shipped in spring and fall, when temperatures are more moderate, to try to make sure that the wine isn't stressed by lack of temperature control in the shipping vehicles and postal hubs.

5 Should I buy wine on eBay?

No. Two factors, in particular, are unpredictable. First, it's impossible to know if the wine has been stored correctly and will be in good drinking condition. More important, if it is a rare or expensive wine, there is no way to know if it is real or one of the millions of counterfeit wines flooding the market.

6 What's the markup on wine in a store?

This varies by class of store and whether a wine is on sale. In general, stores multiply the wholesale price by 1.4, so a wine that runs $10 at wholesale will cost $14 in the store (see also entry 31).

7 How much to spend for a good bottle

To paraphrase Plato, beauty is in the eye of the beholder. One thing is certain, though: The correlation between quality and price in the world of wine is very nearly zero. There are wonderful wines for $8 and terrible wines for $800. Perhaps the best answer is that if you want a simple wine to enhance the flavors of a meal and aid digestion, there are hundreds of perfect wines from about $4 to $10 a bottle. For a wine that rewards a few extra minutes of sniffing and sipping, $10 to $20 is plenty. Anything more than that is for the pure pleasure of the drink. That doesn't mean there aren't perfectly glorious wines that are bargains at much higher prices. A great bottle of Champagne will run at least $40 and a memorable one twice that or more. Wines with a price tag that resembles a monthly mortgage payment are great fun to try, but more often than not the enjoyment comes from the rarity of the experience rather than from the taste of the wine.

8   Are big brands bad?

Many of the largest wine producers make mass-produced wines whose principal attraction is their low price. Thankfully, there are a few huge wine companies that care about making strong wines in several price categories, and these wineries have some built-in benefits that are useful to wine lovers. Their massive buying power can keep the prices of bottles and barrels as low as possible; they can afford to hire (and in fact require) the best of winemakers; and their huge distribution networks mean the wines are widely available. These producers have figured out how to continually make and market pleasurable wine in vast quantities, while staying both profitable and respected.

What sets the producers listed below apart from most of the other megawineries is that they are jealous enough of their reputations to have rigorous quality standards and are aware of the value of trying new ideas to stay ahead of the marketplace. There is a strong correlation between cost and quality on these wines, so don't expect A+ wines for $6, but at each price range, you will find value for money. Try all with full faith.

- Banfi
- Baron Philippe de Rothschild
- Chateau Ste. Michelle (and its sister company, Columbia Crest)
- Gallo Family Vineyards
- Freixenet
- Joseph Drouhin
- Kendall-Jackson
- Maison Louis Jadot
- Moët et Chandon
- Penfolds
- Veramonte

9   Questions to ask in a wine shop

It's important to get a little guidance from a salesperson on your first visit to a wine store. Find one who looks trustworthy and ask a few questions, such as:

1. How is the store organized?
2. Are the best buys placed together somewhere, or spread all around?
3. Is there any kind of a discount program, like case prices or club discounts?
4. What is the shop's specialty?
5. What's on sale today?

DOUG FROST, MS, MW

Wine and spirits writer and one of only three people in the world who is both a Master Sommelier and Master of Wine
www.dougfrost.com

Like most wine professionals, Doug Frost has been asked thousands of times about his favorite wines. "Heck, it all depends upon my mood, upon the season, upon what I'm eating, and maybe even on what I've already consumed that day," he explained. "I drink just about anything that has good flavor and a sense of balance. But…I gotta be honest. I say that I don't have favorites, but a visit to my cellar might suggest otherwise. One wall is entirely devoted to an enormous pile of German estate Rieslings: Zilliken, Fritz Haag, JJ Prüm, Maximin Grünhäuser, Künstler, Gunderloch, and Robert Weil, among others. On any given night, one of those is likely to be on my table. The rest of the cellar expresses my solidarity with so many other places: Oregon, Washington State, the Rhône Valley, Australia, Argentina, the entirety of Spain and Italy—including Campania and Sicily—South Africa, and, yes, even Burgundy and Bordeaux, though I can scarcely afford them anymore."

Notice he left California out of that list. "Did I leave out California? My buying preferences don't include much California anymore, with one very large exception. A cursory inspection of my cellar will reveal more wine from Ridge Vineyards than any other single winery in the world."

10   How to help the staff help you

Wine shop folks are much the same as sommeliers and waitstaff, so you can use similar terminology for both (see entry 27). The best policy is to search out one or two salespeople you trust, then give them all your business. That way, they learn what you like and can start giving you recommendations that are more daring.

1. Tell them if you prefer the Old World or New World style (see Introduction).
2. Tell them the price range you're working with.
3. Specify the grape you'd like.
4. Tell them the purpose of the wine (a party, a gift, dinner at home) and, if possible, what you'll be eating.
5. Tell them your honest evaluation of what they've sold you lately. Even better, take your notes with you (see entry 248). Be as specific as possible, such as: "I loved the flavor of that Zinfandel you sold me. It was really rich, and the blackberry flavor was great, but the alcohol was so high I couldn't taste my dinner."
6. Let them in on your tastes, but do it casually, while walking around the store. How often do you drink whites, and which ones? How often do you drink reds and which ones? What do you buy most often? What wine do you buy when you want to celebrate?

11 What if they don't carry what I want?

If you buy a full twelve-bottle case and pay at least half the cost in advance, most stores will be happy to order a wine if they have an existing account with the distributor. Some stores will waive the case or payment requirements for regular customers. If the wine is obscure, it helps to identify the importer or distributor. For rare or collectible wines, the store might have to limit quantities and ask for full payment up front. If your store can't help, depending on what state you live in, you may be able to order the wine online (see entry 3).

12 Who should I seek out for wine recommendations?

Many wine shops, and even some grocery stores, offer written staff recommendations. They usually show up in the form of a three-by-five card mounted on the wine's bin. Wander the store looking at the recommendations, and hopefully one or two will pop up that you agree with, based on having tasted that wine. Find out who wrote them and ask to talk to that person. This is a great first step to finding your own local wine guru. Often, too, you'll find a description of a wine on a "shelf talker" provided by the winery or distributor (see entry 13), although it's important to remember that these are marketing pieces. Finally, some wine shops have a newsletter or recommendations on their Web site that might be helpful.

13 Navigating wine scores

In the early 1980s, the wine magazines *Wine Advocate* and *Wine Spectator* introduced the 100-point scale to give a shorthand evaluation of how a particular wine compared to a standard. This was meant as a service to the consumer, to make wine buying easier. To this end, wine scores are used in magazines, advertisements, and in wine shops on the "shelf talker," a wine industry marketing tool that you may find attached to the wine's bin or box. Wineries go to the expense of printing eye-catching shelf talkers when one of their wines gets a particularly good score (usually 90 or above on a 100-point scale) or critique from a publication. If price matters to you, it may be best to avoid these wines. It's not that the scores aren't accurate—the people who rate the wines work hard to give consistent and fair scores, and the wines may well be spectacular—but a high score sets the law of supply and demand against the customer. Demand for the wine may rise dramatically based on its score, but most often the amount of that wine produced each year cannot be increased, so the price rises accordingly. Also, a high score is not a truly objective comparison because the person awarding the score has his or her own standards. The best solution is to find a reviewer whom you generally agree with and pay more attention to their scores and evaluations (see entry 14 and also entry 198).

14 Who are the best-known critics?

The most famous American critic is Robert Parker (*Wine Advocate,* www.erobertparker.com), a retired Maryland attorney whose taste for ripe, assertive wines has changed an entire industry. His 100-point scale for wine scoring is shorthand for thousands of buyers, and winemakers have struggled to make their wines to Parker's taste, which tends toward high-intensity wines. In fact, there is a whole cottage industry of consultants whose sole task is to help create Parker-friendly wines. Ditto the *Wine Spectator,* a magazine whose critics' reviews and 100-point scores are posted in most wine shops in America. Since *Wine Spectator* uses several reviewers, their tastes are a bit more difficult to pin down.

Other widely read Americans include Eric Asimov (*New York Times*), Dorothy J. Gaiter and John Brecher (*Wall Street Journal*), Andrea Immer Robinson (author and TV personality), Leslie Sbrocco (author and *Today* show contributor), Jerry Shriver (*USA Today*), and Stephen Tanzer (*International Wine Cellar*). Other well-liked publications include *Wine Enthusiast, Imbibe, Food & Wine,* and *Wine & Spirits.*

Jancis Robinson, Michael Broadbent, Clive Coates, Oz Clarke, and Hugh Johnson are English critics who are popular throughout the world. James Halliday is renowned in his home of Australia, and Frenchmen Michel Bettane and Thierry Desseauve (*Le Classement des Meilleurs Vins de France*) are also quite influential.

15 Finding bargains

There are a few ways to find bargains. Look for big stacks of boxes of a single wine and the more obscure the wine, the better. All those boxes of wine mean someone in the store loved it enough to take a big gamble, and the quantity means the distributor gave them a great price. Store owners often pass a steeply discounted price on to their customers because it keeps them coming back. Selling through a large quantity of a single wine means the distributor is more likely to give the store even more great deals in the future. This is one example where everyone wins. The only exception is in stores that jam through hundreds of cases of wine per day, treating it as just another commodity (see entry 2).

Along the same lines, most stores put minidisplays at the ends of the rows. The owner or buyer will put things there that they want you to notice. Why? Could be any of a number of reasons, but if it's a store you trust, the likelihood is they think it is great wine and want to bring it to your attention. Some stores display their sale wines this way. Always be on the lookout for wines either made from odd grapes, such as Aglianico and Rkatsieteli, or sourced from areas other than the United States, France, Italy, Spain, and Australia, such as Argentina, New Zealand, and South Africa. Obscurity equals value. If the buyers devote precious floor space to obscure wines, then there is something about the wine that lit their rockets. Also, since the managers know that customers won't buy these wines without some encouragement, they will have educated the sales staff, so ask for guidance.

Lastly, look for the "bargain bin." Stores devote space to wine in twelve-bottle increments—that is, by the case. Whether it is a bin, a row, or a shelf, it will hold wine in multiples of twelve. Any number of benign things can conspire to leave just a couple of bottles sitting, lonesome, waiting to be bought. At the same time, the owner wants that valuable space to be filled with wine bottles. So what does he do? He puts the stragglers into a basket or bin and prices all of them at a discount.

16   What sizes do bottles come in?

The majority of bottles in an American wine shop are .375-, .750-, or 1.5-liter bottles, although they are available in sizes up to 30 liters. Wines in larger bottles age more slowly, but the main reason for very large sizes is the splash they make at a celebration, which explains why most ultralarge bottles—the ones with biblical names—are for Champagnes. Here is a list of wine bottle sizes and their names.

SIZE IN LITERS	NAMES	HOW MANY 5-OUNCE GLASSES
.187	Piccolo, quarter bottle, snipe, or split	1.25
.375	Demi or half-bottle. Frequently, but incorrectly, called a split	2.5
.500	No exact name, but used frequently for dessert wines	3.3
.750	Standard bottle	5
1.5	Magnum or double bottle	10
3.0	Double magnum or Jeroboam	20
4.5	Rehoboam	30
6.0	Impérial or Methuselah	40
9.0	Salmanazar	60
12.0	Balthazar	80
15.0	Nebuchadnezzar	100
18.0	Melchior	120
20.0	Solomon	133.33
30.0	Melchizedek	200

17   Why buy a half-bottle?

Half-bottles should be more popular than they are. Most wines start to pass their peak a few hours after opening, so it's always better to finish a half-bottle tonight than be stuck with a leftover half of a standard bottle tomorrow. A half-bottle provides just the perfect amount—two and a half glasses—for a single person. Or a couple might like to have a glass each of Champagne, rather than two. For cooks who like to serve multiple courses, half-bottles allow an individual wine to be matched with each dish. Half-bottles also allow more people to sample really expensive wines. Half-bottles have only two problems: they don't age well, and they cost more than half of a whole bottle.

18   Why buy wine in a box?

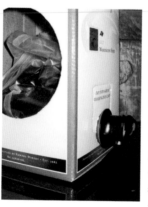

The bottle has a couple of problems as a wine vessel: it allows light and air in, both of which damage the wine. Once the bottle is opened, more air gets in, which causes the wine to start to oxidize. Wine in an open bottle deteriorates in a matter of hours, so saving leftovers overnight is seldom a good idea—yet how many of us want exactly five glasses every time we open a bottle? The Australians and Europeans solved these problems several years ago by putting the wine in a flexible, inert, flavorless, vacuum-sealed plastic bag and dropping it into a box with a perforated hole to hold a spigot. Protected from light and air, the wine lasts for months. Winemakers love the bag-in-a-box concept because the wine is easier and cheaper to ship, and they never have to worry about cork taint (see entry 279). Boxes have become so popular that 54 percent of all the wine sold in Australia is sold in a box. In the United States, the boxes have had an image problem because the majority of the box wine sold here early on was not very high quality. That is changing quickly, and for a person who wants a single glass of wine to drink, a box is a good solution.

19   What are wine futures?

Wine futures (also called buying *en primeur* in France) allow consumers to buy wines at a lower initial price prior to bottling—an investment strategy that bets on the value of the wine rising once it is on the regular market. Futures may enable the buyer to land hard-to-find wines or get in on a great vintage before other consumers discover it and the price rises as a result of demand. Investing in wine futures can be a good idea, but you should stick with a dealer who understands the business and knows which wineries are dependable. Sherry-Lehmann is one of the best futures dealers in the United States. They've been in the business long enough that you can count on them to stand by you if problems arise, and they have the contacts (especially for French wines) to dig out obscure but great wines that are undervalued because they are less known.

If you live close to a thriving wine region, do as the French do and buy futures locally. Even if your favorite winery doesn't have a futures program, they should appreciate your interest enough to give you a first shot at their new releases. And if you go pick up the wine yourself, you'll save on shipping and you'll know the wine hasn't been jostled, overheated, or frozen in between the winery and your home. See also entry 4.

CHRIS ADAMS

Executive Vice President, Sherry-Lehmann, Inc.

Chris Adams is one of the great experts on Bordeaux wine futures. He counts Château Latour's 1961 vintage as the greatest wine he's ever had and drinking it, an experience he hopes he might be able to match someday. "I am convinced that 2005 is the special vintage so many Bordeaux lovers claim it to be," he says. "For the next few years my wife, Becky, and I will be enjoying the *petits châteaux* of Bordeaux, like Lascaux and Mayne Vieille, while we wait for our cru classe wines to age. In the meantime, I admire wineries that can produce good wines, even in the difficult vintages. Like Domaines Barons de Rothschild. They own Lafite Rothschild, Duhart-Milon, L'Evangile, and Rieussec in Bordeaux, and these properties are hallmarks of excellence, even in less cooperative years. They also own Los Vascos in Chile, Quinta do Carmo in Portugal, Aussières in the South of France, and Bodegas Caro (with Nicolas Catena) in Argentina, all of which offer wonderful quality-to-price ratio, and who doesn't appreciate that?"

20 Can I return a bad wine?

There are a number of reasons why wine bought in a shop might be bad. Most often, wine with legitimate flaws can be returned or exchanged at the shop with your receipt. See entry 34 for a complete list of possible flaws.

21   What makes wine kosher?

For a wine to be considered kosher in Orthodox Judaism, it must be produced under strict rabbinical supervision to ensure that Jewish food purity laws are followed (for instance, that no animal product comes in contact with the wine—egg white or gelatin are sometimes used during the production of nonkosher wines), and only Orthodox Jews may physically make the wine. There are rules concerning the grape-growing process as well. Conservative Judaism relaxes these rules somewhat, with the result that any wine made in the United States or Canada is considered kosher. Still, most synagogues use only wines with a hechsher (seal of approval).

22 Is pronunciation important?

Probably not, given the fact that the server's tip is based on keeping you happy. Still, if the thought of pronouncing foreign words is troublesome, just point to the wine's name and say, "I'll take this." People who are anxious to learn will ask, "How do you pronounce that?" Often, the server won't know how to pronounce the wine's name either. In any case, you want to buy and they want to sell, so don't let the small formality of pronunciation disturb the interaction. See also entries 72 and 73.

23 Which first: food or wine?

Most people look at the menu first, then, once everyone at the table has announced their intentions, pick a wine off the list. But should you always pick a wine after you've decided on the food you're ordering, or should it be the other way around? The solution is to take a look at the wine list and see if it has any wines that you've always wanted to try, or that are consistent favorites. If so, choose the wine, and then look through the menu for something to go with it.

24 What the wine list tells you about a restaurant

Wine lists are odd things, usually a reflection of the restaurant's wine buyer's personality. A quick perusal of the list should tell you whether wine is an important part of the restaurant's scope. If the wine list is chatty, with anecdotes and tasting notes, the buyer is most likely an excited wine lover anxious to share his or her passion. That kind of enthusiasm is infectious and usually hits the kitchen and waitstaff as well. Other times, the list has a corporate look, with unchanging offerings and only a modicum of information. Any restaurant with an unchanging wine list has little interest in wine, and probably not much more in food. Restaurants that stitch together phone book–size lists may or may not actually have all those wines in the cellar—kudos to them if they do, but some simply try to attract customers by creating a "prestigious" list. Finally, restaurants with an interesting range of wines by the glass are generally keen on inviting the customer to discover new wines. See also entry 35.

25　How is the wine list organized?

Restaurants and wine bars use various strategies for organizing a wine list. The most common is to separate the wines first into sparkling, white, red, and dessert wines, then into either countries or grape varieties. To help with food and wine pairings, some restaurants will break the wines down into flavor categories, such as light versus dense and dry versus fruity (though everybody categorizes differently). Sorting by price is common, too. If you're uncertain about how they categorize the wines, ask your waiter or the sommelier.

Some restaurants have a separate "reserve" wine list. There are two approaches to the reserve list that you might encounter. The wines on the first type of list are all rare and very expensive. These are manna for folks who have always wanted to taste an extraordinary old vintage, but the cost can be breathtaking. The other type will come from a wine buyer or sommelier who is out looking for incredible value-priced wines. Some wines on this list will inevitably cost a lot of money, but most will be in the regular customer's sweet spot (see entry 29) and worth a good deal more than their price.

The following samples show some of the many ways a wine list can be organized:

By the Glass

WHITE

Pinot Grigio, Lagaria, Italy, 2008	$9
Pinot Blanc, Marc Kreydenweiss, Alsace, France, 2005	$13
Grüner Veltliner, Macherndl, Wachau, Austria, 2007	$12
Albariño, Fillaboa, Rias Baixas, Spain, 2007	$12
Sauvignon Blanc, J.F. Merieau, Loire, France, 2007	$9
Verdejo, Martina Prieto, Rueda, Spain, 2007	$12
Chardonnay, Independent Producers, Washington, 2008	$9
Chardonnay, Baileyana, Firepeak Vnyrd., Edna Vally, 2006	$13

FEATURED SELECTION

Hanzell Chardonnay, Sonoma Valley, 2006	$18

Considered by many to be one of the best Chardonnays in California, Hanzell spares no expense to deliver complex, age-worthy Chardonnay that rivals the world's best. A focused wine of intense fruit and power owes itself to some of California's oldest Chardonnay vines as well as meticulous farming and honest winemaking. Truly an honor to offer this by the glass.

In a place with a list this interesting, a featured selection is worth paying attention to.

By Flight

CHARDONNAY	$14
Independent producers, Washington, 2008	
Albert Grivault, Bourgogne, France, 2006	
Baileyana, Firepeak Vineyard, Edna Valley, 2006	

PINOT NOIR	$16
Wild Rock, Central Otago, New Zealand, 2008	
Ch. De Puligny Montrachet, Monthelie, 2005	
Soléna Cellars, Willamette Valley, 2007	

CABERNET SAUVIGNON	$15
Château de Parenchère, Bordeaux, 2006	
Penley Estate, Coonawarra, Australia, 2007	
Amavi Cellars, Walla Walla, Washington, 2006	

This list offers a mini tasting of two-ounce pours of three wines that totals six ounces, just an ounce more than the average pour. Since none of the wines are well known and this is a fine restaurant, you can infer that the sommelier works hard to find undiscovered gems.

By the Half Bottle

WHITE

Sauvignon Blanc, Duckhorn Vineyards 07 (Napa Valley, CA)	$26
Pinot Grigio, Collio, Livon 06 (Friuli Venezia Giuia)	$28

RED

Merlot, Le Vigne di Zamo 01 (Friuli Venezia Giulia)	$18
Sangiovese, Chianti Classico, Dievole 05 (Tuscany)	$25
Sangiovese, Vino Nobile di Montepulciano, Avignonese 05 (Tuscany)	$28
Cabernet Sauvignon, Clos du Val 05 (Napa Valley, CA)	$33
Zinfandel, Lytton Springs, Ridge Vineyards 06 (Sonoma Valley, CA)	$38
Sangiovese, Chianti Classico, Fontodi 04 (Tuscany)	$42

With half bottles, a single person can have his or her own bottle, or a party can share small servings, and there's no concern about a restaurant by-the-glass program serving wine that is too old.

By Price

RED WINE

Negroamaro, Li Veli 07 (Apulia)	$24	
Sangiovese-Canaiolo-Malvasia, Chianti, Poggio Vignoso 06 (Tuscany)	$25	
Primitivo Salento, Sigillo Primo 06 (Apulia)	$34	
Lambrusco Grasparossa, Tenuta Pederzana 07 (Emilia-Romagna)	$38	
Dolcetto D'Alba, Gianni Gagliardo 07 (Piedmont)	$39	
Barbera D'Asti, Tasmorcan, Elio Perrone 06 (Piedmont)	$40	
Prugnolo-Aglianico, Ramitello, Di Majo Nortante 05 (Molise)	$43	SWEET SPOT
Merlot-Cabernet Sauvignon, Brentino Rosso, Maculan 05 (Veneto)	$48	
Spanna, Colline Novaresi, Dessilani 05 (Piedmont)	$50	
Sangiovese, Vino Nobile de Montepulciano, Avignonesi 05 (Tuscany)	$52	
Barbera D'Alba, Bricco della Olive, Palladino 05 (Piedmont)	$56	
Pinot Nero, Leopoldo, Marchesi Incisa della Rochetta 06 (Piedmont)	$57	
Gamay, Frères Grosjean 07 (Valle d'Aosta)	$58	
Nebbiolo, Barbaresco, Produttori Del Barbaresco 04 (Piedmont)	$75	
Pinot Noir, Cumberland Reserve, Berström 06 (Willamette Valley, OR)	$90	
Sangiovese Grosso, il Duemilatre, Argiano 03 (Tuscany)	$96	

The sweet spot (see 29) is located in the middle third of a list organized by price.

By Varietal

MERLOT

Cycles Gladiator 2006 (California) $22
Dark, richly extracted merlot with currant and spice.
Hogue Genesis 2005 (Washington) $26
Smooth and easy drinking with ripe plum and currant.

SYRAH/SHIRAZ/RHONE

Dead Letter Office Shiraz 2005 (McLaren Vale, Padthaway) $28
*Rich, dark cherry, hints of mulberry and vanilla notes pair well
with lush tannins and a touch of eucalyptus.*
Terre Rouge "Les Côtes de L'Ouest" Syrah 2005 (California) $24
*Dark in color with rich, silky wild raspberry fruit flavors laced
with pepper, tar, and herb tones.*
Côtes du Rhône, Domaine de La Solitude 2006 (Rhone) $24
*Dark fruited and spicy, with currant, cedar and leather,
Grenache-based blend. 91 Wine Spectator*

This chatty, informative, and very inexpensive list provides a great learning opportunity.

With Varietals Categorized by Old World and New World

SYRAH/SHIRAZ

Old World

Château de St. Cosme, Gigondas (Rhone, France) 2005	$54
Paul Autard, Chateauneuf du Pape (Rhone, France) 2005	$72
Château de Beaucastel, Chateauneuf du Pape (Rhone, France) 2004	$125
René Rostaing, Puech Nole (Languedoc, France) 2005	$58
Pierre Gaillard, St. Joseph, "les Pierres" (Rhone, France) 2006	$57
Alain Graillot, Crozes-Hermitage (Rhone, France) 2006	$51
E. Guigal, Côte Rôtie, "La Mouline" (Rhone, France) 2002	$250
Betts & Scholl, Hermitage (Rhone, France) 2001	$90
Jean Louis Chave, Hermitage (Rhone, France) 2004/2005	$260

New World

Paraiso, Syrah (Santa Lucia Highlands) 2005	$42
Favia, Syrah, "Quarzo" (Amador County) 2005	$88
John Duval, Shiraz, "Entity" Barossa Valley, Australia) 2006	$67
Penfolds, Shiraz, "Grange" (Barossa Valley, Australia) 2002	$285

Note the division of Old World and New World wines.

26   Who can help me?

You can choose among the server, sommelier, or wine buyer, but not every restaurant will have all of these. Ninety-eight percent of servers pick a few wines on the list that they like and recommend them repeatedly. The other 2 percent will let you know that they are the most knowledgeable person in the house, and they very well might be. Still, ask to talk to a sommelier or wine buyer, who will be intimate with all the wines on the list. Here's the dialogue: "What a fascinating bunch of wines. I know wines fairly well, but this list has so many interesting wines that are new to me. Is your wine buyer here tonight?" The buyer may be the restaurant owner, the sommelier, or the server who knows the most about wine. If that person isn't in, ask who in the house knows the most about wine. The goal is to find the person who can best answer your questions and point you to the wine you want. If you are worried about hurting your server's feelings, start by asking his or her opinion on the best appetizers, then ask who knows the most about wine.

27   Talking to the sommelier: ten tips

1. Always first: tell them if you are a New World– or Old World–style drinker (see Introduction).
2. Always second: price range. This is a business transaction, not an audition, so don't be afraid to talk about price (see entry 30). Otherwise the sommelier will have to feel you out, and that will waste both your time and his.
3. Get the guesswork out of the way by giving them a quick, honest evaluation of your knowledge.
4. Let them know what food each person at the table will order.

5. Tell them what level of acidity you like in a wine (see entry 272).
6. Ask for wines that they think are amazing bargains, wines that, at the end of the night, they are stunned that no one bought.
7. Tell them wines that have pleased you in the past, such as, "Normally, I really love Rhônes with a steak, but I wanted to try something new. Any recommendations?" or "I usually like big, fruity California wines with Italian food. Could you show me some that I may not know about?"
8. If you like specific aromas or flavors in your wine, let them know. For instance, target either red berry (strawberry, raspberry) or black fruit (plum, blackberry) flavors for reds; for whites it's tropical fruits (pineapple, passion fruit), citrus, or pome fruits (apple, pear). Other aromas may include black pepper, vanilla, caramel, flint, flowers—or anything that strikes you.
9. If you can't find a wine on the list that you were hoping to see, tell them. They usually have wines in back that aren't on the list (for instance, the last bottle of something that was just removed from the list), and if not, they can recommend something similar to what you were looking for.
10. If you order a wine and they don't have it in stock, ask them what they have, and if the alternative is more expensive, ask if you can have it for the same price.

28 Should I order a bottle or a glass?

This is a simple question of math and consumption. A standard 750 milliliter bottle of wine is 25.4 ounces. While a few restaurants serve 6 ounces or 4 ounces per glass, the majority use a 5-ounce pour. That means a bottle of wine will contain five glasses. Most restaurants price their wines by the glass higher than one-fifth the cost of a bottle, so if there is a good chance that you'll consume five glasses, buy the bottle.

On the other hand, if you want only a few glasses, either because that's all your party wants or needs, or because you want a different wine with each course, then buying by the glass makes good sense.

Keep in mind, though, that restaurants are often stuck with open bottles left over at the end of the night. Those wines end up being served the following day, and sometimes for several days thereafter. A wine that has been open overnight won't necessarily taste bad; it just won't taste lively. Always ask how long the bottle has been open if you're ordering by the glass, and if the answer is anything before "earlier today," pick a different wine, or ask for a small sip of the leftover wine to make sure it is up to your standards. See also entry 35.

One 750 ml bottle
serves five glasses

29 Finding the "sweet spot" on the list

Wine lists can be like minefields filled with dangerous big-ticket items aimed at the low-information expense-account crowd. These wines are carefully allocated to protect profit margins, and the truth is, there is often no correlation between price and quality. The main haven of expense-account wines is the steak house, but they show up everywhere. In general, stay away from celebrated wineries and famous places. There are wonderful wines such as Kistler and Silver Oak that are so well known by the expense-account set that their prices get pushed up beyond reason. You may be paying for high-quality wine, but you may also be paying for expensive PR and basic rarity. Instead, look for the weird places and little names. Those wines are very likely on the list because the buyer couldn't live without them, and searching them out will pay cash dividends. Even better, if you end up talking to the wine buyer, he or she may be so enchanted with your choice that they will show you all the other hidden gems. As for price, pick a wine about a third of the way up the price list scale. This is the price range where the wine buyer is picking wines not just for you—these are the wines they'd buy for themselves.

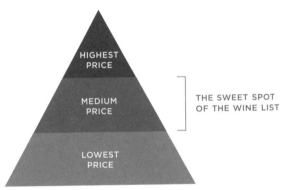

30   How to talk about price

When customers get coy about how much they want to spend, both the server and the customer are doomed to a dance where no one leads. Customers often are afraid the server will look down their nose at them, and unfortunately, sometimes that happens. Still, you are buying, and they are selling, so stick to your guns. Arrive at a dollar amount you'd like to spend and, if you don't want to announce it to the table, point to the price on the wine list and say to the sommelier, "I'd like something in this range. Can you recommend a wine that will complement our food?" See also entry 29.

buying wine

31 What's the restaurant's markup?

This varies. The most expensive places tend to be steak houses and hotels, where they may charge three times retail or higher. That's close to five times the wholesale price, and restaurants usually pour about a fifth of a bottle if you order by the glass. That means that every time you buy a glass of wine in one of these restaurants, you've paid for their whole bottle. In restaurants that love wine lovers, the markup will be much smaller, sometimes less than twice the retail price. When you go to a restaurant for the first time, though, it's hard to know what the markup is until you actually see the list and compare the price of a familiar wine with the price you pay at your wine store. If markup matters to you, see if the restaurant posts their wine list on their Web site, and research prices in advance.

32 Will just one wine work for everything?

Yes. Champagne and many other sparkling wines work with virtually everything, but the style you choose is important (see entry 210). A wine made mostly from Chardonnay is better for light dishes and a wine made mostly from Pinot Noir, or a rosé, is best for heavier dishes. For the heaviest of red meat dishes, a sparkling red wine such as Shiraz works best.

33   When nothing looks familiar

Be excited about having the chance to try something new. Usually, seeing no familiar wines indicates an interesting list and a thoughtful buyer. Places with lists like this usually give their staff extensive training, which means that even if the buyer is not there, someone should still be able to give knowledgeable help. If not, pick a grape or growing area that you like and pick a wine about a third of the way up the pricing scale (see entry 29). If the restaurant offers any wines by the glass that interest you, ask for a taste. Restaurants generally pour 4-, 5- or 6-ounce glasses, so there will always be enough in a 25.4 ounce (750 milliliters) bottle to give a sip to a potential customer.

34   Sending it back

You should definitely return a bad wine in a restaurant, but let's define "bad." If you just don't like the wine and *they* recommended it, just politely say that you don't like the wine and would prefer something else. If you don't like the wine and *you* chose it, you may have to chalk it up to a learning experience. If the wine seems to actually have something wrong with it—if it's "corked" (smells even a little like old, wet cardboard) or has some other weird smell or taste—politely tell the person serving it that you think there is something wrong with the wine. The best time to do this is when they offer you a taste before pouring (this is the whole purpose of this procedure) or very shortly thereafter. Don't try to return a wine after much of the first round has been drunk. Here is information on the six main flaws in wine and how to recognize them.

NAME	CAUSE	AROMA/FLAVOR	SEND BACK OR RETURN TO SHOP?
Corked	TCA (see entry 279)	Wet cardboard or old gym socks	Yes
Cooked/ Madeirized	Excessive heat in storage or shipping	Stewed prunes or Madeira (see entry 161)	Yes, unless you're responsible for the poor storage
Oxidized	Poor bottling or poor storage	Nutty, like sherry (see entry 165)	Yes, depending on wine style and age
Sulfur	Too much sulfur used as a preservative (see entry 46)	Rotten eggs or car tires	Sometimes a sulfur odor will disperse when the wine is poured; if not, return it.
Volatile acidity (VA)	Abnormal levels of acetic acid	Nail polish remover or vinegar	Yes, if very obvious
Brett	*Brettanomyces* yeast in winery	Sweaty horse or funky barnyard	There is some gray area, as *Brett* is not always considered bad; it depends on the style of wine. If it's overwhelming, return it.

If you feel guilty about returning a wine in a restaurant, know that it won't cost them one penny. The restaurant simply gets a credit from the wholesaler, who passes the loss back to the winery. The only exception to this is restaurants with long lists of very old and rare wines. When one of those bottles is bad, the restaurant suffers the loss. Restaurants serving old, rare wines will usually have a sommelier who will smell and taste the wine to make sure it is okay before ever pouring it for you.

35 How do restaurants choose wines to sell by the glass?

In most cases, restaurants offer wines by the glass because many customers don't want a whole bottle but would still like a nice wine. Usually, the wine buyer picks wines by the glass because they provide good profit margin and work well with the restaurant's cuisine, and the best restaurants will pass some of the savings on to their customers.

However, this is an area where wineries will do almost anything to influence the wine buyer. Very few things make a winery happier than a restaurant agreeing to place one of their wines on the by-the-glass menu. In a store, a shopper might buy a case of a particular wine and drink it over time with their spouse. That means two people now know how good the wine is. If those same twelve bottles are at a restaurant, then twelve tables of two to four people (a total of twenty-four to forty-eight people) will know how good that case of wine is. The best marketing for the winery is when the restaurant sells those twelve bottles by the glass, which means sixty people (five glasses per bottle times twelve bottles) will experience the wine. For this reason, wineries and distributors will offer discounts to restaurants that promise to sell the wine by the glass. These slots are so coveted that the distributor's sales staff will frequently get bonuses for winning these positions on the wine list—sometimes the distributor will share the bonus with servers and sommeliers, and that impacts where the servers and sommeliers steer the customer. The important point is that the consumer may be led to these wines for reasons other than quality. Most restaurants are scrupulously honest, but caveat emptor.

36   Why does the sommelier show me the bottle?

This is your opportunity to confirm that they have brought you what you ordered. Servers live demanding lives and have a large number of orders to juggle, so they can occasionally make a mistake. Always check the bottle to confirm the name of the winemaker, grape (if it's on the label), and vintage. Once you have accepted the wine, it's yours, unless you discover a defect when the taste is poured (see entry 34).

37   Why am I given the cork?

There are three reasons.

1. To allow you to see that it is intact and not defective. Determine this by looking at it to make sure the wine didn't leak up the sides too far (the cork should be wet at one end, mostly dry on the sides, and dry on top), and/or squeezing it to make sure it is solid, not crumbly. If you encounter a problem, it is a signal for you to be alert to the possibility of oxidation or another fault (see entry 34) when your taste is poured. This brief check applies only to real corks, not plastic ones, which won't tell you anything.
2. So that you can look at the cork and make sure any writing on it matches the bottle. This is important only for very old and expensive bottles, which have been known to be counterfeited.
3. Tradition.

38   When should I be given an ice bucket?

It is said that Americans drink their red wines too warm and their white wines too cold. That also holds true with the storage in most restaurants and wine bars. Your wine should start out a bit colder than you like it, with enough poured so that when you finish the glass, it's just as you like it. If the wine is served too warm to allow following that procedure, it's time to ask for an ice bucket, or ask the server to chill the wine for you by whatever method the restaurant uses. This goes for both red and white wines. People may stare at you when you plop a red wine in the ice—even if only for a few minutes—but you will bring it closer to the proper temperature and enjoy the wine more. See also entry 285.

39   How should I order dessert wine?

Order dessert wine by the bottle if there are enough people in your party and you can reach a consensus. Ordering it by the glass really depends on the restaurant. If you trust the restaurant's wine program, ask how long the bottle has been open, or ask for a taste. Most restaurants don't offer nonfortified dessert wines by the glass because they oxydize too quickly (unless the restaurant uses a gas preservation system) and sell too slowly. People who love an after-dinner tipple of Port or any of the world's other great fortified wines (see entry 181) may be disappointed in many restaurants by how long the bottle has been open. These wines are just as sensitive to oxygen and heat as any other wine, and while they may still taste rich and sweet, the freshness and vitality are gone by the second or third day.

buying wine

40 When to tip the sommelier

If your server has been helping you with the wine, you should absolutely show your appreciation in his or her tip. If a sommelier or wine buyer has been especially helpful, you might want to consider leaving him or her a tip as well. The appropriate method of doing this varies by restaurant, but secretly handing them a little cash (anywhere from $10 to $100) will be a well-appreciated kindness.

41 How does BYOB work?

Depending on state laws and local customs, some restaurants will allow patrons to bring their own wines. There are three problems with this from the restaurant's point of view. First, wine is a major profit center in most restaurants, one that disappears if someone brings their own. Second, the waitstaff depends on the tips they get from selling wine. Third, BYOB doesn't cover the cost of labor for opening the wine, filling and refilling the glasses, and washing the glasses (to say nothing of broken glasses).

For all these reasons, restaurants that allow BYOB will charge a "corkage fee." Sometimes the fee is very reasonable and sometimes less so, to encourage customers to order from the wine list. If you're interested in bringing your own bottle, call the restaurant in advance to find out if they allow it and what the corkage fee is.

GREGG HARRINGTON, MS

Master Sommelier and owner of Gramercy Cellars,
Walla Walla, Washington

Gregg Harrington currently makes what he calls "small lot, high acid, old oak wines." Before that, he ran wine programs for food industry professionals such as Wolfgang Puck and Emeril Lagasse. We asked where he recommended people start learning about wine. "A good way is to find a domestic region you like and then stick with it for a while," he stated. "If you like Zinfandel, then ask yourself where they make it best. The answer: Sonoma. For international wines, find a bottle you like, then look on the back for the name of the importer, and buy other wines from that importer. Three I like are Neal Rosenthal, Eric Solomon, and Jorge Ordoñez. The importers themselves usually have a consistent taste profile. Also, go to your favorite wine retailer, tell them what you like, and ask them to point you to wines they consider to be amazing bargains. It's very rare I spend over $20 on a bottle of wine in a retail store. Currently, I'm really enjoying Bodegas Borsão wines from Jorge Ordoñez, pretty much anything from Chianti Classico or Rosso di Montalcino, Domaine Jean-Paul Droin Chablis, and Kouros Roditis from Greece."

buying wine

39

Reading the Label

Wine labels can carry a wealth of information if you know how to decipher them. In most countries, the information on the label is prescribed by either the government or a quasi-governmental agency. European wineries put a lot more information on their bottles, albeit in a language foreign to most of us. Luckily, things are so tightly controlled in Europe that we only need to remember a few terms to be able to at least broadly understand their labels. Once outside of Europe, the labels get a lot easier to use.

Why are European labels so hard to read?

This difficulty often comes down to the differences between New World (North and South America, Australia, New Zealand, South Africa) and Old World (European) labels. By tradition, Europe's labels refer to vineyards, geographic areas, and wine producers—information the local customers consider of the utmost importance. And since most wine-making areas in Europe allow only specific grapes in the wine, putting the grape name on the label seems redundant. The challenge for anyone not from the region is knowing which grapes are associated with which growing areas. New World wine labels, on the other hand, almost always emphasize the grape.

NORTHSTAR

MERLOT

COLUMBIA VALLEY

2 0 0 5

ALC. 14.7% BY VOL.

NEW WORLD

DR. LOOSEN

2007

Wehlener Sonnenuhr

Riesling Spätlese

PRÄDIKATSWEIN · PRODUCE OF GERMANY
ERZEUGERABFÜLLUNG: WEINGUT DR. LOOSEN · D-54470 BERNKASTEL/MOSEL
A. P. NR. 2 576 162 32 08 · ENTHÄLT SULFITE

alc. 8.5% vol   Mosel   750 ml ℮

OLD WORLD

Notice the simplicity of the American label on the left versus the complexity of the German label on the right.

43   Can I predict how a wine tastes from its label?

A wine label offers an abundance of data that an experienced taster can use.

1. The juxtaposition of grape and location can tip you off to the wine's most likely flavors. For example, see entry 179.
2. Another piece of the puzzle comes from knowing the winery. Most wine producers have a house style because one person is in charge of the wine making.
3. The quantity of alcohol tells how ripe the grapes were when picked (higher alcohol equals riper grapes; see entry 48). Riper grapes equal richer wines and less of an impression of acidity. See also entry 272.
4. The Old World terms that specify amounts of residual sugar, grape ripeness, types of barrels, and length of aging give the consumer a fighting chance at guessing what the flavors in the glass will be like. Some of these terms are further defined in entry 55, entry 65, and entry 71.

44   Is vintage important?

Yes, but relative to location. The vintage refers to the year on the bottle label, which is the year in which the grapes were harvested. Each grape-growing region has different climatic and other conditions every year during the growing season that affect the quality and quantity of the grapes for that year. A good vintage is one in which growing conditions were optimal; a bad vintage is one in which some event endangered the quality or quantity of the grapes. Most of the New World (countries other than those in

reading the label

Europe) is blessed with good weather and a minimum of government restrictions on the wine-making process. This allows winemakers to minimize the effects of a less-than-perfect harvest, so it is rare to find a truly bad vintage. The converse is true in Europe (the Old World). Having good enough weather to produce usable grapes at harvest is a constant problem, and with government regulations covering every possible aspect of wine making, it is more difficult to correct problems in the winery. That's why in the Old World, vintages really do matter. It's also important to realize that vintages provide only a broad framework for considering quality: some wineries do better than others in "poor" vintages.

One other aspect of vintage is very important. When a great vintage comes along, such as 2005 in Burgundy, people tend to neglect the very good vintages surrounding that year. Both 2004 and 2006 were good years in Burgundy, and their wines are drinkable far younger than the highly structured 2005, so be on the lookout for vintages surrounding the great ones.

45 What is "Appellation d'Origine Contrôlée"?

The AOC is a system that started in France and is now imitated through much of the European Union. Its more than five hundred regulations are an attempt to protect the unique qualities of the agriculture of specific areas by requiring that certain minimal standards be met (the system is in use for wine as well as cheese and other regional products). The system sets distinct terminology that can be used on wine labels according to how closely the wine conforms to the production laws for each level. The least restrictive laws merely set out standards for places and grapes, while the most restrictive may actually tell the winemaker the days they may harvest. In general, the main areas controlled are the geographical area, the grapes grown, viticulture methods, wine-making techniques, total yields, and the ripeness level of the grapes at harvest. New World countries also use geographical appellations, but with far fewer restrictions. The table below gives the control terminology you'll see on wine labels for each of five countries, usually along with the appellation, or geographical area, the wine came from (for example: Appellation Alsace Contrôlée). The most basic level, table wine, has been left off the chart because such wine is rarely exported to the United States. See also entry 113.

EUROPEAN WINE QUALITY STANDARDS

	France	Italy	Spain	Portugal	Germany
Most flexible	Vin de Pays	Indicazione Geografica Tipica (IGT)	Vino de la Tierra	Vinho Regional	Deutcher Landwein (uncommon in the U.S.)
	Vin Delimité de Qualité Superieur (VDQS)			Indicação de Proveniencia Regulamentada (IPR)	Qualitätswein bestimmter Anbaugebiete (QbA)
	Appellation d'Origine Contrôlée (AOC)	Denominazione di Origine Controllata (DOC)	Denominación de Origen (DO)	Denominação de Origem Controlada (DOC)	Prädikatswein or Qualitätswein mit Prädikat (QmP)
Most restrictive		Denominazione di Origine Controllata e Garantita (DOCG)	Denominación de Origen Calificada (DOCa or DOC) or Denominoció d'Origen Qualificada (DOQ)		

46 What is sulfur and why is it in wine?

Sulfur dioxide is used in the vineyard as a natural fungicide. It is also used in wine making, when it is added to most wine to help prevent the effects of oxidation and promote freshness in the end product, and to restrain troublesome bacteria and yeasts. (It is used in many foods as a natural preservative as well, such as dried fruits.) Sulfur dioxide can be harmful to people with asthma, which is the reason for the warning "Contains sulfites" on wine sold in the United States.

47 What does "estate-bottled" mean?

It is a strictly American term that means the grapes were grown on grounds owned or under long-term lease by the winery; that the grapes come from where they say they come from; and that the wine is made and cellared at the winery. Similar terms appear (in the language of origin) on wines produced outside the United States based on wording and restrictions existing in each country.

48 Why do I want to know the alcohol level?

The first (perhaps obvious) reason is to know how potent the wine is. The difference in alcohol between three glasses of a light German Riesling and three glasses of an Amador Petite Sirah is equal to two quick shots of tequila. Alcohol level also lets you know how ripe the grapes were at picking. A wine with alcohol higher than 13.5 percent was made from very ripe grapes, which tend to produce fruitier wine. Unfortunately, if the grapes are overripe, the wine can taste like dried fruit: plum flavors will turn to prune. A lower alcohol level, say, less than 10 percent, tends to indicate less-ripe grapes or a variety with lower natural sugar content. Generally these wines will have higher acidity. See also entry 208.

49 What are old vines?

Older grapevines produce fewer clusters of grapes, but those grapes have greater intensity and stronger flavors. Of course, the older a grapevine the more likely it is to die from any of dozens of different maladies, so vineyards with really old vines, say fifty to a hundred years old, are uncommon. In most countries, "old" is not legally defined, and winemakers use a rather free definition of what it means.

HINT *In English the term is "Old Vine"; you may also see* Vieilles Vignes *(in French) or* Alte Reben *(in German) on wine labels.*

reading the label

47

50   What does *frizzante* mean?

In Italian, it refers to a wine with very light bubbles. For more-bubbly wines, similar to Champagne, the Italian term is "spumante." The bubbliness of sparkling wine is based on the pressure of the carbon dioxide in the bottle. "Sparkling" is the term in English for wines with the highest pressure, including Champagne, Asti (made in Piedmont, see entry 152), and Cava (made in Spain). See the table for terms that describe the levels of pressure in five languages. See also entry 178.

BUBBLE INDEX

Lanaguage	Term
French	mousseux
English	sparkling
Italian	spumante
Spanish	espumoso
French	crémant
French	pétillant
English	semi-sparkling
German	spritzig
Italian	frizzante
French	perlant
German	perlwein
Italian	frizzantino
Spanish	vino de aguja

More intense bubbles ↑

Less intense bubbles ↓

51 How to read an American label

Labels from the United States are simple to read. Most of the important items are on the label: the producer, grape, appellation, vintage, and alcohol level. More so than their Old World counterparts, New World wineries put additional information on the back label, such as which grapes are in the blend, what barrels were used, and how long to age the wine.

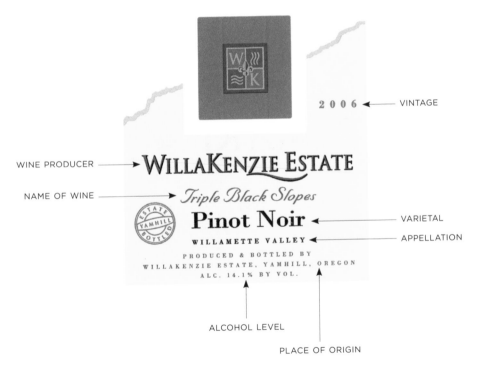

2 0 0 6 ◄——— VINTAGE

WINE PRODUCER ——► **WILLAKENZIE ESTATE**

NAME OF WINE ——► *Triple Black Slopes*

Pinot Noir ◄——— VARIETAL

WILLAMETTE VALLEY ◄——— APPELLATION

PRODUCED & BOTTLED BY
WILLAKENZIE ESTATE, YAMHILL, OREGON
ALC. 14.1% BY VOL.

ALCOHOL LEVEL

PLACE OF ORIGIN

52 How to read an Argentine label

Argentina's labels fall somewhere between the New World and Old World styles (see Introduction)—they give more information than they used to. The most highly regarded wine-growing area in the country is Mendoza. As quality improves, the Argentines are finding that certain areas within Mendoza are growing better fruit, and dividing them into government-controlled appellations, so expect to start seeing those names on Argentine labels soon.

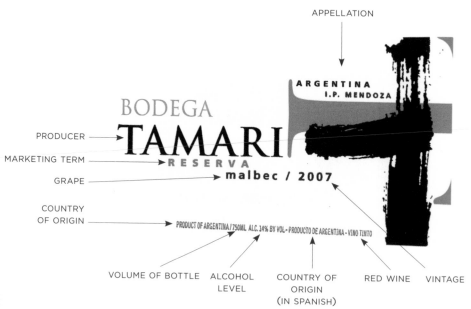

APPELLATION

ARGENTINA
I.P. MENDOZA

BODEGA
PRODUCER → TAMARI
MARKETING TERM → RESERVA
GRAPE → malbec / 2007

COUNTRY
OF ORIGIN → PRODUCT OF ARGENTINA / 750ML ALC. 14% BY VOL - PRODUCTO DE ARGENTINA - VINO TINTO

VOLUME OF BOTTLE   ALCOHOL LEVEL   COUNTRY OF ORIGIN (IN SPANISH)   RED WINE   VINTAGE

53   How to read an Australian label

Australia generally follows the convention of naming the grapes in big, easy-to-see letters, although this information occasionally appears in smaller letters below a madcap name that may be easier for the consumer to remember, such as Suckfizzle, The Broken Fishplate, Swagman's Kiss, Love Grass, The Ball Buster, or The Feral Fox. The label shown is from a joint venture between an American family and a French family that is much more reserved.

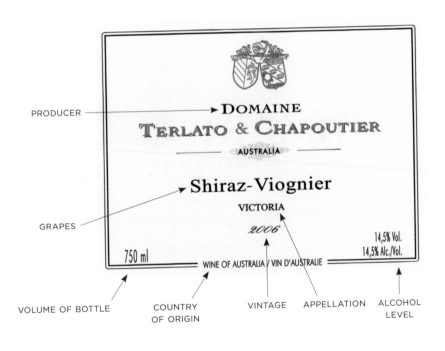

PRODUCER ───── ▶ **DOMAINE**
TERLATO & CHAPOUTIER
AUSTRALIA

▶ **Shiraz-Viognier**

VICTORIA

2006

14,5% Vol.
14,5% Alc./Vol.

750 ml

GRAPES

WINE OF AUSTRALIA / VIN D'AUSTRALIE

VOLUME OF BOTTLE   COUNTRY OF ORIGIN   VINTAGE   APPELLATION   ALCOHOL LEVEL

54 How to read an Austrian label

People are generally divided into two groups when it comes to Austrian wine labels. One believes that the quantity of information is a gift to consumers that helps them determine what is in the bottle before plunking down their euros. The other group sees the labels as confusing, filled with arcane jargon, resembling a contract with too much small print. The truth is, as usual, in between.

The most important items to notice are the wine producer, the grape, the wine's sweetness level, and the growing area. Beyond that, put yourself in the hands of a person at a restaurant or wine shop who understands Austrian wine's charms. See also entry 55.

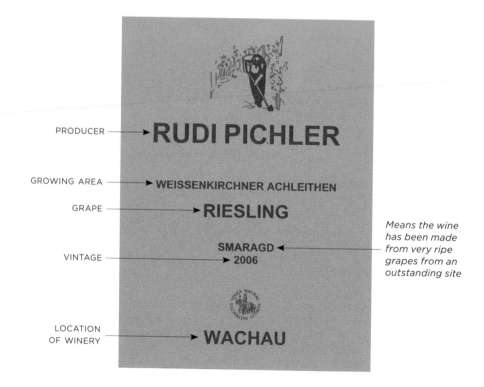

PRODUCER ──► **RUDI PICHLER**

GROWING AREA ──► **WEISSENKIRCHNER ACHLEITHEN**

GRAPE ──► **RIESLING**

VINTAGE ──► **SMARAGD** ◄── Means the wine
2006 ── has been made
from very ripe
grapes from an
outstanding site

LOCATION
OF WINERY ──► **WACHAU**

55 What are Steinfeder, Federspiel, and Smaragd?

These are wine classifications in the Wachau area of Austria. In order, each has a higher sugar content at harvest and thus higher potential alcohol in the bottle. Steinfeder, which is named after the local feather grass, has alcohol below 11 percent. These can be charming wines, but they are quite inexpensive and seldom exported. In fact many Austrians believe Steinfeders will disappear due to global warming. Federspiel wines, named for falconry, run from 11.5 percent to 12.5 percent alcohol. Smaragd is the highest quality wine of the Wachau. Named for a green lizard that runs through the Wachau vineyards, these wines must be more than 12.5 percent alcohol and are generally rich and more expensive.

56 How to read a Chilean label

Chilean wines have the standard New World information on their labels, but since they are in a rush toward the top of the pricing market, expect to see more complicated labels soon, especially in terms of newly developed subappellations.

WINERY OWNER — DOMAINES BARONS DE ROTHSCHILD (LAFITE)

VINTAGE — 2005

WINE PRODUCER — LOS VASCOS

VARIETAL — CABERNET SAUVIGNON

APPELLATION — COLCHAGUA

VOLUME OF BOTTLE — 750 ml. MIS EN BOUTEILLE AU DOMAINE

PRODUCED BY VIÑA LOS VASCOS - PERALILLO - CHILE — COUNTRY OF ORIGIN

ALCOHOL LEVEL — Red Wine Alcohol 14.0% by Volume Contains Sulfites — PASTERNAK Wine Imports — Imported by Pasternak Wine Imports Harrison, NY.

PRODUCTION STATEMENT

LOCATION OF WINERY

MEANS BOTTLED AT THE ESTATE

57 How to read an Alsace label

The word *Clos* means the grape vines are (or were once) behind a
wall, usually one to delineate church property. Like other Old World
wines, Alsace wines are regulated by the AOC system (see entry 45),
which sets standards. One other important point about this label
is the statement "Vignerons en biodynamie." It stipulates that this
winemaker uses biodynamic principles in farming (see entry 192).

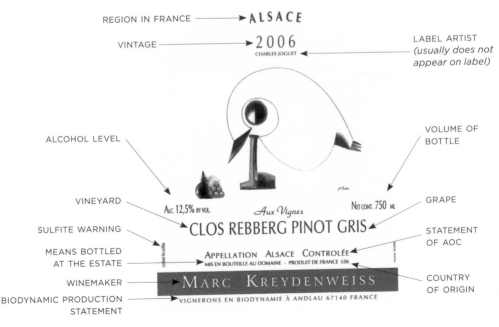

REGION IN FRANCE ⟶ **ALSACE**

VINTAGE ⟶ **2006**
CHARLES JOGUET

LABEL ARTIST
*(usually does not
appear on label)*

ALCOHOL LEVEL

VOLUME OF
BOTTLE

VINEYARD

Alc 12,5% by vol.   *Aux Vignes*   Net cont. 750 ml

GRAPE

SULFITE WARNING

CLOS REBBERG PINOT GRIS

STATEMENT
OF AOC

MEANS BOTTLED
AT THE ESTATE

APPELLATION ALSACE CONTROLÉE
MIS EN BOUTEILLE AU DOMAINE - PRODUIT DE FRANCE L06

WINEMAKER

MARC KREYDENWEISS

COUNTRY
OF ORIGIN

BIODYNAMIC PRODUCTION
STATEMENT

VIGNERONS EN BIODYNAMIE À ANDLAU 67140 FRANCE

reading the label

58 How to read a label from Graves, in Bordeaux

The labels of different regions within Bordeaux are similar, except for the possible indication of the winery's inclusion in one of the various regional wine classifications that have been constructed over the years. The wines of the Graves were classified in 1953 and 1959 (similar to the 1855 classification of the Médoc, see entry 139), but the system was eviscerated in 1987 when many of Graves' best vineyards were included in a newly created AOC, Pessac-Léognan. (The producer below does not figure in the classification.)

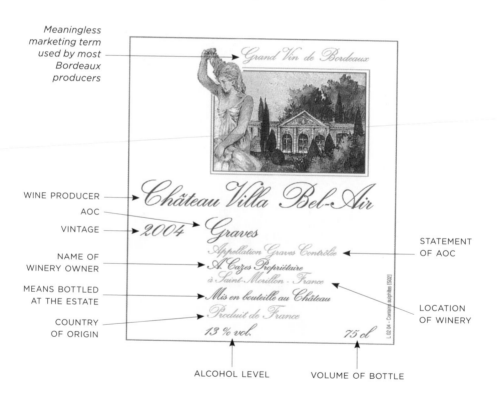

Meaningless marketing term used by most Bordeaux producers

WINE PRODUCER
AOC
VINTAGE

NAME OF WINERY OWNER

MEANS BOTTLED AT THE ESTATE

COUNTRY OF ORIGIN

STATEMENT OF AOC

LOCATION OF WINERY

ALCOHOL LEVEL   VOLUME OF BOTTLE

JAMES TIDWELL, MS, CWE

Master Sommelier; Beverage Manager and Sommelier, Four Seasons Resort and Club at Las Colinas, Dallas, Texas

Here are twenty recommendations from James Tidwell, most of which are fairly priced and available from better wine merchants.

WHITES

Grüner Veltliners: Bründlmayer or Leth

Albariño: Martín Códax ("delicious and straightforward")

Italian Moscato: Saracco or Ceretto

New Zealand Sauvignon Blanc: Tupari or Kim Crawford

White Burgundy: Château de Chorey Jacques Germain Beaune Domaine de Saux, Guy Amiot Bourgogne, or Henri Boillot

Riesling (Tidwell's favorite): from Germany, Robert Weil; from Alsace, Domaine Weinbach; from Australia, Jeffrey Grosset; and from Austria, Emmerich Knoll

REDS

Crozes-Hermitage: Alain Graillot or Domaine Gilles Robin Crozes

Pinot Noir: from Oregon, Ken Wright; and from Burgundy, Domaine Méo-Camuzet Bourgogne

SPARKLING

Prosecco: Trevisiol Prosecco di Valdobbiadene Extra Dry

DESSERT

Australian stickies: Chambers Muscat

reading the label

59 How to read a label from the Médoc, in Bordeaux

The Médoc portion of Bordeaux is home to many of the most expensive and highly regarded wines in the world. In 1855, the Médoc popularized the concept of putting wineries into quality categories. The wines that made it into the classification (see entry 139) fall into one of five Grand Cru categories referred to as "growths," first growth through fifth growth. Much has changed over time, and some wines ranked then are now better and others worse, but the system hangs on bullishly.

Note that the term "Grand Cru" has a different meaning in the Médoc than in other parts of France, and even the other Bordeaux AOCs. In much of France, if the term Grand Cru is used at all, it applies only to the best wines. In the Médoc, a wine that is classified Grand Cru could be at any of the five levels of classified wines.

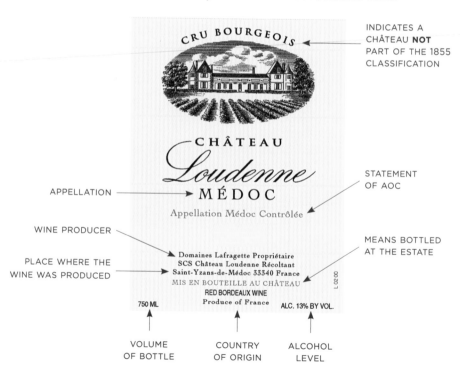

INDICATES A CHÂTEAU **NOT** PART OF THE 1855 CLASSIFICATION

STATEMENT OF AOC

APPELLATION

WINE PRODUCER

PLACE WHERE THE WINE WAS PRODUCED

MEANS BOTTLED AT THE ESTATE

VOLUME OF BOTTLE

COUNTRY OF ORIGIN

ALCOHOL LEVEL

60 How to read a label from St. Emilion, in Bordeaux

St. Emilion is an AOC in the eastern part of Bordeaux. The wineries of St. Emilion were classified in 1955, and those results have been revisited four times since. The 2006 survey raised the ire of a number of winemakers because of what they considered politically motivated downgrading. St. Emilion has three classifications, with two wines rated Premiers Grands Crus Classés A, eleven Premiers Grands Crus Classés B, and fifty-three Grands Crus Classés. Note the term "1er" in the Angelus label below—it's in the B category—and means "premier."

FORMAL CLASSIFICATION

WINE PRODUCER

NAME OF WINERY OWNER

VINTAGE

AOC

ANGELUS
1ᴇʀ GRAND CRU CLASSÉ
CHATEAU
ANGELUS
2002
DE BOÜARD DE LAFOREST & FILS
SAINT-ÉMILION

D. C. FLYNT, MW

Master of Wine and proprietor, D. C. Flynt MW Selections

D. C. Flynt is one of America's smartest Burgundians, a man with such a passion for those wines that he imports many of them himself. His zeal is infectious and it's a rare person who doesn't leave Mr. Flynt's seminars as a convert. Thankfully, he has a straightforward strategy for learning about the wines. "For white wines, if you are just beginning, I would stay with areas like Marsannay, St-Aubin, Pernand-Vergelesses, Mâcon, or Chablis," he recommends. "AOC [Appellation d'Origine Contrôlée] Chablis is still grossly underpriced and the value is terrific. If you want a bit of oak, you can get a Premier Cru St-Aubin for under $25. In the warmer years, Marsannay and St-Aubin can be superior to the Montrachet wines that can run hundreds, even thousands of dollars.

"For reds, look at a couple of appellations. St-Romain is a little-known appellation, but the wines are very typical Côte de Beaune. Savigny-lès-Beaune is the best bargain in all of AOC Burgundy. These are wines with violet, white pepper, and truffle aromas, and work incredibly with cassoulet or cheaper cuts of meat. Another terrific value, because no one knows about it, is Bourgogne Passetoutgrains, a blend of Pinot Noir and Gamay."

Mr. Flynt's picks for relatively inexpensive, but consistently wonderful Burgundies are:

La Chablisienne Chablis
Domaine Jean Chartron Aligoté Clos de la Combe
Domaine Huguenot Père & Fils Marsannay,
  both blanc and rouge
Domaine Pierre Gelin Fixin, Bourgogne Passetoutgrains, and
  Bourgogne Aligoté
Domaine Philippe Girard Savigny-lès-Beaune "Vieilles
Vignes"

61 How to read a Burgundy label

Burgundy wine labels and classifications are so difficult that even many Burgundians don't understand them. The important point to know about Burgundy's labels is that the words in large letters will almost always be the vineyard's location. Sometimes the name of the wine producer will also be writ large, especially if it is one of the famous négociants (companies that produce wines from grapes bought from various growers in an area). This Bâtard-Montrachet is a Grand Cru, which in the hands of the best winemakers can be a transcendent wine. The reason Burgundy stumps so many people is that the laws of inheritance in France have left some tiny sites with dozens of owners, which potentially means dozens of winemakers and dozens of viticultural schemes—even within each Grand Cru. That makes buying a Burgundy like negotiating a minefield. So much so that it is frighteningly easy to find a $30 Burgundy that is much better than a $300 Burgundy. The easiest solution is to find a few pleasing producers and check for their wines in your price range.

MEANS BOTTLED AT THE ESTATE

COUNTRY OF ORIGIN

AOC

FORMAL CLASSIFICATION

ALCOHOL LEVEL

PRODUCER

STATEMENT OF AOC

Product of France

Mis en bouteilles à la propriété

Bâtard-Montrachet
GRAND CRU
APPELLATION BÂTARD-MONTRACHET CONTRÔLÉE

ALC 14% BY VOLUME

WHITE WINE

CONTENTS 750 ml

DOMAINE LEFLAIVE
PROPRIÉTAIRE A PULIGNY-MONTRACHET (CÔTE-D'OR)

L 08 1 08 0

LOCATION OF WINERY

VOLUME OF BOTTLE

62 What does Grand Cru mean? Premier Cru?

These are terms that have the most meaning in Burgundy, though they are also used in Alsace, Bordeaux, and Champagne. The term Grand Cru doesn't translate neatly into English—*Grand* means wonderful or large, and *Cru* means wine, vintage, or vineyard. Burgundy grants its Grand Cru (and its subaltern Premier Cru) classification based on the vineyard, not the producer, which means several winemakers owning land in the same vineyard can be making wines of different quality, depending on the owner's growing and wine-making practices. This means that, with Burgundy, it pays to be familiar with the reputation of the winemaker, not simply the vineyard status.

Alsace's winemakers frequently don't even put the term "Grand Cru" on their labels because more than fifty vineyards in Alsace are listed as Grand Cru, and not all of them are good—some winemakers feel the term has limited value.

In Bordeaux, it is the winery that is classified, and the term Grand Cru will mean one of two things. In the Médoc, it is a term given to any wine that was ranked in the top five classes of the Official Classification of 1855 (the top class, called "first growths," will say "Premier Grand Cru Classé" on the label), while in St. Emilion, across the river, Grand Cru indicates the wine was considered one of the sixty-six best.

Champagne, too, awards Grand Cru and Premier Cru, based on vineyard quality. The rank was originally established as a way of pricing grapes from different vineyards heading to the wineries—the seventeen Grand Cru vineyards were allowed to charge 100 percent of the prevailing rate, and the Premier Crus were allowed to charge 98 to 99 percent. There has been a movement to change this system because it rewards historic excellence and punishes improvement. See also entry 139.

63 How to read a Champagne label

The most important item on a Champagne wine label is the name of the producer. Most Champagnes are carefully crafted for consistency by blending wines from multiple years, grapes, and vineyards. The goal is to have a brand with consistent flavors year to year. If the wine is made solely from Chardonnay, the words "Blanc de Blancs" will be on the label. That means "white of white," that is, a white wine made from the white Chardonnay grape. If the label says "Blanc de Noirs" ("white of black"), it is a white wine made from a black (red) wine grape, Pinot Noir. If the label has neither term on it, the wine is a blend of grapes. The third thing to notice is the sweetness level. Two styles dominate—Brut and Extra Dry (or Extra Sec). Ironically, Brut is the drier wine and Extra Dry is slightly sweeter. Finally, the term "rosé" on the label refers to the pretty color achieved by adding some red juice to the white wine. See also entry 143.

REGION — CHAMPAGNE

Brut 1997 — VINTAGE

VINEYARD

VOLUME OF BOTTLE

COUNTRY OF ORIGIN

SULFITE WARNING

S

SALON
BLANC de BLANCS
Le Mesnil

750 ml. PRODUCE OF FRANCE 12% vol.
ÉLABORÉ PAR A.S. LE MESNIL S/OGER - FRANCE
NM-300-00 CONTAINS SULPHITES

PRODUCER

Literally "white of white," wine made from Chardonnay grapes

ALCOHOL LEVEL

64 How to read a Rhône label

The Rhône is another region where the producer's name is the most important information on the label. Knowing which grape is in the bottle will take memorizing the location and rules for almost twenty AOCs (see entry 45), all of them different. This particular Jaboulet wine is from Crozes-Hermitage, which won't help most people. The name Jaboulet is well respected and has been for a couple of centuries, even though this particular Jaboulet winery is new, but just the name is tantamount to a guarantee of quality. People who take the time to learn about Rhône wines will know from the AOC on the label that it is in the northern part of the Rhône region and that its wines are made from Syrah, although up to 15 percent of the blend can be from Marsanne and Rousanne, which are white grapes. Côtes du Rhône and Côtes du Rhône Villages are two other common designations for Rhône wines. Though both have AOC status, they are harder to predict because they can use any of fourteen grapes. See also entry 144.

LOCATION OF WINERY

STATEMENT OF AOC

NAME OF WINE

NAME OF WINERY

MEANS BOTTLED AT THE ESTATE

Crozes-Hermitage

APPELLATION CROZES-HERMITAGE CONTRÔLÉE

2007 — VINTAGE

Nouvelère

MARQUE DÉPOSÉE

D O M A I N E

Philippe & Vincent
JABOULET

MIS EN BOUTEILLE À LA PROPRIÉTÉ

SHAYN BJORNHOLM, MS
Master Sommelier

Shayn Bjornholm is deeply in love with Washington wines and is one of the most knowledgeable folks in the state about them, but I asked him to step outside his comfort zone and talk about other wines. He complied, mostly. We started with learning strategies. "Money is always such an issue, and getting wine can be expensive. So the best way to learn is to search for free tastings at restaurants, wine shops, classes, etc. The best wine shops have lots of tastings. Buy whenever you can, but taste, taste, taste. When I was first learning, I also started reading things like Jancis Robinson's *Oxford Companion to Wine*."

Mr. Bjornholm considers Washington Merlots to be among the wine world's great bargains, but urged trying some others. He added, "For myself, for home consumption, I always look in the $15 to $20 range. I like Côtes du Rhône from Guigal or Beaucastel's Perrin, both of which are very affordable. In Spanish wines, I look for anything imported by Jorge Ordoñez. And of course, I'm in love with German Rieslings, especially anything by Prüm or Robert Weil."

reading the label

65 How to read a German label

German labels provide both the greatest challenges and the most useful information. The first term to look for is "Qualitätswein mit Prädikat," or its newer counterpart "Prädikatswein." The best indicator of quality is the name of the producer. The second most important piece of information is the ripeness level of the grapes. In order from least to most ripe, the terms for this are: Kabinett, Spätlese, Auslese, Beerenauslese, and Trockenbeerenauslese. It is important to remember that the term "Auslese" on this label refers to the grapes' ripeness at harvest, not the sweetness of the wine, although unless the term "trocken" is on the bottle, the wine will be sweet. Knowing the growing region provides little help until a wine drinker becomes familiar with the characteristic differences among the wine-making areas. Lovers of German wine should make friends with a knowledgeable and trustworthy seller in order to avoid expensive mistakes.

MEANS "WINE ESTATE"

WEB SITE

RIPENESS LEVEL OF GRAPES AT HARVEST

Means "small castle in the town of Gimmeldingen," the vineyard's location

VOLUME OF BOTTLE

GOVERNMENT APPROVAL CODE

FOUNDED IN 1744

WINE PRODUCER

MEANS BOTTLED AT THE ESTATE

LOCATION

VARIETAL

VINTAGE

ALCOHOL LEVEL

Means it is one of Germany's top wines (though it doesn't assure great taste)

GROWING REGION

How to read an Italian label

Although Italy is a classic Old World wine country with an ever-expanding set of regulations, the labels are still easy to read. Italy doesn't require a listing of the grapes on the label, since the producer and geographical area are the more important pieces of information. Most wines will have one of three quality levels emblazoned somewhere on the label: DOC ("Denominazione di Origine Controllata"); DOCG ("Denominazione di Origine Controllata e Garantita"); or IGT ("Indicazione Geografica Tipica"); see entry 45. In Italy, though, the quality levels don't necessarily mean much. For instance, the label below is from a rare and very high-priced wine considered to be of the highest standard, yet it carries the medium level, DOC. On the other hand, Langhe's immediate neighbors make Asti Spumante, an inexpensive and ubiquitous wine that carries the higher quality designation, DOCG. IGT is a kitchen-sink category that allows winemakers to use unapproved grapes. Some of Italy's best and worst wines carry IGT on their label.

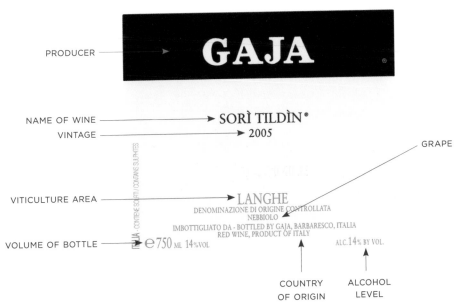

PRODUCER

GAJA

NAME OF WINE → SORÌ TILDÌN®
VINTAGE → 2005

GRAPE

VITICULTURE AREA → LANGHE
DENOMINAZIONE DI ORIGINE CONTROLLATA
NEBBIOLO
IMBOTTIGLIATO DA - BOTTLED BY GAJA, BARBARESCO, ITALIA
RED WINE, PRODUCT OF ITALY

VOLUME OF BOTTLE → e750 ML 14%VOL. ALC.14% BY VOL.

ITALIA CONTIENE SOLFITI / CONTAINS SULPHITES

COUNTRY OF ORIGIN   ALCOHOL LEVEL

reading the label

SERGIO ESPOSITO

Author of *Passion on the Vine* and CEO and founder of NYC's Italian Wine Merchants

"I'm sitting in Hong Kong right now," Sergio Esposito said over the phone. "And I'd love to know Cantonese, but it's not going to happen—it's too complicated. But as they say here, you can't eat an elephant all at once, you can only do it one bite at a time. So if a person really wants to learn about Italian wine, the only way to do it is to take one bite at a time. You start with either a favorite varietal, a favorite region, or a price point. With wine, it is all about the enjoyment. Or you can make it a serious endeavor. Just remember, you can't eat an elephant all at once.

"Italian wine is a sine qua non with food. You don't drink it as an aperitif. You don't sip wine overlooking the Tuscan hillside. An Italian would grab you by the arm, sit you down, and at least pull out some salami. Any Italian wine is food-friendly. One more thing to keep in mind is that Italian wines are good for a long time after opening. Weeks. If a wine goes bad after a couple of days, it was crap in the beginning."

Mr. Esposito provided some specific recommendations. "Italy has so many wonderful wines to offer. But in the under-$30 range, I love the Movia wines. They are from Collio, but on the Slovenian side of the border. Villa Mangiacane makes a great Chianti Classico. And all of Valle dell'Acate's wines from Sicily are wonderful."

67 Why are there roosters on Chianti labels?

The rooster was first used as a trademark for Chianti Classico more than 300 years ago. It was reinstituted in the twentieth century as a commercial trademark. Since 2005, it has been a trademark for the growers and winemakers of Chianti Classico, proving the wine has been grown, made, and aged according to law. There are three levels of Chianti, with the simplest being called Chianti, followed by Chianti Classico, and finally Chianti Classico Superiore (the most complex and expensive of the three).

The traditional black rooster, "gallo nero" in Italian

How to read a New Zealand label

Like other New World wine-producing countries, New Zealand puts the emphasis on the names of the grape variety and winemaker rather than on the location. The country has comparatively limited rules for wine making or labeling, so it's possible to simply list the winemaker, grape variety, vintage, alcohol level, and volume, but most exporting winemakers are intent on developing New Zealand's reputation as a maker of serious wines, so they often give more information than necessary, as with this Felton Road wine.

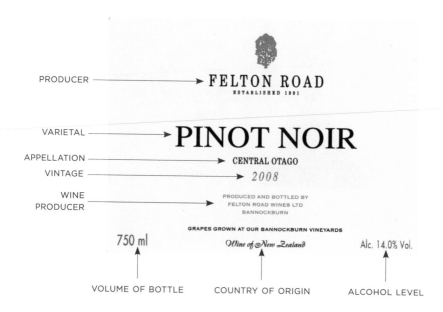

PRODUCER → **FELTON ROAD**
ESTABLISHED 1991

VARIETAL → **PINOT NOIR**

APPELLATION → CENTRAL OTAGO

VINTAGE → *2008*

WINE PRODUCER → PRODUCED AND BOTTLED BY
FELTON ROAD WINES LTD
BANNOCKBURN

GRAPES GROWN AT OUR BANNOCKBURN VINEYARDS

750 ml — *Wine of New Zealand* — Alc. 14.0% Vol.

VOLUME OF BOTTLE — COUNTRY OF ORIGIN — ALCOHOL LEVEL

69 How to read a Portuguese label

Portugal was one of the first countries in Europe to set up a system delineating areas for fine wine production (appellations). The Douro area has been providing the world—especially Great Britain and its colonies—with sweet, long-aging wines ever since. That connection is part of the reason why Portugal's labels are easier to understand than other Old World labels. Although some newer dry table wines are specific about which grapes are used, the majority of wines, especially Ports, are made from old vineyards containing a jumble of multiple varieties. See also entry 158.

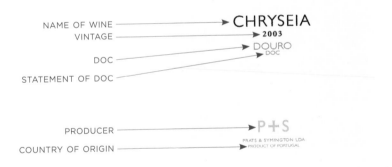

NAME OF WINE ──────────────► **CHRYSEIA**
VINTAGE ──────────────► **2003**
────► DOURO
DOC ──────────────► DOC
STATEMENT OF DOC ──────────►

PRODUCER ──────────────► P+S
PRATS & SYMINGTON LDA
COUNTRY OF ORIGIN ──────────► PRODUCT OF PORTUGAL

70　How to read a Spanish label

Spain's labels follow European standards (see entry 45), so you will
have to know an area and/or maker that appeals to you, or learn
which of your favorite grapes come from which Spanish region.
One term to look out for on a Spanish label: Spain is one of the only
countries where the term "Reserve" ("Reserva" in Spanish) carries a
legal meaning (see entry 71).

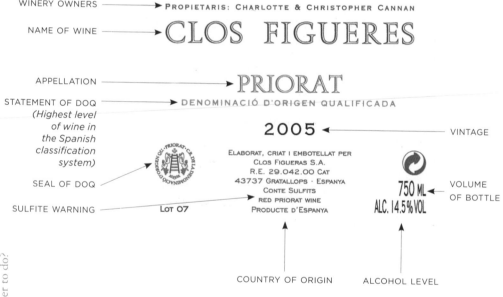

WINERY OWNERS ⟶ PROPIETARIS: CHARLOTTE & CHRISTOPHER CANNAN

NAME OF WINE ⟶ **CLOS FIGUERES**

APPELLATION ⟶ **PRIORAT**

STATEMENT OF DOQ ⟶ DENOMINACIÓ D'ORIGEN QUALIFICADA
(Highest level
of wine in
the Spanish
classification
system)

2005 ⟵ VINTAGE

ELABORAT, CRIAT I EMBOTELLAT PER
CLOS FIGUERAS S.A.
R.E. 29.042.00 CAT
43737 GRATALLOPS · ESPANYA

SEAL OF DOQ

CONTE SULFITS
RED PRIORAT WINE
SULFITE WARNING ⟶ LOT 07 PRODUCTE D'ESPANYA

750 ML ⟵ VOLUME
OF BOTTLE
ALC. 14.5% VOL

COUNTRY OF ORIGIN　　ALCOHOL LEVEL

71 What is Reserve or Reserva?

Reserve is a term used mostly by New World winemakers (see Introduction), and Old World winemakers that sell to New World consumers. It has no controlled meaning and, unless you already know the integrity of the winery, should be considered puffery. "Reserva" does, however, have a specific meaning in Spain, where many geographical areas group red wines into one of four age categories.

1. Vino Joven (young wine) doesn't have to spend any time in oak and can be sold shortly after it's made.
2. Crianza wines spend twelve months maturing in oak.
3. Reserva wines have to spend three years aging, one of which must be in oak.
4. Gran Reserva wines are made only when the quality of the harvest warrants it. They go through a minimum of five years aging with at least a year and a half of the aging in oak.

Grapes

Widely grown around the world, Chardonnay, Merlot, and Cabernet are only three of the hundreds of grapes used to make wine. Here we will go through the main wine grapes and identify the best versions. But we also offer options for those with a more adventurous nature, such as Cortese, Grüner Veltliner, Torrontés, Aglianico, Malbec, or maybe even Xinomavro.

In this section, recommendations are priced as follows: $ = $15 and less; $$ = $15–$30; $$$ = $30–$75; $$$$ = $75 and up.

How to say it: white grapes

Just remember, it's not as important to be able to pronounce the names of the grapes as it is to be charming when you ask the person selling you the wine how to pronounce it.

GRAPE	PRONUNCIATION
Albariño	al-buh-REE-nyo
Alvarinho	al-var-EEN-ho
Chardonnay	shar-duh-NAY
Chenin Blanc	SHEH-nin blawnk
Gewürztraminer	geh-VURZ-trah-min-er
Grüner Veltliner	GROO-ner VELT-lee-ner
Malvasia	mal-VAH-zee-uh
Marsanne	MAR-san
Müller-Thurgau	MULE-er TUR-gow
Muscat	MUSS-cat
Pedro Ximénez	PAY-dro him-EN-ez
Pinot Gris / Pinot Grigio	PEE-noe GREE / PEE-noe GREE-jhee-oh
Riesling	REE-sling
Rousanne	ROO-san
Sauvignon Blanc	SAW-vin-yon blawnk
Sémillon	sem-e-YONE
Torrontés	tore-ohn-TACE
Viognier	vee-ohn-YAY

How to say it: red grapes

GRAPE	PRONUNCIATION
Cabernet Franc	kab-er-NAY FRANK
Cabernet Sauvignon	kab-er-NAY SAW-vin-yawn
Carignan	care-in-YAN
Carmenère	car-men-YARE
Cinsault	sin-SO
Dolcetto	dole-CHET-oh
Gamay	GAM-ae
Grenache	gre-NOSH
Malbec	MAL-bek
Merlot	mer-LOW
Mourvèdre	moor-VED-ruh
Nebbiolo	neb-ee-OH-low
Pinot Noir	PEE-noe NWAR
Sangiovese	san-gee-oh-VAY-seh
Syrah / Shiraz	sih-RAH / shi-RAZZ
Tempranillo	tem-pra-NEE-yo
Zinfandel	ZIN-fan-dell

grapes

74 What is the world's most common grape?

At roughly 800,000 acres of plantings—almost all in Spain—the most widely grown wine grape in the world is Airén. A simple white grape, it makes a light, tart wine. The grape's highest calling is as the base for Spanish brandy, but in recent years Spanish farmers have been pulling their Airén and replanting the vineyards with Tempranillo because the latter is higher quality and much more profitable. Italy's Trebbiano (known as Ugni Blanc in France) is the second most grown grape and will likely take over as number one in the next few years.

75 Is wine made only from grapes?

Any sweet juice can make a wine, whether from fruits, grains, flowers, or even more creative ingredients. In many northern states, fruit wines are common, usually from tree fruit or berries. Folks in the southern United States make wine from watermelons, blackberries, and citrus fruits. Flowers such as dandelions are also used. In Asia, the Japanese make sake from rice, and the Chinese use everything from plums to crushed snakes to make wine.

76 What are the different styles?

Chardonnay profiles range along a continuum from the bright, light, and elegant style of Burgundy's Chablis area to the dense, fruity, and rich approach in California. The grapes' ripeness at harvest and the winemaker's use of oak have the largest effect on Chardonnay's final flavors.

The timing of harvest is important because as Chardonnay gets riper, it also gets fruitier, but it loses its acidity. Picked too early, it has abundant acidity but not much fruit flavor. Another factor to consider: the riper the grapes, the higher the alcohol level of the wine (see entry 48). Local tastes play into the equation as well. Here are three examples. In middle and southern Burgundy, Chardonnay is harvested on the early side, partly to protect it from early frosts but also because the French value acidity in wines, since they inevitably drink the wine with food (see entry 208). The northernmost part of Burgundy—Chablis—picks even earlier, so their wines have the most vibrant acidity. Most California Chardonnay is drunk as an aperitif (see entry 203), in which case riper fruit is a positive and too much acidity tastes sour. California's climate allows farmers to really ripen their grapes, which yields fruitier wine with more intense flavors and higher alcohol.

Oak is used very differently, too, in these three regions. In Meursault, for instance, in central Burgundy, winemakers use oak both during fermentation and for aging, which lends a caramel and marzipan aroma to the wines. In Chablis, most winemakers avoid oak to put all the focus on the Chardonnay's flavor. The intensely ripe, fruity flavors of California Chardonnay can stand up to oak's strong aromas, although some wineries produce a lighter-tasting "unoaked" version (see entry 194). Outside these three regions (for instance, in Italy, Chile, or Washington State), the tendency is to make

grapes

Chardonnay in a style that falls somewhere between the engaging intensity of California's version and the structured sophistication of Burgundy's.

See also entries 186, 193, and 196.

77 How to find unoaked Chardonnay

The world wine market is experiencing a backlash against the use of oak for Chardonnay—in spite of centuries of great Chardonnays from Burgundy that were fermented or matured in oak barrels. For people who disliked the recent surge in super-oaky Chards that tasted of burnt toast, cinnamon, vanilla, and even the lumberyard, unoaked Chardonnay has become a hot product. So hot that most wineries that don't oak their Chardonnays find some way to communicate "unoaked" on the bottle, and in most shops the person selling you wine will immediately be able to point you to a few examples. Some of the easier-to-find brands are Iron Horse or Sebastiani from California, and Kim Crawford from New Zealand. And one geographical area specializes in unoaked Chardonnay: Chablis, in France. See also entry 194.

78 Getting high-quality Chardonnay in the States

The best North American Chardonnays are from Washington and California. These are two distinctly different styles, depending on the growing conditions and the winemaker's use of new oak barrels. Hot growing conditions, such as in Napa or Washington's Columbia Valley, tend to produce fruity, fleshy, high-alcohol versions that work well with the caramel and vanilla aromas in new oak barrels. Cooler areas such as Santa Barbara, Carneros, and the west end of the Russian River Valley produce Chardonnay that has more acidity and lower alcohol, and tends to have subtler oak flavors. Of these areas, try focusing on Washington's Columbia Valley and California's Russian River Valley. Washington's Columbia Valley AVA (American Vitacultura Areas) has areas of desert with daytime temperatures in the hundreds, but the dry air allows rapid cooling after dark (a difference called the diurnal temperature swing), so the grapes become intensely fruity yet retain enough acidity to be refreshing. In the Russian River Valley AVA, the style changes as the river moves west because the climate gets progressively cooler. Neither Columbia Valley nor Russian River Valley wines try to be like the lean, austere French Burgundies. Both areas produce robust, American New World–style wines (see Introduction and also entry 211).

RECOMMENDED WINERIES

Washington

Abeja $$$
Canoe Ridge Vineyard $$
Chateau Ste. Michelle
 Ethos $$$
Columbia Crest Grand
 Estates $

California

Buehler Vineyards $
Hess $
Rochioli $$$$
Williams Selyem $$$
Walter Hansel Winery $$

grapes

BOB BETZ, MW

Master of Wine and co-owner of Betz Family Winery

Bob Betz spent the majority of his professional life at Chateau Ste. Michelle, where he was in charge of its two prestige co-owned brands, Col Solare and Eroica. He has traveled widely in wine-growing areas since 1968 and has developed a strong preference for Grenache-based wines. "For our house wines, we drink more Grenache wine than any other single variety, from France, Spain, Italy, the U.S.," he said. "I love the U.S. versions because they are so inviting and extraordinarily drinkable. For whites, our house wines are usually either Grüner Veltliner or Riesling, although we also have the occasional Sauvignon Blanc and Chardonnay. One wine that's worth a splurge, and always a good wine, is Phelps Insignia. Likewise for Ernst Loosen's wines in Germany, which are the ultimate in terms of Riesling expression and penetration." Mr. Betz's number-one recommendation is to drink the wine where it is made. "I'm a real fan of wine tasting in context, like on a trip. That's always the best way to learn."

79 Finding Chardonnay bargains

Chardonnay is grown worldwide, and many areas can come close to the expensive benchmarks of Burgundy and northern California. The more obscure the growing region, in general the lower the price must be to get any market share. If you prefer the generous fruit flavors of Sonoma and Napa Chardonnays, the best places to look are elsewhere along the U.S. Pacific coast. From Santa Barbara north to Monterey, stellar Chardonnays are made, as well as in Washington State (see entry 78). South American Chardonnays are generally quite well made, especially those from Argentina and Chile. Australia's McLaren Vale and Adelaide Hills have gained enough fame that their prices are climbing, but both still produce plenty of bargains. Those who prefer the Burgundy style without the price tag should look for wines from New Zealand's South Island, especially from the areas of Waipara Valley and Central Otago. See also entry 167.

CHARDONNAY BY ANY OTHER NAME

White Burgundy (Bourgogne Blanc), Mâcon Villages, Corton Charlemagne, Pouilly Vinzelles, and Beaujolais Blanc are all code for Chardonnay, as well as:

- Blanc de Blancs Champagne
- Chablis
- Pouilly Fuissé
- Bâtard-Montrachet
- Meursault

80 Why ABC ("Anything but Chardonnay"?)

During the late 1990s and through the first decade of the new millennium, the acronym ABC was common. It had a dual meaning, "Anything but Cabernet" or "Anything but Chardonnay." The viral spread of the term had to do with the dominance of varietal wines from these grapes both in stores and on wine lists, along with just a touch of superciliousness on the part of wine lovers who wanted access to dozens of other worthy varieties. It became code for everything from a straightforward request for something different to a sort of secret handshake indicating the buyer considered himself more sophisticated than someone who relies on the tried and true. In any case, the issue should be about avoiding bad Chardonnay, not all Chardonnay, but ABBC takes longer to say.

81 How to talk Chardonnay

Chardonnay is a chameleon. Plant it in cool climates, such as Chablis, with short sunlight and it will taste of citrus (lemon, grapefruit, lime) or minerals (wet rocks or flint). Add more sun and warmth, as in Napa, and you'll get tropical fruit (pineapple, mango, banana), stone fruit (apricot, peach), tree fruit (apple, pear), and melon (cantaloupe, honeydew). Let it rest in a new oak barrel, and nonfruit aromas pop out of the glass, including coffee, toasted bread, butterscotch, and vanilla. Chards from cool areas can be described generally as steely or austere, whereas those from warmer areas may be big, ripe, or luscious.

82 Where to look for quality Riesling in the States

Riesling loves a cool climate. In the warm areas, it makes a dense wine that can come out flabby (lacking acidity). The closer the grapes get to the cool coast of California, the better. Mendocino's coastal area is just about ideal. In Michigan, the Lake Michigan shore, and in New York State, the Finger Lakes area both produce wonderfully acidic Rieslings. Given the ideal climate of both, and their push for constant improvement, either could end up making the top Rieslings in the United States. Right now, though, the best-quality Riesling is coming from Washington, where the grape grows in the eastern part of the state. See also entry 215.

HINT *Washington proved its preeminence as Riesling country when the famous German winemaker Dr. Ernst Loosen came to the United States looking for an ideal place to make Riesling. He picked eastern Washington and approached Chateau Ste. Michelle about a joint venture. The result, named Eroica, is consistently one of the best Rieslings in America.*

grapes

83   Why does Riesling grow so well in Germany?

Riesling loves Germany's cool weather, a factor that encourages the grape to retain its signature acidity. The threat of a cold early winter wind blowing down the Rhine and Mosel rivers worries grape growers into picking the grapes when they are less ripe than their New World counterparts, who can get the same sugar levels in their fruit by late September that the Germans get in early November. Less ripeness means lower alcohol and more acidity in the wine. German Riesling is one of the world's top food wines because its low alcohol won't interfere with foods' flavors and its high acidity guarantees a palate cleanser with each sip. Similar climatic conditions in Alsace (France) and Austria also make for great Riesling; Alsace's version is denser, higher in alcohol, more fragrant, and stout enough to stand up to pork stews and sauerkraut, while Austria's falls in between the German and French styles. See also entry 149.

RECOMMENDED WINERIES

California
Arrowood $$$
Handley Cellars $$
Navarro Vineyards $$

Michigan
Fenn Valley Vineyards $$
Peninsula Cellars $$$

New York
Dr. Konstantin Frank $$$
Hermann J. Wiemer $$

Washington
Chateau Ste. Michelle
  Eroica $$
Columbia Winery $$
Milbrandt Vineyards $

84 Is Riesling always sweet?

No. Riesling has such abundant acidity that it can taste delicious as a sweet wine, a dry wine, or anywhere in between. For years, New World wine drinkers avoided wines with bracing acidity, so most of what we imported was sweeter wines whose sugars offset acidity's sourness. Germany, France, and Austria have always produced stellar bone-dry Rieslings; they just kept most of them at home. The best New World Riesling producers, especially those in Washington State, are learning to balance acidity and sweetness so that neither is noticeably too powerful. See also entries 186 and 271.

85 What flavors best describe Riesling?

Apples, apples, and apples. Green, red, pink, you name it: apples. After that, lemon, orange peel, flowers (especially paperwhite narcissus), and honey. Some Old World Rieslings can also exhibit lime aromas and aromas of kerosene or wet stones.

86 Is Welschriesling the same as German Riesling?

No, they have nothing in common other than eight letters. Welschriesling is frequently encountered in Eastern European and Austrian wines. It generally makes simple, dry, or off-dry white wines meant to be drunk early and cheap, although a few high-quality examples exist. The exception to the rule is in years when the grapes develop botrytis (see entry 182). Then it becomes a decadently rich and expensive wine, particularly in Austria.

87 Finding Riesling bargains

Because Riesling has yet to achieve its rightful popularity, even the best wines of the Old World are priced below their quality level. The great German wines are labeled Prädikatswein (the older term was Qualitätswein mit Prädikat; see entry 45). While it's possible to find good values in this category, bargains are elusive. If you have a trustworthy seller, ask if they have a killer Qualitätswein bestimmter Anbaugebiete (QbA wine, the next category down in the quality scale). Many of the historic wineries of Germany and Alsace have reputations to protect and are offering very good Rieslings at lower prices. In Alsace, the bargains will be harder to find, although Trimbach's Riesling is both widely available and reasonably priced. Bargain American Rieslings come from Washington State and Mendocino County, California. Chateau Ste. Michelle and Handley are two brands worth trying.

88 Finding quality Sauvignon Blanc in the States

California Sauvignon Blancs tend to have both minerality (like wet flint) and distinct tropical fruit (pineapple and grapefruit) aromas. Several of the California makers use oak barrels to add richness to the wine, referring to the oaked versions as Fumé Blanc (see entry 89). As always, the cooler the weather (that is, the closer to the coast), the more acidic the wine, and vice versa. So in the cold regions of Santa Barbara and the western Russian River Valley, the wines are tart with abundant tropical fruit aromas, while in the warmer areas such as eastern Paso Robles or Napa, the wines tend to be more luscious and exhibit more generous alcohol. And for a wine that truly approaches the minerality of France's Sauvignon Blanc–based Sancerre, there is a tiny estate vineyard in Texas whose terroir seems to match up perfectly. See also entry 216.

RECOMMENDED WINERIES

California

Chateau St. Jean Fumé Blanc $$
Dancing Bull $
Flora Springs Soliloquy $$
Gainey Vineyards $$
Peter Michael Winery $$$

Texas

Spicewood Vineyards $

89 Is Sauvignon Blanc made with oak barrels?

Sometimes. Generally, when the wine is made solely from Sauvignon Blanc—as in Sancerre, New Zealand, Friuli (Italy), and Chile—winemakers eschew oak. The exception is wine with the name "Fumé Blanc." Where there's no law to stipulate, the tradition is that these wines will have been aged in oak. In areas where winemakers blend Sémillon with the Sauvignon Blanc—Bordeaux and Australia—it's more common to age and sometimes even ferment the wine in oak.

SAUVIGNON BLANC BY ANY OTHER NAME

Any of these terms on the label are code for Sauvignon Blanc.

- Sauvignon (Italy)
- Sancerre
- Pouilly Fumé
- Saint-Bris
- Fumé Blanc

90 Where is Sauvignon Blanc grown?

Sauvignon Blanc grows well throughout the world. In the Old World, it does best in France and Italy. In both places the wines are well balanced, light, and elegant. The Old World's polar opposite in style is New Zealand, where the wine has a shocking amount of grapefruity acidity. In the Americas—particularly the Central Coast of California and the Casablanca Valley of Chile—the wine tends to have more tropical fruit aromas, a denser texture, and less acidity. Good examples also come from Australia and South Africa.

OTHER WHITES

91 Getting quality Pinot Grigio in the States

American winemakers usually shoot for one of two styles with this grape. If it is light, fruity, and low in alcohol, they use the Italian name: Pinot Grigio. If it is a more profound wine with higher alcohol and more intense flavor, they use the French term Pinot Gris. California got a head start on the Italian style from immigrants in the last century, but the French style is gaining ground. Oregon is aiming at the French style, and the state may someday be as famed for its Pinot Gris as for its Pinot Noir. See also entry 214.

grapes

RECOMMENDED WINERIES

California
Etude $$$
Palmina $$
MacMurray Ranch $$

Oregon
Chehalem $$
Elk Cove $$
Ponzi $$

92 How to find quality Viognier in the States

Viognier's original home is in Condrieu in the northern part of France's Rhône Valley. There it makes an intense, steely wine with peach aromas and cleansing acidity. In most of the United States, Viognier is grown in hot areas where farmers have to carefully manage the sugar and acids in the grapes to prevent flabby and overly alcoholic wines (see entry 187). Washington's Walla Walla Valley and California's Paso Robles AVA grow the best Viognier on the Pacific coast. Both Virginia and Texas are also home to top-notch versions. In fact, if the United States ever takes a fancy to the grape, Texas could end up as well known for Viognier as Oregon is for Pinot Noir. At a blind tasting a couple of years back for New York wine and food writers, comparing a French Condrieu (about $60 a bottle) to Brennan Vineyards Viognier from Texas ($16), a majority of the writers preferred the Texas wine! See also entry 217.

93   What does Chenin Blanc taste like?

Although the American public has never developed much of a taste for Chenin Blanc, it is a dominant white grape in the French Loire Valley and in South Africa. Part of its appeal lies in its versatility. It can work well as a dry wine, a sweet, long-lived wine, an aromatic fortified wine, or as a dry or off-dry sparkling wine. Its flavors derive mainly from the climate in which it is grown. In cool areas, like the Loire's Anjou, Vouvray, Savennières, and Saumur regions (the regions you'll see on the label) the acidity will be refreshingly high, and the wines may have apple, mineral, honey, and forest undergrowth aromas. In warmer areas the grape tends to grow in huge quantities, increasing the potential for mediocre wines. Two good versions of New World Chenin are from Dry Creek Vineyards in Sonoma and Mulderbosch in South Africa. See also entry 145.

94 Where is Pinot Blanc grown?

Pinot Blanc (known as Pinot Bianco in Italy and Weissburgunder in Germany and Austria) is a beautifully aromatic white wine that is best known in the Old World areas of Alsace (France), Alto Adige, and Friuli (Italy), and throughout Austria. The best versions develop pungent apple and melon aromas. Although the grape makes lovely wine in France and Italy, it is often overshadowed by more renowned grapes such as Pinot Gris, Gewürztraminer, and Riesling. The Italian brand Tiefenbrunner as well as Alsace's Leon Beyer both make good, inexpensive versions. The Austrians celebrate the grape for its ability to make an enchanting late-harvest wine. In the New World, much of the Pinot Blanc goes into a number of jug wines, but in its few great areas such as British Columbia's Okanagan Valley and California's Monterey County, it is used for premium wines. No one in the New World seems to have cracked Pinot Blanc's code like California's Chalone Vineyard, whose version is rich, distinctive, and comparatively long-lived.

95 Finding Cabernet Sauvignon in the States

Where can you get it? The easy answer is Napa. Unfortunately, everyone is in on that secret. That means prices have exploded, and when that happens, opportunists pour in. The result is a minefield of very expensive wines, some of which are overpriced disappointments. There's also a matter of style. Napa Cabs tend to be opulent, jammy, powerful drinks. For someone who loves a more food-friendly French Cabernet, such as Bordeaux, Napa's version will taste like a big fruit bomb. Still, there is something wonderful about the high alcohol, berry flavors, and caramel aromas of a Napa Cab that goes very nicely with a grilled rib-eye steak. Given the fact that some Napa Cabs are pushing the $500 mark on release, the public will soon start looking for more reasonably priced wines. The place that is poised to overtake Napa's hegemony is Washington's Columbia Valley. If the wine comes from one of three AVAs in the Columbia Valley—Horse Heaven Hills, Walla Walla Valley, or Red Mountain—you are almost guaranteed a worthy bottle of wine. And while the prices are high, they are bargains compared to Napa. See also entries 98 and 219.

96 How to talk Cab

Cabernet Sauvignon is popular all over the world both with consumers, who love the flavors and aromas, and winemakers, who love its hardiness and decent yields. Its main requirement is enough sun and warmth to ripen fully. Underripe Cabernet smells like bell peppers and artichokes. When fully ripened, the aromas change to blueberries, cassis, and blackberries (along with black cherries and black plums, this is referred to generically as "black fruit"). Cabernet's thick, pungent skins mean that if the maceration isn't watched carefully, the wine can end up with too many tannins, which gives the wine a mouth-puckering quality. When the tannins are properly balanced—called smooth tannins—they are barely detectible, and then mainly as a light grip as the wine slides along the palate. Cabernet is almost always aged in oak, and it's also frequently fermented in oak barrels, which lends the finished wine butterscotch and vanilla aromas. New World Cabernets, as well as most other New World red wines, are often referred to as "highly extracted," meaning they feel thick in the mouth and are jumping with rich fruit flavors. The wines get the massive extraction from their ripeness at harvest and extended maceration (see entry 185). See also entry 219.

RECOMMENDED WINERIES

Napa
Beringer $-$$$
Chateau Montelena $$$
Flora Springs Winery $$$
Lokoya $$$$

Columbia Valley
Betz Family Winery $$
Cayuse $$$$
Chateau Ste. Michelle $-$$$
Isenhower Cellars $$
Januik Winery $$

97 Why is Cabernet so often a blend?

Cabernet's original home is in Bordeaux, where growers have traditionally had trouble getting the fruit fully ripe. Since most people don't like the aromas or harsh tannin of underripe Cabernet, the time-honored fix has been to blend in other grapes (most often Merlot and Cabernet Franc) to offset Cabernet's weaknesses. In the New World, Cabernet is most often raised in areas where it can attain near perfect ripeness, so it shows up more often as a straight varietal wine.

98 Finding Cabernet bargains

While there are occasional bargains on good Cabernet in both Napa and Bordeaux, the wines are so expensive overall that you'd have to waste a lot of time hunting, time better spent drinking. The best bargains currently come from eastern Washington, California's Central Coast, Coonawarra in Australia, the north island of New Zealand, and Chile. For folks intent on capturing some Old World subtlety and elegance, France's Languedoc region delivers great wines for much less than a Bordeaux. See also entry 147.

99 Are Cabernet Sauvignon and Cabernet Franc related?

Yes. Cabernet Franc and Sauvignon Blanc are the genetic parents of Cabernet Sauvignon. Cab Franc tends to be earlier ripening, lighter in tannin, and somewhat more aromatic than its progeny, and it is often used for blending with Cabernet Sauvignon (see entry 97). It can be found as a varietal wine in Chinon and other areas of the Loire Valley in France, as well as from selected growers in the New World. See also entry 145.

100 Where to look for quality Syrah/Shiraz in the States

American winemakers are still trying to tease out a national style that honors this grape variety. Syrah's popularity in the United States is a relatively new phenomenon, so there's still no true idea of what an American Syrah should taste like. There's the French Rhône style, which is firm, with massive tannic grip, huge concentration, and aromas of blackberries, violets, and black pepper. Then there's the Australian version—where they call the grape Shiraz—which is a big mouthful of decadently fruity wine, all plums, berries, and caramel. Think of it as the classical strains of Debussy versus the hard rock of Australia's AC/DC.

Washington's Cayuse Vineyards and California's Saxum are at the pinnacle of the Syrah trade in the United States, and they couldn't possibly taste more different. While both have the fruit wallop of the Aussie version and a hit of tannin like the Rhône version, they differ substantially in their minerality and earthiness. Unfortunately, both wines are impossible to get unless you wait for years to get on their mailing list (which is worth doing), so try a Cline versus a Columbia Crest Grand Estates. Both will run about $12 and give a fast lesson on the effects of terroir (see entry 190). See also entries 144 and 227.

RECOMMENDED WINERIES

California
Cline $-$$
Copain Wines $$-$$$
Hess Collection $$-$$$
Saxum $$$$
Shafer Vineyards $$$$

Washington
Cayuse Vineyards $$$$
Columbia Crest $-$$$
Isenhower Cellars $$
K Vintners $$-$$$
Reininger Winery $$$

Colorado
Balistreri Vineyards $$

GUY STOUT, MS
Master Sommelier and wine educator

Guy Stout is a widely loved figure in the Court of Master Sommeliers, and though he's tasted some of the world's most renowned wines, he doesn't equate cost and enjoyment. "I have been blessed to enjoy greats like Lafite, Petrus, Romanée-Conti, and Grange," just to mention a few. "Yet my most memorable experience has very little pedigree. I was staying at a youth hostel in Barcelona. I had an empty two-liter plastic water bottle, and one of the people at the front desk sent me to a bodega where I could get it filled with wine. I paid thirty-two cents for two liters of *vino tinto* and I still remember how wonderful it tasted."

So what does he like to drink at home? "We like lighter unoaked whites like Albariño, Riesling, Fiano di Avellino, Grüner, Pinot Grigio, and Sauvignon Blanc. We enjoy drinking a sparkling wine like a Prosecco or a nonvintage Champagne with

grapes

pistachios and crackers and a slice of cheese. For reds, Chianti and Rosso di Montalcino are our current passion, along with ripassos from the Veneto, Barbera from Piedmont, and Nero [d'Avola] from Sicily. It's always fun finding the best wine for the price!"

SHIRAZ BY ANY OTHER NAME

Any of these terms on the label are code for Syrah/Shiraz.

- Hermitage*
- Crozes-Hermitage*
- St.-Joseph*
- Côte-Rôtie*
- Cornas

Syrah is blended with the white Viognier, Marsanne, or Roussanne in these wines.

101 What flavors best describe Syrah/Shiraz?

Syrah's flavors vary widely by terroir (see entry 190). It can be anything from an impressively austere and tannic Rhône Hermitage to an oaky, fruit-laden wine from Australia's Barossa Valley. Syrah will always be inky dark and will have anywhere from muted to explosive blackberry aromas. In varying levels, tar, bacon, black pepper, leather, and earthy aromas are also common.

PINOT NOIR

102 What are the different styles of Pinot Noir?

Pinot Noir is an elegant wine no matter where it's made. The question is: are you getting Cate Blanchett or Angelina Jolie? (Pinot Noir is generally referred to in the feminine.) Those who prefer the lean, cool, and intelligent Ms. Blanchett may go for the style of wine invented in Burgundy and taken up in Oregon and the south island of New Zealand, while fans of Ms. Jolie's earthy, lusty, more direct draw may prefer wines from California, Italy (where the grape is called Pinot Nero), and Australia. Such is its impact that mostly romantic terms are used to describe Pinot Noir, phrases like "roses strewn across fields of wild strawberries with just a hint of your lover's postprandial aromas."

grapes

103 Getting quality Pinot in the States

Duels have been fought over less contentious subjects. People who love Burgundy wine gravitate to Oregon Pinot Noirs. In fact, when the Drouhin family, one of the most famous of Burgundy winemakers, decided they wanted to start a winery in the United States, they went straight to Oregon's Willamette (pronounced Will-AHM-ette) Valley and pronounced the terroir the equal of Burgundy's. Oregon's style has not only plenty of fruit but also the type of intense acidity that announces it is truly a wine to drink with food. Of course, the French, who wouldn't dream of drinking wine (other than Champagne) as an aperitif, would approve. California's winemakers create equally elegant wines but with a bit more generosity in the fruit. Pinot Noir prefers a cool climate, so California areas such as the Russian River Valley, Monterey Bay, the Central Coast just north of Santa Barbara, and the Carneros AVA at the southern tip of Napa and Sonoma are ideal places. See also entries 122 and 225.

RECOMMENDED WINERIES

California
Domaine Carneros $$
Etude $$-$$$$
Kistler $$$$
MacMurray Ranch $$
Rex Goliath $
Rochioli Vineyards
  $$$-$$$$
Williams Selyem $$$$

Oregon
Benton Lane $$-$$$
Domaine Serene $$$
Domaine Drouhin $$$
King Estate $-$$$$
Ponzi $$-$$$$
Sokol-Blosser $$$

Any of these terms on the label is code for Pinot Noir.

- Pinot Nero (Italy)
- Spätburgunder (Germany)
- Blauburgunder (Austria, Switzerland)
- Burgundy/Bourgogne

104 Finding Burgundy bargains

Bargains exist everywhere, even among the infamously posh Pinot Noirs from the Côte d'Or of Burgundy, where a single bottle of Domaine de la Romanée-Conti "Romanée-Conti" wine can run as much as $10,000. It's best to start with a reputable négociant, a company that produces wine from grapes bought from various growers in an area (Louis Jadot, Joseph Drouhin, and Louis Latour are good choices). There is a greater likelihood that you'll get good value your for money buying Burgundy wines produced by a négociant of long standing. For instance, Louis Jadot's Jacques Lardier is a masterly winemaker capable of making top-notch wines at many levels, whether it's a $500 Bonne Marres or a $30 Fixin. Pick a comfortable price range and try a few wines. Remember, Burgundies are named after their location, not their grape (see entry 61), so when you find one you like, try another négociant's version from the same location to see whose you prefer.

grapes

HINT *In the United States the best bargains tend to cluster around California's Central Coast from Santa Barbara County through Paso Robles and up to Monterey. And while Pinots from both Australia and New Zealand have shown rapid price growth, there are still bargains available. Try focusing your search in South Australia or Canterbury, New Zealand.*

MERLOT

105 Where to look for quality Merlot in the States

Merlot likes the same growing conditions as Cabernet Sauvignon, so you'll frequently find them camped together. In both California and Washington, the best versions tend to be high in alcohol, round, plummy, and rich, but lacking the structure of Bordeaux's multi-thousand-dollar Pomerols. Merlot isn't as attached to one place as Cabernet is to Napa. Some of the best Merlots are from Washington's Columbia Valley. The trio of Horse Heaven Hills, Walla Walla Valley, and Red Mountain are the AVAs to look for on the labels. Good to great Merlot comes from all over California, from Paso Robles all the way up to Mendocino, with a special emphasis on Napa and Sonoma. See also entry 223.

106 Why did Merlot become unpopular?

Merlot went through a period of enormous popularity in the 1980s and 1990s. To meet the demand, a lot of farmers tried to expand what they had by planting new vines and by forcing the grape vines they already had to produce extra fruit. The result was a huge run of insipid, overpriced wines notable for having been "made" in the winery rather than the vineyard—and the winery's work focused mostly on adding sugar, acidity, and oak to compensate for badly grown grapes. It became fashionable for connoisseurs to turn up their nose at these wines, a fact translated into fiction in Paul Giamatti's memorable rant in the movie *Sideways*. Thankfully, Merlot's brush with ostracism has left it less expensive and almost solely in the hands of farmers and winemakers who care. All widely available wines go through popularity cycles (see entry 80). Hopefully, during its next wave of popularity, Merlot will fare better.

PAUL GREGUTT

Author of *Washington Wines & Wineries: The Essential Guide,*
Northwest Editor for *Wine Enthusiast, Seattle Times* columnist
www.paulgregutt.com

Paul Gregutt ranks as one of the reigning experts of the
Washington wine world. His advice on Washington wine was
succinct: "You have to come here and visit the wineries," he said.
"The vast majority of the wines up here can only be had at the
winery or at a local shop. That being said, for wines that have
more national distribution, Kung Fu Girl by Charles Smith Wines
or Randall Grahm's Pacific Rim are both great Rieslings."

His passionate pick for Washington's best grape is Merlot.
"Washington Merlots can be great. I mean, starting at eight
dollars, the Columbia Crest wines are excellent. And in terms of
the Leonetti at eighty dollars—and I don't think anyone in the
New World, maybe in the whole world, does better Merlot than
Leonetti. We do well with Cabernet, too, especially the Sineann
Old Block Cabernet from Champoux Vineyard and Betz's Cabernet
from Ciel du Cheval Vineyard. But you don't have to spend a lot of
money. Both Columbia Crest and Milbrandt put out great wines in
the lower price ranges."

107 What flavors best describe Grenache?

Once the most planted red wine grape on earth, Grenache has now lost the marketing war to Cabernet Sauvignon and Merlot. In its four best locations (the Rhône, Priorat, South Australia, and Paso Robles) the grape is rich, fruity, and spicy. Because it lacks palate-cleansing acidity and tannin, it is generally blended with other grapes capable of lending some structure, such as Syrah, Carignan, and Mourvèdre. Grenache is also seldom made as a single-varietal wine because of its tendency to oxidize quickly. On its own it tastes of raspberries, black cherries, and black pepper. Grenache makes a spectacular rosé wine that most often has flavors of strawberry and black pepper. See also entry 220.

108 What's so special about Zinfandel?

Zinfandel is extravagantly fruity, rich, and highly alcoholic. Winemakers have noticed Zinfandel's popularity and have been pushing the intensity higher and higher, with alcohol levels of 15 percent, ultrafull body, concentrated dark fruit flavors, and lots of caramel barrel character now the norm.

The vast majority of the Zinfandel in the world is grown in the United States, and Americans have a fondness for the grape. Plant Zinfandel where the weather is hot and dry, steal its leaves, and cut off most of its grape clusters, and it rewards the winemaker with luscious juice. The hot lowlands of Napa, Sonoma, and Paso

grapes

Robles offer some of the best growing conditions. For those who love the grape, both Ridge and Rosenblum offer a panoply of Zins, which allows you to try several wines from the same winemaker and will amply prove the effects of terroir (see entry 190). The Oregon contingent, sitting out in the hot eastern deserts, are showing incredible promise, too. The problem is that few growers ever thought of Oregon as Zinfandel country, so little is planted—but that is sure to change. See also entry 229.

RECOMMENDED WINERIES

California
Cline $-$$
Rancho Zabaco $-$$$
Ridge Vineyards $$-$$$
Rosenblum Cellars $-$$$
St. Francis $$-$$$

Oregon
Sineann $$$
Troon Vineyard $$$$

109 How can I expand my tastes?

Use this chart to discover the less-known grapes of the world, based on what you already like. Read down the left side for your favorite grapes, then read across the row to find recommendations of others that might interest you, country by country.

. . . try these

If you like these . . .	FRANCE	ITALY	SPAIN	SOUTH AMERICA	OTHER
CHARDONNAY	Pinot Blanc	Soave (primarily Garganega grape) or Grillo	Albariño		Sémillon (Australia)
SAUVIGNON BLANC		Gavi (Cortese grape) or Fiano			dry Grüner Veltliner (Austria)
RIESLING	Muscat, Chenin Blanc (off-dry to sweet)	Arneis		Torrontés (Argentina)	semisweet Grüner Veltliner (Austria)
MERLOT		Valpolicella (a blend of three grapes) or Nero d'Avola	Tempranillo	Bonarda (Argentina), Carmenère (Chile)	
PINOT NOIR	Cabernet Franc				
SYRAH/ SHIRAZ		Aglianico, Nero d'Avola			Xynomavro (Greece), Dão (a blend; Portugal)
ZINFANDEL	Carignan	Primitivo		Malbec (Argentina)	
CABERNET SAUVIGNON		Barolo (Nebbiolo grape)			

Wine Regions

Here we cover the main wine regions of the world, describing the grapes they grow best and what their most famous wines are. Have an interest in the cuisine of a specific country? Read on to find matching wines as well as information about regional growing conditions, the best grapes, and most dependable wineries. This is also where to find the answers to general questions about a region. Like, what "classified growth" in Bordeaux means. Or why did Yellow Tail get so popular?

110 What are the top five wine-producing countries?

France, Italy, and Spain are the largest producers, although their production numbers are diminishing, a fact most winemakers attribute to Europe's newly stringent drinking and driving laws. The United States and Argentina follow a distant fourth and fifth. China doesn't share its figures. It is guessed to be in sixth place, but Chinese health officials are trying to get the populace interested in the health benefits of drinking red wine, so there is little doubt China will soon be in the top five.

111 Is wine made in every U.S. state?

Yes. California, New York, Washington, and Oregon account for 97.8 percent of U.S. wine production, but every state now has a winery, and many of them are taking advantage of the agritourism trade (see entry 314). Many northern states do not have a thriving grape-growing industry, so they make wine from grape juice or must (juice along with the pulp, skins, seeds, and stems) purchased from another state. To find wineries in your state, check out www.allamericanwineries.com.

112 What are the top five wine-producing states?

This is a contentious issue. Everyone agrees that California is first. No other state even comes close. New York and Washington follow, and these, too, have huge wine industries. In fact, in the most recent report from the Tax and Trade Bureau, California, New York, and Washington account for more than 96 percent of the wine produced in the United States. And as big and respected as fourth-place Oregon is, it accounts for less than 1 percent of America's production. The problem comes with fifth place. Texas, Virginia, Pennsylvania, New Jersey, and Ohio all claim that spot.

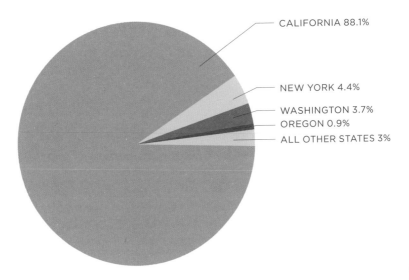

CALIFORNIA 88.1%

NEW YORK 4.4%

WASHINGTON 3.7%
OREGON 0.9%
ALL OTHER STATES 3%

Does not total 100% due to rounding.
Source: Persis J. Ramroth, Industry Analyst, Trade Analysis and Enforcement Division, Alcohol and Tobacco Tax and Trade Bureau, 2009

113 What is an AVA?

An AVA is an American Viticultural Area, a designation by
the federal government that the area has definable geographical
boundaries and that the land within is somehow special in terms of
its impact on winemaking. The AVA system is much less rigorous
than Europe's Appellation of Origin system (see entry 45), which
also designates types of grapes that may be grown, vineyard yields,
and several other specifics aimed at managing quality. AVAs range in
size from something larger than the state of Rhode Island to an area
as small as a single winery, and sometimes overlap.

what's a wine lover to do?

114 Why is California the primary wine state?

California is blessed with the perfect climate range, ideal soil, the best viticulture and enology university in the country, and a population that loves to drink wine. Spanish and Italian immigrants to California brought centuries of tradition along with cuttings from their vines. Other than the temporary setback of Prohibition, California's wine industry has thrived and maintained its spot as the top wine-growing area in the country. The state has every type of climate imaginable, so all types of grapes can find someplace in California to grow successfully. But Washington and Oregon are nipping at California's quality monarchy, and they have the same division of cool maritime and dry, hot inland climates that has been California's weapon in the international wine wars. Of course, that competition is keeping California winemakers on their toes, which is good for all of us.

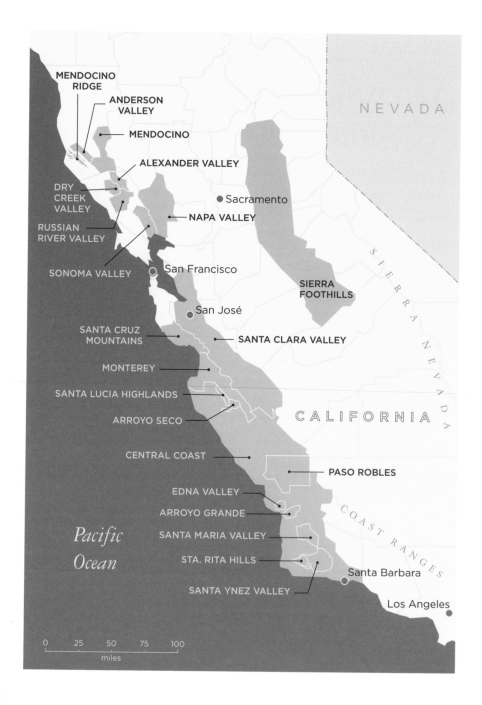

MENDOCINO
RIDGE

ANDERSON
VALLEY

MENDOCINO

ALEXANDER VALLEY

DRY
CREEK
VALLEY

RUSSIAN
RIVER VALLEY

SONOMA VALLEY

NAPA VALLEY

● Sacramento

NEVADA

SIERRA

NEVADA

San Francisco

SANTA CRUZ
MOUNTAINS

MONTEREY

SANTA LUCIA HIGHLANDS

ARROYO SECO

CENTRAL COAST

EDNA VALLEY

ARROYO GRANDE

SANTA MARIA VALLEY

STA. RITA HILLS

SANTA YNEZ VALLEY

San José

SANTA CLARA VALLEY

SIERRA
FOOTHILLS

CALIFORNIA

PASO ROBLES

COAST RANGES

Santa Barbara

Los Angeles

*Pacific
Ocean*

0   25   50   75   100
miles

what's a wine lover to do?

115 Where to look for California whites

While white grapes grow throughout the state, it is the cooler coastal areas that lend the requisite snappy acidity that rescues potentially soft grapes such as Chardonnay and Viognier. Even wines with generous acidity such as Riesling and Sauvignon Blanc do better in the western part of the state. The Central Coast is good for Chardonnay, Sauvignon Blanc, Viognier, Pinot Blanc, Marsanne, and Roussanne. In Sonoma, Chardonnay reigns, although the Russian River Valley is also good for Pinot Grigio. Western Mendocino has a much cooler climate and therefore shines with Riesling and Gewürztraminer. Most of Napa's prime white grapes were long ago pulled in favor of Cabernet Sauvignon, but those willing to make the investment create some gorgeous Sauvignon Blanc. All that being said, the area within seventy-five miles of the coast and between Santa Barbara and Mendocino is such perfect grape country that farmers can raise pretty much whatever they like.

WHAT ARE THE BEST-QUALITY CALIFORNIA SPARKLING WINES?

Domaine Carneros
Domaine Chandon
Gloria Ferrer
Iron Horse Vineyards
J Vineyards
Korbel

Laetitia Vineyard
Mumm Napa
Piper Sonoma
Roederer Estate
Scharffenberger Cellars
Schramsberg

116 Napa versus Sonoma: what's the difference?

For years, wine lovers looked upon Sonoma as Napa's country bumpkin cousin. Sonoma had farmers, but Napa had *winemakers.* Consumers in the know loved this dichotomy because it meant that Sonoma's best wines were available for a fraction of the cost of Napa's. But, of course, Sonoma's winemakers and grape growers took umbrage at the characterization and at the loss of revenue. Things have changed. Sonoma's Russian River Valley is home to many of the best Pinot Noirs in America (although the Oregon contingent would disagree; see entry 121). Ditto for Sonoma's Chardonnays. Sonoma's Dry Creek area also produces renowned Zinfandels. The Alexander Valley's Cabernet Sauvignon and Merlot don't get the press of its Napa brethren, but they frequently beat Napa's when you consider the ratio of cost to quality. And for those who like pineappley Sauvignon Blanc, Sonoma is home to some of the best in the land. On the other hand, Napa's reputation is well earned. Almost every grape grows beautifully in some part of Napa; whether it's the cool Carneros in the south or the hot lowlands in Oakville, disparate grapes from sensitive Pinot Noir to hardy Cabernet Sauvignon grow happily.

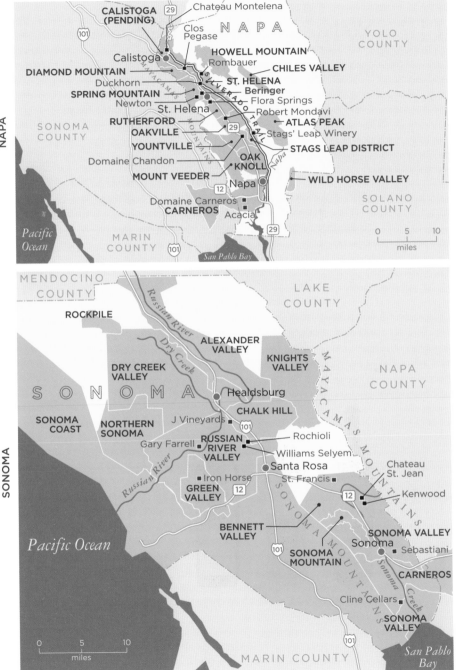

NAPA

CALISTOGA
(PENDING)

Chateau Montelena

N A P A

YOLO
COUNTY

Clos
Pegase

Calistoga

HOWELL MOUNTAIN

Rombauer

CHILES VALLEY

DIAMOND MOUNTAIN

Duckhorn

ST. HELENA

SPRING MOUNTAIN

Beringer

Newton

Flora Springs

St. Helena

Robert Mondavi

RUTHERFORD

ATLAS PEAK

OAKVILLE

Stags' Leap Winery

YOUNTVILLE

STAGS LEAP DISTRICT

Domaine Chandon

OAK
KNOLL

MOUNT VEEDER

Napa

WILD HORSE VALLEY

SOLANO
COUNTY

Domaine Carneros

CARNEROS

Acacia

SONOMA
COUNTY

MACACAMAS

SILVERADO TRAIL

MOUNTAINS

Napa

Pacific
Ocean

MARIN
COUNTY

San Pablo Bay

0   5   10
miles

SONOMA

MENDOCINO
COUNTY

LAKE
COUNTY

ROCKPILE

Russian River

Dry Creek

ALEXANDER
VALLEY

KNIGHTS
VALLEY

DRY CREEK
VALLEY

NAPA
COUNTY

S O N O M A

Healdsburg

CHALK HILL

SONOMA
COAST

NORTHERN
SONOMA

J Vineyards

Gary Farrell

RUSSIAN
RIVER
VALLEY

Rochioli

Williams Selyem

Chateau
St. Jean

Russian River

Santa Rosa

Iron Horse

St. Francis

Kenwood

GREEN
VALLEY

BENNETT
VALLEY

SONOMA VALLEY

Sonoma

Sebastiani

SONOMA
MOUNTAIN

CARNEROS

Cline Cellars

SONOMA
VALLEY

Pacific Ocean

MARIN COUNTY

San Pablo
Bay

0   5   10
miles

MAYACAMAS MOUNTAINS

SONOMA MOUNTAINS

Sonoma Creek

117 Why are Napa Cabs so expensive?

Anyone growing Cabernet Sauvignon in Napa should create a symbolic reliquary to André Tchelistcheff, Robert Mondavi, and Warren Winiarski and genuflect nightly. These men worked hard to let the world know what a great place Napa was for making Bordeaux-style wines. Tchelistcheff was a renowned wine consultant who placed his imprimatur on the land in the 1940s; Mondavi was a tireless champion of the area, talking it up all over the world; and Winiarski took his Cabernet to the "Paris Tasting" in 1976 and proved that California wine could go toe-to-toe with the best and win.

Once the quality was known, wealthy Californians looking for a little wine-country lifestyle began to buy Napa land, pushing prices in the valley over $300,000 per acre. In a good year, that $300,000 acre will produce 2,400 bottles. Of course, you can amortize the cost of land over a long period, but there are finance, production, and marketing costs on top of that. The more important question becomes, is the wine worth it?

118 Who are the Rhône Rangers?

Back in the 1980s, when America seemed interested only in Chardonnay, Merlot, and Cabernet Sauvignon, a few renegade wineries, particularly Bonny Doon Vineyards, Qupé, and Joseph Phelps, decided to expand the boundaries and pay more attention to the main grapes of the Rhône Valley in France: Syrah, Grenache, Marsanne, Roussanne, Viognier, and Mourvèdre. They dubbed themselves the Rhône Rangers and swore fealty to Rhône wines such as Châteauneuf-du-Pape, Côte-Rôtie, and Hermitage. The movement gained strength when importer Robert Haas joined with France's Perrin family, owners of Rhône stalwart Château de Beaucastel, to create Tablas Creek winery in Paso Robles. Today, the Rhône Rangers have attracted three hundred other wineries to their cause and become a force in American wine making. See also entry 144.

119 What are California's up-and-coming regions?

Almost all of California is capable of growing grapes, but some areas that aren't yet famous are growing world-class fruit. In the northern part of the state, near Sacramento, the Sierra Foothills AVA has average high temperatures in the nineties, but those highs make ideal growing conditions for extracted, high-alcohol, behemoth Zinfandel and Syrah, perfect for folks who love everything big. South of San Francisco, the Santa Cruz Mountains are geographically craggy and tough to work, but a few diligent winemakers have cracked the code. Ridge regularly pierces the $100-a-bottle mark with its long-lived Cabernet-based Monte Bello, and its Santa Cruz

Mountains wine is a somewhat more affordable option from the area. Mount Eden Vineyards is at a higher elevation in a perfect spot for Chardonnay and Pinot Noir. Just to the south, most of the Monterey Bay AVA is flatter and warmer, but even its highlands are warm and sunny. It excels in riper versions of Chardonnay from makers such as Mer Soleil and Chalone.

Still farther south, Paso Robles's wine business is booming. On the east side of Highway 101, the flat ground, sunshine, and abundant heat lead to huge, dense, high-alcohol wines. Cabernet, Merlot, Zinfandel, Syrah, Chardonnay, Petite Sirah, and Sauvignon Blanc all do well in this area. The west side is in the Santa Lucia range and the climate is much cooler, which yields acidity and subtle flavors. Between the high-quality wines and the fact that the area is still relatively undiscovered, Paso Robles has the best wine values in California. And in the cool Santa Barbara area, home to the Santa Maria Valley, Santa Ynez Valley, and Santa Rita Hills AVAs there are dozens of small family wineries producing tasty wines from Pinot Noir, Chardonnay, Syrah, Grenache, and Sauvignon Blanc.

120 What's "Meritage"?

It is a term owned by the Meritage Association to describe American wines based on the Bordeaux blend of grapes. Back in 1988, a few winemakers were looking for a distinctive term that could be used industry-wide for these wines. In Bordeaux, they blend Cabernet Sauvignon, Merlot, Cabernet Franc, Malbec, and Petit Verdot and label it according to maker and location. American winemakers have always created Bordeaux blends, but haven't had a way to express that fact on the label, since the word *Bordeaux* is restricted to French wine from that region, and under U.S. law, a grape name can't be used on the front label of the bottle unless at least 75 percent of the wine is made from that grape. Now American producers can pay a licensing fee to the Meritage Association to use this relatively recognizable term.

121 What is Oregon's signature grape?

Pinot Noir. In 1979, the late David Lett of Eyrie Vineyards boldly went to France for the Wine Olympics and his 1975 South Block Reserve (the winery's last bottle is pictured below) was the world's top-scoring Pinot Noir. Understandably, this was a cause célèbre among the French, who believe in the natural supremacy of Burgundy. The following year, Burgundian Robert Drouhin challenged Lett to a rematch. This time Lett placed second, but Drouhin was impressed enough to come to Oregon and buy land. Since then, Oregon, especially the Willamette Valley, is synonymous with Pinot. See also entry 103.

LESLIE SBROCCO

Author of *The Simple and Savvy Wine Guide* and *Wine for Women* and an Emmy Award–winning television personality
www.lesliesbrocco.com

Leslie Sbrocco is an outrageously funny person to share wine with, but behind that humor is a staggering amount of knowledge. And though she likes to say that her favorite wine is the one in the glass in front of her because she gets to drink it, if she had her druthers, she'd be drinking a 1919 Château Haut-Brion. But she does mention a strategy: "Since I can't drink Haut-Brion regularly (and who can?), I pick up easy-drinking house wines to share with neighbors and friends. These days I find myself looking for Latin lovers such as hearty Argentine Malbec, spicy Chilean Carmenère, and a racy white called Albariño from Spain. But, I also gravitate toward the elegant whites from Alsace in France, the beautiful Pinot Noirs from Oregon, and lusciously sweet tawny ports from Portugal. Oh, did I mention rosé Champagne is my ideal wine to begin and end an evening? As the song says—love the one you're with."

122 What makes Washington a state to watch?

Washington has perfect growing conditions, an excited bunch of young winemakers willing to take chances, and a supportive state government. Most of the wine is grown east of the Cascade Mountains, where the weather is hot in the day (over a hundred degrees in the summer) and drops forty to fifty degrees at night. Grapes love to work all day and rest at night, so that diurnal temperature swing is ideal. Most of the area sees sparse rainfall (see picture at left of Red Mountain AVA). All this warm sun and precise irrigation leads to some of the country's richest, most highly concentrated wines.

Right now, Washington winemakers are concentrating on Chardonnay, Cabernet Sauvignon, Merlot, Riesling, Syrah, and Cabernet Franc, but they are still searching for their best grapes. Washington Syrahs are richer than the Rhône version and more potent than Australia's. Most places in the United States have trouble getting Cab Franc ripe enough to taste like something other than bell peppers, but the Washington version is a luxurious wine. As for Riesling, German wine superstar Dr. Ernst Loosen, a man who knows everything about the grape, picked Washington for his first foray into American wine. Others will follow. See also entry 321.

wine regions · washington

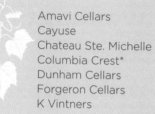

THIRTEEN WONDERFUL WASHINGTON WINERIES

Amavi Cellars
Cayuse
Chateau Ste. Michelle
Columbia Crest*
Dunham Cellars
Forgeron Cellars
K Vintners

L'Ecole No 41
Novelty Hill
Pepper Bridge Winery
Powers Winery
Reinenger
Seven Hills

Consistently the best budget wines in the United States

123 What are some top wines from other states?

Every state in the country produces wine (see entry 111), but these dozen superb producers from six states will give you a place to start investigating U.S. wines off the beaten track.

TOP-NOTCH OUT-OF-THE-WAY WINERIES

Colorado	Boulder Creek Winery, Guy Drew Vineyards
Michigan	Chateau Grand Traverse, Peninsula Cellars
New Mexico	Black Mesa Winery, Gruet
New York	Dr. Konstantin Frank, Paumanok Vineyards
Texas	Becker Vineyards, Fall Creek Vineyards
Virginia	Blenheim Vineyards, Horton Vineyards

124 What are Argentina's best-known grapes?

Argentina's greatest wine is made from Malbec, originally a Bordeaux grape, which grows to perfection around the northwestern city of Mendoza. Argentine Malbec is a rich, chewy, full-bodied wine with tooth-staining fruit that still somehow seems elegant. It is also relatively unknown, so Malbecs are still great bargains. Torrontés is the most commonly grown white wine, and its floral fragrance, velvety mouthfeel, and delicious acidity should appeal to wine lovers all over the world. Argentina's winemakers are always trying to perfect popular international grapes such as Chardonnay, Cabernet Sauvignon, and Merlot. Some wineries have had great success and are experimenting with pricing their wines at the level of French wines.

125 Any up-and-coming regions to watch?

Eighty-five percent of Argentina's exported wine comes from grapes grown in the Mendoza area, but two areas have a lot of potential. The Rio Negro region of Patagonia is far south and has as much as sixteen hours per day of sunshine during the growing season. A trickle of important winemakers are starting to plant there. North of Mendoza, the high-altitude area of Salta is already making excellent Torrontés and Cabernet Sauvignon. See also entry 322.

EIGHT GREAT ARGENTINES

Achaval Ferrer
Altos Las Hormigas
Bodegas Salentein *(all three lines)*
Bodega Catena Zapata *(all four lines)*
Bodega Familia Zuccardi *(all four lines)*
Cheval des Andes
Viña Cobos

126 What are the best-known regions to look for?

Australians are experimenting with grapes all over the country, though in general grapes do best in the southern half, along the coasts. Here is a list of Australia's best regions as well as a few of their top grapes and producers.

CREAM OF THE AUSTRALIAN CROP

Region	Specialties	Producers to look for
Hunter Valley	Chardonnay and Sémillon	Margan Family, McWilliam's, Tyrrell's Wines
Barossa Valley	Shiraz	Penfolds, Peter Lehmann, Torbreck
McLaren Vale	Chardonnay and Grenache	d'Arenberg, Wirra Wirra
Coonawarra	Cabernet Sauvignon	Balnaves of Coonawarra, Parker Coonawarra Estate
Adelaide Hills	Pinot Noir and Chardonnay	Ashton Hills Vineyard, Henschke
Rutherglen	stickies (see entry 131)	R. L. Buller Premium Fine, Chambers Rosewood Vineyards

127 Where to find hidden gems

Tiny Kangaroo Island is making very promising Cabernet Sauvignon. Western Australia is huge, covering almost a third of the country. Its most interesting wine area is Margaret River, home to some of Australia's best Cabernet Sauvignon, Sémillon, and Sauvignon Blanc. Tasmania is verdant, with enough rain to assure the island plenty of water to make excellent Chardonnay and Pinot Noir.

SEVEN GEMS FROM DOWN UNDER

Cape d'Estaing
 (Kangaroo Island)
Ferngrove Vineyards (WA)
Goundrey (WA)
Houghton Wines (WA)

Leeuwin Estate (WA)
Pipers Brook Vineyard
 (Tasmania)
Pirie Tasmania (Tasmania)

128 Any Australian bargains to be found?

Due to exchange rates and aggressive backing by the government, Australian wines are relative bargains in the marketplace. Unfortunately, winemakers there have fought an uphill battle against consumer perception that cheap Australian wine is less desirable than its European counterparts. The truth is, especially in the $10 to $20 price range, Australian wines generally offer some of the best bargains in the world. While Australia makes competitive versions of standards such as Chardonnay, Cabernet, and Merlot, its strongest offerings relative to the worldwide competition in that price range are Shiraz (as well as anything blended with Shiraz), Grenache, Sémillon, and stickies (see entry 131). A few brands you can always trust are Peter Lehmann, d'Arenberg, Penfolds, and R. L. Buller & Son.

129 What white wines come from Australia?

Australia has every imaginable climate and grows all of the popular white grapes. Chardonnay dominates all the other white varieties. In fact, if you added together all of the Australian white wines other than Chardonnay, it would just about equal the amount of Chardonnay grown. Chardonnay lovers can find good wine all over the country, but the Adelaide Hills offers some of the best. Aussies prize Sémillon—especially from the Hunter Valley—but since most of the world doesn't know what a varietal Sémillon wine tastes like, the Aussies end up getting to keep most of it for themselves. Look for Peter Lehmann's and Wyndham Estate's versions if you want to try it. Sauvignon Blanc from McLaren Vale and Riesling from Clare Valley are also well respected.

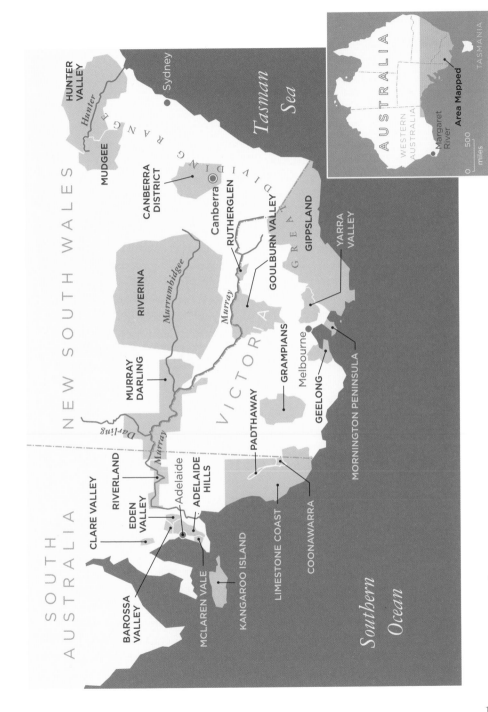

wine regions · *australia*

EVAN GOLDSTEIN, MS

Author, founding board member of the Court of Master Sommeliers, and president and chief education officer of Full Circle Wine Solutions, Inc.

Evan Goldstein is widely considered one of the wine world's great experts on pairing food and wine. And while his job allows him access to a never-ending array of valuable and obscure wines, he does have a few bargain suggestions. "I have a few go-to wineries that are dependably good. Navarro in Mendocino's Anderson Valley is right up at the very top and has been consistent for decades," he mentions. "In Australia, I love D'Arenberg's range and consistency. Finally, for the money, you'd be hard pressed to find a winery that does a better job year in and year out than Chateau Ste. Michelle . . . really. We also drink (more due to my wife) a lot of Spanish wine, especially the great values from Rioja, Galicia, Jumilla, and La Mancha, as well as Washington State wines and in Rhônes, value wines like Côtes du Ventoux and Côtes du Rhône. The wines of Alsace are also great value for the money."

130 Why is Yellowtail so popular?

This is a question that will form the core of more than a few MBA case studies. It isn't the first, but it is the most successful venture into branding in the wine business. The wine is made by what was a small winery owned by the Casella family. They recognized there was a need in the United States for oaky, fruity wines in the $8 range. Making it was easy enough, but how to get it recognized in a sea of other wines? In 2001, they bought a label design from Barbara Harkness, a designer in Adelaide, Australia. The cute kangaroo on the label caught on almost immediately. The Casellas made a first run of 25,000 cases to try out the market. By the next year, they sold more than two million cases and today they are selling more than nine million cases annually. Yellowtail has a 13.4 percent market share of all imported wines in the United States. The brand's success fostered a surge in the use of "critter labels" on wines, as consumers learned to recognize their wine by the easy-to-spot animal on the label.

131   What are "stickies"?

"Sticky" is the generic term for Australia's famous fortified dessert wines. Prime examples come from two grapes: Muscat Blanc à Petits Grains and Muscadelle. Aromas can range from floral to raisins and orange zest to caramel. The Australians borrow sherry's solera system of mixing vintages (see entry 164) and Madeira's warm storage (see entry 161), but come up with something completely different from either precedent. With the exception of Pedro Ximénez sherry (see entry 165), Australia's stickies from the Rutherglen area are the greatest sweet wine bargains on earth. Granted, some push over $200 for a half-bottle, but R. L. Buller (the "Premium Fine" line) and the Chambers Rosewood Vineyards stickies give you 95 percent of the quality at less than $15. See also entry 243.

132 What are the two main wine regions in Canada?

One is in Ontario along the Niagara Peninsula just west of Niagara Falls. Ontario is mainly known for its decadent ice wines (see entry 133) but also produces dry table wine, including Riesling, Chardonnay, Cabernet Franc, Merlot, and Pinot Noir. The other main area is British Columbia's growing region around the Okanagan Valley (shown here), located on the Canadian border with Washington, placed longitudinally between Yakima and Spokane and extending north for 120 miles. The Okanagan is on the same latitude as Bordeaux. The region produces terrific Pinot Blanc with the density of a California Chardonnay, the acidity of an Italian white, and all the lovely pear aromas expected from an Alsace Pinot Blanc. The other Alsace varieties grown in the Okanagan Valley are Pinot Gris and Gewürztraminer, and while they don't scale the heights like the Pinot Blanc, the best versions are marvelous. There is also very good Merlot, Pinot Noir, Cabernet Sauvignon, and Chardonnay.

133 What is ice wine?

Ice wine can be made only when the grapes have stayed on the vine long enough to be fully frozen, and making it is a difficult and dangerous business. The temperature has to get below seventeen degrees Fahrenheit, and the grapes are usually picked in the middle of the night in December and January to make sure they remain frozen until they are pressed. With the water content of the grapes bound up in ice, the juice is correspondingly sweeter, and the result is an extraordinary richness in the wine, and in the best examples, enough acidity to make the sugar and fruit dance on your palate. The key, of course, is that the grapes must have high sugar levels before they freeze, and be fully ripe but not rotten, a difficult balance. Riesling is the grape most often used for ice wine, but it is also made from Vidal Blanc, Gewürztraminer, Chardonnay, Pinot Gris, Cabernet Franc, and Merlot. Ontario is the most consistent producer of ice wine (trademarked as "Icewine") because the producers of the region have focused on it as a specialty. Germany and Austria make the most famous and expensive ice wines (*Eiswein* in German), but they can be made anywhere ripe grapes freeze on the vine.

TOP TEN CANADIAN WINERIES

British Columbia
Burrowing Owl
CedarCreek Estate Winery
Hawthorne Mountain Vineyards
Inniskillin Okanagan Vineyards
Sandhill Wines

Ontario
Cave Spring Cellars
Daniel Lenko Estate Winery
Inniskillin Niagara Peninsula
  Vineyards
Sanson Estate Winery
Thirty Bench Wine Makers

134 Does Chile have a signature grape?

Yes, Carmenère. The country's wine business is more than four hundred years old, but it wasn't until the nineteenth century that French wine stock began to pour into the country. From then on, the standard international grapes—Chardonnay, Sauvignon Blanc, Cabernet, and Merlot—dominated the landscape. The winemakers planted hundreds of acres of what they thought was French Merlot, only to find out later (much later, in the 1990s) that it was really Carmenère, a grape that became virtually extinct in Europe following the phylloxera epidemic (see entry 191). The grape thrives in Chile, which, since it has most of the world's supply, has worked to perfect it.

EIGHT EASY-TO-FIND CHILEAN WINERIES

Almaviva
Casa Lapostolle
Concha y Toro
Cousiño Macul

Errazuriz
Montes
Santa Rita
Veramonte

ACONCAGUA
VALLEY

Aconcagua

■ Errázuriz

Valparaíso

CASABLANCA
VALLEY

■ Veramonte   Santiago
             ■ Cousiño
MAIPO   Macul
VALLEY

Maipo

*Pacific
Ocean*

Rapel

RAPEL
VALLEY

Los   ■ Montes
Vascos ■   *Tinguiririca*
       ■ Casa
COLCHAGUA Lapostolle
VALLEY

CURICÓ
VALLEY

● Talca

MAULE
VALLEY (5)

ITATA
VALLEY

BÍO BÍO VALLEY

(5)

A N D E S

ARGENTINA

C H I L E

0   25   50
     miles

● Santiago

area mapped

135 What regions in Chile are important to know?

Most of Chile's wine grapes are grown in the areas surrounding Santiago and south. The fastest growing and most exciting area is Casablanca Valley, just west of Santiago and home to top Sauvignon Blancs and Chardonnays. The most famous Cabernets and Merlots come from Maipo Valley, which directly surrounds the capital, although local winemakers are betting on Rapel Valley to the south as the place for the best high-end red wines. Curicó Valley is known mostly for one winery, Torres, but its international reputation is enough to lend some fame to the region. See also entry 325.

FRANCE

136 What are Alsace's best known whites?

Although some red grapes are grown in Alsace, the Alsaciènnes (the name of the residents; Alsatians are dogs) consider Riesling, Gewürztraminer, Pinot Gris, and Muscat to be the noble grapes of Alsace, and, indeed, when you find any of these grapes from a reputable maker, you are in store for a treat. These are dense wines with strong aromas, rich flavors, and the stoutness to stand up to pork trotters or a halibut steak.

GILLES DE CHAMBURE, MS

Master Sommelier and Director of Wine Education at Meadowood, Napa Valley

"No matter where I am, I always drink the local wine," explains Gilles de Chambure, who has three houses, one in the Napa Valley, one on the Sonoma coast, and one in Gascony in the southwest part of France. While the peripatetic lifestyle could create problems finding good wines, not so for Mr. Chambure. "When I'm in California, I want a Zinfandel or a Petit Sirah. The one difference is in the summer, when my favorite wines are a Champagne or aged Pinot Gris or Riesling from Alsace.

"When it comes to learning about a region with a broad range of wines, I recommend you use a single brand as a guide, like Jadot or Drouhin in Burgundy, or Hugel, Trimbach, or Weinbach in Alsace. That will give you an opportunity to focus on a wine style and place, and experiment across prices so you can see how important the terroir and the winemaker are to the final wine."

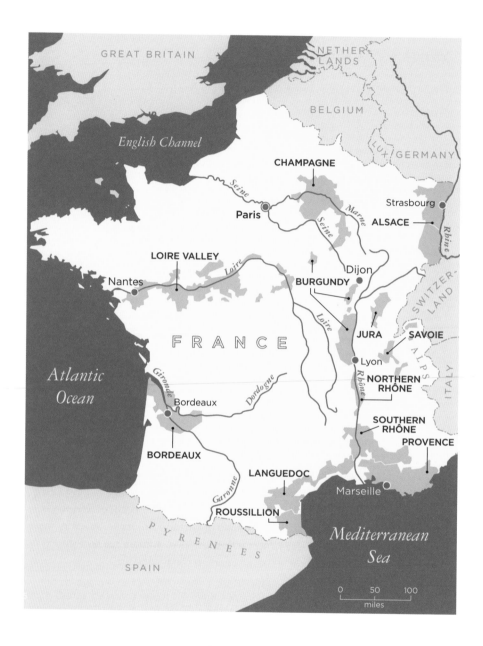

GREAT BRITAIN

NETHER-
LANDS

BELGIUM

English Channel

LUX

GERMANY

CHAMPAGNE

Strasbourg

Seine

Marne

ALSACE

Paris

Seine

Rhine

LOIRE VALLEY

Dijon

SWITZER-
LAND

Nantes

Loire

BURGUNDY

F R A N C E

Loire

JURA

SAVOIE

Lyon

ALPS

*Atlantic
Ocean*

Gironde

Dordogne

**NORTHERN
RHÔNE**

Rhône

ITALY

Bordeaux

**SOUTHERN
RHÔNE**

PROVENCE

BORDEAUX

Garonne

LANGUEDOC

Marseille

ROUSSILLION

P Y R E N E E S

*Mediterranean
Sea*

SPAIN

0   50   100
miles

137 Bordeaux versus Burgundy: what's the difference?

Despite being in the same country, speaking the same language, and sharing astronomical pricing for their rarest wines, the two have little in common. Bordeaux is much warmer, to start with. The two AOCs offer recognition based on the winery in Bordeaux, versus the vineyard in Burgundy. They use different grapes and different shaped bottles. There is more inexpensive Bordeaux than inexpensive Burgundy. And finally, the two areas have very different terroirs.

	BORDEAUX	BURGUNDY
Main red grapes	Merlot Cabernet Sauvignon Cabernet Franc Petit Verdot Malbec	Pinot Noir
Main white grapes	Sémillon Sauvignon Blanc	Chardonnay Aligoté Sauvignon Blanc
Climate	Maritime (near a large body of water, shows relatively little variation in temperature between summer and winter)	Continental (surrounded by land, shows broad variation in temperature between summer and winter)
Topography	Flat	Hilly
Labeled by	Château name and location	Vineyard name and producer
Vineyard size	Large. Many of the classified wineries have more than 100 acres.	Tiny. Many vineyards are fewer than ten acres, some as small as a single row of grapes.
Producer term	Château	Négociant

wine regions • france

Atlantic
Ocean

MÉDOC

Gironde

ST. ESTEPHE

PAUILLAC

HAUT-
MÉDOC

ST. JULIEN

RIGHT BANK

MARGAUX

LEFT BANK

POMEROL

B O R D E A U X

ST. EMILION

Dordogne

Bordeaux

ENTRE-DEUX-MERS

PESSAC-
LÉOGNAN

GRAVES

Garonne

SAUTERNES

0   50   100
miles

138 Right bank versus left bank

The Bordeaux wine region is about the size of Connecticut, and to distinguish among regional styles, wine lovers tend to separate it into the large geographical areas of right bank, left bank, and Entre-Deux-Mers (which translates as between-two-seas, although it's really two rivers). The left bank is the west side of the Gironde Estuary and the Garonne River; the right bank is the eastern side of the Dordogne River, and Entre-Deux-Mers is between the Garonne and Dordogne. Each of these large regions contains various appellations. The left bank wines are the most famous and tend to use more Cabernet, although this area also produces wonderful Sémillon- and Sauvignon Blanc–based wines; the right bank wines are not as well known but include some of the world's most expensive wines, traditionally based more on Merlot and Cabernet Franc. Entre-Deux-Mers wines are mostly inexpensive wines, both white and red.

139 What is the 1855 classification?

In 1855, the Bordeaux wine merchants rated the wines of the Médoc based on their historic prices (and, by extension, perceived quality) and designated four as First Growth wines (Château Lafite-Rothschild, Château Margaux, Château Latour, Château Haut-Brion), fourteen Second Growths, fourteen Third Growths, ten Fourth Growths, and eighteen Fifth Growths. In 1973, Château Mouton-Rothschild was added to the First Growth list after a relentless campaign on the part of the family that owned the property; otherwise, the classification has never been revised. Today, the five First Growth wines are punishingly expensive, especially in good vintages. It is important to remember, though, that overall the 1855 classification hasn't been updated since then, in spite of numerous changes in ownership and wine quality. The sweet white wines of Sauternes and Barsac were also rated in 1855, with Château d'Yquem given the top designation.

140 Bordeaux stars on a beer budget

The geniuses at Domaines Barons de Rothschild make wines of every price point. You could start with the First Growth Château Lafite-Rothschild at $1500 and its second label, Carruades de Lafite at $200. Too much? Try the lower priced Château Duhart-Milon for $75, or its second label, Moulin de Duhart for $38. Still too much? Then look to Chile for Los Vascos at $10. At any point along the line, you can get at least a glimpse of the real thing.

141 What is the Côte d'Or?

Bourgogne (Burgundy in English) is composed of six geographic areas: Beaujolais, Chablis, Mâconnais, Côte Chalonnaise, Côte de Beaune, and Côte de Nuits. The last two are also collectively referred to as the Côte d'Or. The word *Côte* translates variously as coast, slope, or hill, and you will frequently find Côte d'Or translated as Golden Slope, which is incorrect. In fact, the second word is a shortened form of *Orient,* so that Côte d'Or actually translates as Eastern Slope. The Côte de Nuits is home to many of the world's most expensive Pinot Noirs. Ditto for the Côte de Beaune, although it is also the source of the world's most prized Chardonnays.

142 Is Chablis part of Burgundy?

Yes. White wines—almost all from Chardonnay—are made in all of the six geographic areas of Burgundy (see entry 141), but Chablis tends to be distinctive for two reasons. First, it is farthest north, with the coolest climate. That means the grapes tend to be less ripe at harvest, making them more acidic than in other areas of Burgundy. Second, whereas oak barrels are used for white wine throughout most of Burgundy, in Chablis the Chardonnay is most often fermented and matured in stainless steel tanks rather than in barrels, depriving the wine of the toasty aroma of oak and accenting the green-apple acidity of less-ripe fruit. See also entry 179.

ERIC ASIMOV
Chief wine critic of *The New York Times*

Eric Asimov writes about wine with utter clarity and a generous amount of enthusiasm. His *Wines of the Times* column is one of the most useful and unsnobby wine guides available.

Asked about wine recommendations, he starts: "The best place for recommendations is to find the best wine shop close to where you live, develop a relationship, and then ask that person to give you a case of twelve different wines. Try them over time and decide what you like and don't like." Yet he doesn't recommend the types of tastings he writes about. He adds, "I have a quibble with wine classes for beginners. They have ten wines, taste and spit, and don't learn how to enjoy a wine; they learn how to write tasting notes. Instead, try one per night and enjoy it.

"That being said, I'm a huge fan of Beaujolais, and I think the best are the smaller crus like Louis-Claude Desvignes and Marcel Lapierre. For great Chardonnays, even the basic cooperative wine from the Mâconnais, Macon-Lugny Les Charmes, is delicious, and for $25 or so, I love the Mount Eden Wolff Vineyard from California. I'm also in love with Zinfandel, though not the really overpowering ones. Look for Nalle, Dashe, and Quivira."

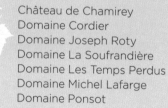

THIRTEEN BURGUNDY LABELS YOU CAN TRUST

Château de Chamirey	Domaine Simon Bize
Domaine Cordier	La Chablisienne
Domaine Joseph Roty	Louis Latour
Domaine La Soufrandière	Maison Bertrand Ambroise
Domaine Les Temps Perdus	Maison Joseph Drouhin
Domaine Michel Lafarge	Maison Louis Jadot
Domaine Ponsot	(especially the Fixin)

what's a wine lover to do?

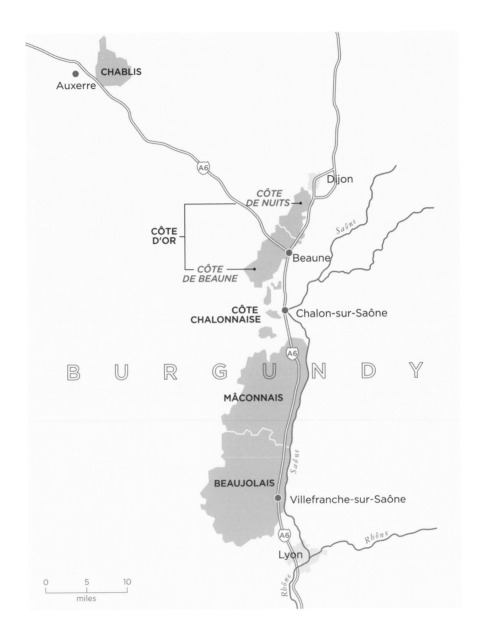

CHABLIS

Auxerre

Dijon

CÔTE
DE NUITS

CÔTE
D'OR

Saône

CÔTE
DE BEAUNE

Beaune

CÔTE
CHALONNAISE

Chalon-sur-Saône

B U R G U N D Y

MÂCONNAIS

Saône

BEAUJOLAIS

Villefranche-sur-Saône

Rhône

A6

Lyon

Rhône

0   5   10
miles

143 Champagne: are the big brands better?

This is a matter of taste and definition. Salon may produce only five thousand cases of wine (a fairly small number), and only in the best years, and Salon is widely considered to be among the handful of very best Champagnes—yet it is a part of the huge Laurent-Perrier group. Dom Pérignon would be in that same handful, yet it is the top wine of the enormous Moët et Chandon corporation. The biggest wineries have the most financial strength and the ability to tie up the best vineyards and distributors in multiyear contracts. That being said, the whole world loves a David and Goliath story, and many wine lovers will swear that the big-name producers trample on the concept of terroir (see entry 190) by buying and blending grapes from all over the Champagne region. Plus, the largest hundred companies account for more than 95 percent of American sales, yet there are more than 15,000 growers in Champagne.

An alternative you will be hearing about in the near future is "grower Champagnes," referring to wine made by the same person or company that grows the grapes, preserving that sense of place. A tiny "RM" on the corner of the label designates a grower Champagne. As to which is better: either. Why choose? Enjoy them all.

EIGHTEEN OF CHAMPAGNE'S BEST

Big Guys		Grower Champagnes
Billecart-Salmon	Pol Roger	Chartogne-Taillet
Bollinger	Pommery	Gaston Chiquet
Gosset	Ruinart	Guy Charlemagne
Krug	Salon	J. Lassalle
Moët et Chandon	Tattinger	Pascal Doquet
Mumm	Veuve Clicquot	
Perrier-Jouët		

144 Northern versus Southern Rhône

The northern Rhône Valley is much cooler and produces wines mainly from Syrah as well as three white grapes: Viognier, Marsanne, and Roussanne. The white grapes are used to blend with the Syrah, although the Condrieu appellation makes wines from straight Viognier, and white-only blends are made as well. The most famous northern Rhône areas are Côte-Rôtie, Saint-Joseph, Hermitage, and Crozes-Hermitage.

The southern part of the valley is warmer and produces wines from a much broader variety of grapes. Syrah, Grenache, Mourvèdre, Carignan, and Cinsault are the main red grapes; for whites it's Roussanne, Marsanne, Viognier, Muscat, Ugni Blanc, Bourboulenc, and Picpoul. Several of the wines, including the famous Châteauneuf-du-Pape, use more than a dozen different grapes—both red and white—in the blend.

TEN TOP RHÔNE WINES

Northern Rhône
Auguste Clape
M. Chapoutier
J.L. Chave
E. Guigal
   (northern and southern)
Jean-Luc Colombo
   (northern and southern)

Southern Rhône
Château de Beaucastel
Château Rayas
Domaine de la Charbonnière
Domaine La Garrigue
Perrin et Fils

KAREN MACNEIL

Author of *The Wine Bible,* and chairman of the Rudd Center for Professional Wine Studies at the Culinary Institute of America

As befits an educator, Karen MacNeil has spent some time pondering how to make wine more accessible and less stodgy. "The big problem with wine is not what part of the pool you get into, it's just that you get into the pool," she said. "Most experts didn't start on prestigious wines; they picked things that were extremely idiosyncratic."

She was also emphatic about not giving specific recommendations. "There's not so much a play list, but there is a good strategy," she offered. "Choose a country and for six months, drink only wines from that country. That way, you reduce the possible wines down to a more manageable number. After six months of doing that, you will have a feel, a kind of taste-memory for a country. Once you've achieved that, move on to a different country. Start with smaller wine countries like Argentina or Spain, and leave France for the end because it is the most difficult."

Her smartest rule: "The best way to learn nothing about wine is to drink what you already know you like."

145 What grapes are grown in the Loire Valley?

A vast variety is grown along the Loire, but this region's gift to the world is Sauvignon Blanc from Pouilly Fumé and Sancerre. These wines avoid the pungent grapefruit and pineapple aromas found in the New Zealand and California versions. Instead, the best versions of Pouilly Fumé and Sancerre have gorgeous, subtle balance between those tropical fruits, but adding subtle berry, smoke, and grass aromas. The region is also famous for its Chenin Blanc. In the Vouvray region the wine is sturdy, with good acidity and nutty aromas. Chenin is also made as an off-dry and a sweet wine. The region's Muscadet, made from the Melon de Bourgogne grape, is a classic pairing with oysters. Red wine fans will enjoy a slightly chilled Chinon, made from the Cabernet Franc grape. Its raspberry and blackberry flavors pair up nicely with chicken or goose.

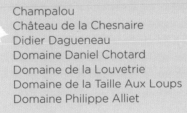

SEVEN OF THE BEST OF THE LOIRE

Champalou
Château de la Chesnaire
Didier Dagueneau
Domaine Daniel Chotard
Domaine de la Louvetrie
Domaine de la Taille Aux Loups
Domaine Philippe Alliet

146 What to expect from Provence

Many people think of Provence as the rosé capital of France, and the region does produce some delicious versions, but there are more poor examples than great ones. The best wines of Provence are those from Bandol and Les Baux-de-Provence, two AOCs that produce big-boned red and dry rosé wines, although wonderfully quaffable and inexpensive wines come from other areas as well. The dominant grapes for both rosés and reds are Grenache, Cinsault, and Mourvèdre, with some Syrah being grown as well. As a red wine, Mourvèdre can be tannic and high in alcohol, so Grenache and Cinsault are often blended in to soften it.

SIX PROVENÇAL TREATS

Château d'Esclans
Château Routas
Domaine de Triennes
Domaine Ott
Domaine Tempier
Mas de Gourgonnier

KERMIT LYNCH

Wine importer and author of *Adventures on the Wine Route, Inspiring Thirst,* and *Wines of the Northern Rhône,* and part-time resident of Bandol

Kermit Lynch called from France one summer morning to talk about how to navigate the maze of European wines. "The important thing to know is the best wines are made at the family domain, and as such, aren't available everywhere. The whole wine world is moving toward simple varietal naming, and European wines are just not simple, you can't get around that. The best thing to do is to develop a relationship with a good wine shop person, describe something you like, and then ask them to recommend a European wine."

So what would be the best strategy for plotting our way toward knowledge? "We all seem to love Chardonnay," he says. "It's my favorite white wine. But my preference is for that from France, which is quite different from the hot-weather New World wines. Look for a wine labeled Chablis or Bourgogne. That's where the grape is originally from, and it's a great opportunity to learn. If you'd like to try something other than a Cabernet Sauvignon, try a Cabernet Franc from the Loire Valley, like a Chinon. I don't think there are any bad Chinons imported to the U.S., so they are almost always a safe bet. And if you like Pinot Noir, my God, you have to try a Burgundy."

147 What to know about Languedoc

The Languedoc region, on the western rim of the French Mediterranean, is a huge wine-growing area whose reputation has grown dramatically over the past decade. Dozens of grape varieties are grown throughout the region, including many international ones such as Cabernet Sauvignon, Merlot, and Chardonnay as well as more traditional regional grapes: Grenache, Syrah, Mourvèdre, and Carignan for reds and Bourboulenc, Grenache Blanc, and Picpoul for whites. A well-chosen bottle of Languedoc wine will generally provide good value.

FIVE LANGUEDOC LEADERS

Calvet-Thunevin
Chapoutier
Domaine de Lavabre
Mas Champart
Yannick Pelletier

GERMANY

148 What grows in Germany besides Riesling?

Riesling, the most common grape in Germany, accounts for one fifth of the vineyard area. It is followed by Müller-Thurgau (a varietal cross of Riesling and Madeleine Royale), Spätburgunder (the German term for Pinot Noir), Dornfelder (red), and Silvaner (white). Müller-Thurgau's major virtue as a grape is astronomical yields. Although a few good wines are made from the grape, it's more likely to show up in branded wines such as Blue Nun or Liebfraumilch. It doesn't age well, and the acidity level seldom measures up to its sweetness. Spätburgunder is the best of Germany's reds, mirroring many of Burgundy's flavors, but with a lighter touch.

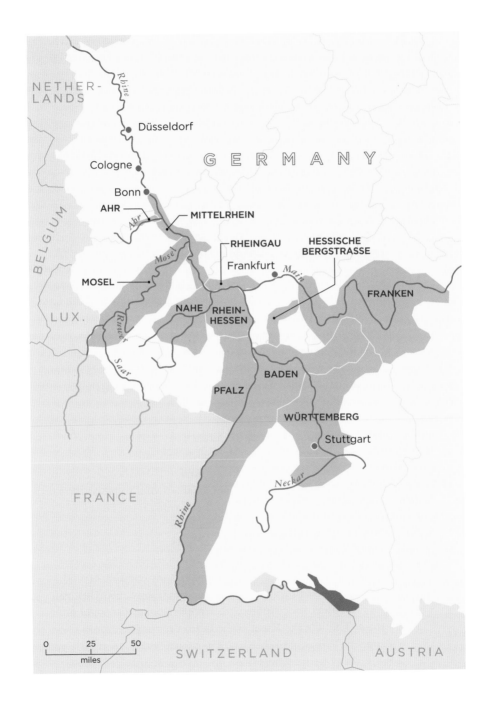

149　What are the German regions to know?

The Mosel and Rheingau, two of the world's great regions for Riesling, are almost totally devoted to the grape. The terraced Mosel vineyards are incredibly dramatic, sloping at angles that would scare most downhill skiers. The vines are planted on the steep slopes to try to maximize sunlight during the short, cool growing season. Every year is a fight for the maximum amount of sunlight—which creates ripeness and sugars—before the freezes come along and destroy the crops. Because of the slope, the vines have to be tended and harvested by hand. It's amazing the wine doesn't cost more. Note that wines labeled Mosel were formerly labeled Mosel-Saar-Ruwer; the name was shortened for the label, but wines labeled Mosel may come from any of the three regions.

Sadly, the winemakers of the Mosel went through a period of diminished profits because of the widely held myth that only dry wines are good. Some responded by vinifying dry their fascinating, unique, time-honored sweet wines, in an attempt to please the world market. This is a case where the old way really is the best. Luckily, some winemakers hold on to the traditions.

There was a time when Mosel and Rheingau wines could be easily differentiated in two ways. First, the Mosel wines came in green bottles, and the Rheingau wines came in brown bottles. Second, where the Mosel wines were elegant and restrained, the Rheingau wines had huge, concentrated green apple aromas that could fill a room. Think of the Mosel as the Beatles to the Rheingau's Led Zeppelin. Things have changed. The brown bottles are mostly gone. Sadly, the powerful aromas have also all but disappeared. There are still a few winemakers clinging to the old styles and making wonderful wines. Unfortunately, economic pressures have forced many of them to feel the need to harvest more grapes per vine at the expense of their characteristic intensity. It's important to find a knowledgeable shopkeeper who will steer you to the wines that still possess Rheingau's historic magic. Rheinhessen and Pfalz (two huge areas) and the smaller Nahe are other quality regions you may see on labels. Riesling is the main grape in these regions, too, but you'll also find a host of other grapes (see entry 148). See also entry 327.

FOURTEEN OF GERMANY'S MOST AROMATIC WINES

Mosel

Dr. H. Thanisch
Dr. Loosen
Egon Müller
Fritz Haag
Joh. Jos. Christoffel Erben
Joh. Jos. Prüm (aka J. J. Prüm)
Karthäuserhof
Maximin Grünhäuser
S. A. Prüm
Selbach-Oster

Rheingau

Franz Künstler
Georg Breuer
Robert Weil
Schloss Reinhartshausen

150 What is a Super Tuscan?

Sangiovese is the most common grape in Toscana (Tuscany in English). All of the region's world-famous wines—Chianti, Brunello di Montalcino, and Vino Nobile di Montepulciano—are made from Sangiovese. Tuscany is also the home of the renegade winemaker who caused the creation of the IGT (Indicazione Geografica Tipica) classification (see entry 45). Mario Incisa della Rochetta of Sassicaia decided in the mid-1960s that he wanted to add Bordeaux grape varieties such as Cabernet Sauvignon and Merlot to his Sangiovese, which was not allowed under DOC rules. After Sassicaia's phenomenal success in the marketplace, other Tuscan winemakers took notice and wanted to use nonnative grape varieties themselves. Eventually, the outcry was sufficient that the government developed a classification that allowed this: IGT. Now most respectable Tuscan wineries make an IGT wine and call it a "Super Tuscan."

151 What unusual whites come from Italy?

A huge number of white grapes are grown in Italy whose names are little known anywhere except at the local viticultural universities. The most common white grapes are Catarratto, Trebbiano, Malvasia, and Pinot Grigio, only the last of which is a household word outside Italy. Italian wine drinkers are generally more interested in where a wine comes from and who makes it than they are in the grape variety, one reason you usually don't see the name of the grape on an Italian bottle. For example, Soave is made from Trebbiano and Garganega grapes, Gavi is made from the Cortese grape, and Orvieto is made from Trebbiano and Grechetto. The Roero DOCG is home to the Arneis grape, which makes a lovely, aromatic wine with peach and apricot aromas. The greatest concentrated areas for Italian whites are north and east of Venice, called Alto Adige and Friuli. There, the producers *do* put the grape's name on the bottle.

Alto Adige has been in Austrian hands as much as Italian, and the culture is largely Germanic. Alto Adige's wines have bright acidity and mesmerizing fragrances. The region's main wines are Gewürztraminer—the most famous wine—plus Pinot Bianco and Sylvaner.

There are only a few places on earth that can match Friuli's white wines. The climate and location by the sea deliver wines that are the very antithesis of New World wines, with emphasis on delicate floral aromas and subtle flavors. Friuli whites taste so clean and so much like the grape they are made from that the international varieties grown there (Gewürztraminer, Riesling, Chardonnay, Pinot Grigio, Pinot Bianco, and Sauvignon Blanc) won't taste like any other version. The most famous local grape is Friulano (once known as Tocai Friulano but renamed because of its similar sound to Hungary's wine Tokaji). Traditionalists also like to make wines from Picolit, Malvasia Istriana, and Ribolla Gialla. The Malvasia, especially, has a beguiling floral aroma.

152 What sparkling wines are made in Italy?

The most famous Italian sparkler is Prosecco (the name of both the wine and the grape used for it), and there are many reputable makers offering quality and value. The great sparkling wine of Italy is Franciacorta, a wine made using the same method as Champagne— and costing as much, too. The other major Italian sparkler is Asti (formerly known as Asti Spumante), a fragrant, lightly sweet, low-alcohol wine made from the Moscato (Muscat) grape. Most areas in Italy make some sort of sparkling wine. Not so common, but worth searching out, are the *frizzante* wines (see entry 50) of Gavi and Asti and the lightly sweet, red sparkling Brachetto d'Acqui.

153 What to expect from Piemonte's reds

Piemonte (Piedmont in English) is one of the best wine districts in Italy. For sheer profundity, the region's famous red grape, Nebbiolo, is up there with Pinot Noir. The most famous Nebbiolo is from the DOCG of Barolo, and it is extraordinarily expensive. Less expensive and almost as good are the Nebbiolos from four other DOCGs: Barbaresco, Gattinara, Ghemme, and Roero.

Nebbiolo is a cranky grape to work with and subject to early flowering before the last frost. Despite its fame, it makes up less than 4 percent of the area's vineyards. In its youth, Barolo's tannins are tough but its aromas—roses, forest floor, smoke—are beguiling. As it ages, and it will age for decades, the tannins soften and the wine becomes more approachable. For those unwilling to wait, pass up the Barolo and concentrate on the other four.

Two other red grapes have achieved DOCG status in Piemonte: The pleasantly fruity Dolcetto is a great food wine with fairly high acidity and soft tannins, meant to be drunk young. The locals' favorite red wine is Barbera, a wine that historically was acidic and lacked tannic grip. Over the past few decades, winemakers have been aging Barbera in French barrels, and the wine has morphed into an inky, muscular wine with black cherry and leather aromas. Fifty percent of the grapes grown in Piemonte are Barbera, and the best versions won't carry the snob appeal of a Barolo, but they cost significantly less and offer more pleasure when young. See also entries 224 and 328.

154 What wines is Sicily known for?

Chardonnay, Grecanico, Fiano, and Grillo are the main white wines. Sicily's most famous grape, the red Nero d'Avola, produces a dark, rich wine with the perfume of an older Barolo, and at a dramatically lower price. Lovers of huge, intense wines should look for a plummy Syrah, peppery Aglianico, or fruity Merlot.

155 What wines are made from the Sangiovese grape?

The major Sangiovese-based wines from Italy come from the central part of the country, and best of all are the wines from Tuscany. The most famous Sangiovese-based wine is Chianti, but others include Vino Nobile di Montepulciano and Morellino di Scansano. The Rolls-Royce of Italian Sangioveses is Brunello di Montalcino, consistently one of the most expensive and sought-after red wines in the world. The best strategy for the cost-conscious may be to find a great Brunello winemaker and buy their Rosso di Montalcino, which is made similarly but is much less expensive. This is especially true if you want to drink the wines within ten years of the vintage, because Rosso is made to drink young and Brunello is made to age.

Chiantis range in price from less than $10 to way over $100. Younger, less-expensive Chiantis will be fruitier and more approachable, while the more expensive wines, such as a Chianti Classico Superiore, will be older upon release and have more layered and complex aromas. Chiantis tend to have a floral aroma, whereas Brunello and Rosso di Montalcino have more blackberry and currant aromas. A decent Brunello will run $75, while the best will run ten times that. See also entry 150.

TEN TUSCAN GREATS

Altesino	Ornellaia
Antinori	Pieve Santa Restituta
Badia a Coltibuono	Poggio Antico
Banfi	Ruffino
Il Poggione	Sassicaia

156 What wines are made in the Veneto?

The Veneto wine region is due west of Venice and extends to the southern shores of Lake Garda. It is home to three of Italy's best wines—Soave, Valpolicella, and Prosecco, a sparkling wine (see entry 152). Soave is a white wine made principally from Garganega with Pinot Bianco, Chardonnay, and Trebbiano di Soave also allowed. Basic Soave is a variable wine that can be extraordinary or characterless. Soave Superiore is more intense, with flavors of almonds, pine nuts, and lime rind. There is also a hauntingly aromatic sweet wine called Recioto di Soave, made from dried grapes (see entry 183).

Veneto's most famous red wine is Valpolicella, which is made mostly from the grapes Corvina, Rondinella, and Molinara. Like Soave, the wine comes in three levels. The basic level is simply called Valpolicella and, again, can be anything from heavenly to boring (hint: ask for a "ripasso" style). The liquid gold of Veneto is Amarone, for which winemakers dry the grapes for at least four months for a bone-dry, hugely concentrated, and long-lived wine. It's expensive but unforgettable. Recioto della Valpolicella is a sweet wine also made from dried grapes. See also entry 328.

SIX OF VENETO'S BEST

Allegrini
Dal Forno
L'Arco
Masi
Tedeschi
Zenato

157 What are the best-known wines of southern Italy?

Southern Italy was long known for producing unextraordinary jug wine, but lately, much of the area has been attracting attention for a growing list of winemakers intent on producing great wines. Some of the best are coming from Campania (the area surrounding Naples) and Apulia (Italy's heel). Campania's principal white grapes are Greco di Tufo, Fiano, and Falanghina. The Greco is perfect with lightly dressed fish, where the mild wine highlights the sea's freshness. Aglianico is the king of Campania's red grapes and the base for Taurasi, a big-boned, acidic, and tannic wine. The wines of southern Apulia are robust reds that would appeal to lovers of Sonoma Zinfandel (see entry 108). The main grapes are Primitivo (which is closely related to Zinfandel), Negroamaro, and Malvasia Nera, all intense, powerful, and aromatic grapes. See also entry 154.

158 What grapes are used for Portuguese dry wines?

In general, Portugal's white wines are light refreshers made from combinations of Alvarinho, Loureiro, Encruzado, Bicla, and Arinto grapes. The best-quality red grapes are Touriga Nacional, Tinta Roriz, Touriga Franca (three of the grapes used for Port), Baga, and Periquita, but Portugal grows a mind-boggling tutti-frutti of red grapes, and each DOC has different preferences. Advising which grapes to search out is difficult because the Portuguese grow dozens of varieties that are unique to the country, and some are so obscure that even many of the vineyard owners can't identify them. If you focus by region, though, Vinho Verde in the far north produces a refreshing white with a light spritz that is meant to be drunk young and casually. The Douro region, where the grapes for Port are grown, produces intensely flavored dry reds from the same grapes.

SEVEN SKILLED PORTUGUESE WINEMAKERS

Alvaro Castro
Broadbent
Herdade do Esporão
Niepoort

Prats & Symington
Quinta de Roriz
Quinta do Crasto

159 Why are so many Port brands British?

Back when England ruled the seas, it imported wine from France. When periodic wars kept the British from their French wines, they turned to Portugal, with whom they had good relations. The British found it necessary to add brandy to the red wines of the Douro region to ensure they would survive shipping in good condition. The addition of brandy began to happen earlier, during fermentation, resulting in a sweet wine similar to the Port of today. It was the names of the shippers at the mouth of the Douro river (around the city of Oporto) that were associated with the wines—thus the British brands Taylor, Sandeman, Cockburn, and others.

160 What are the different styles of Port?

Traditionally port is an after-dinner digestif, drunk from smaller stemmed wineglass. There are two main styles of Port—the rubies or bottle-aged Ports, and the tawnies, or cask-aged Ports—each with various substyles. As the names imply, one style is bottled right away and meant either to be consumed young or aged in the bottle, and the other is matured in wooden casks for various lengths of time before being bottled ready to drink. Basic ruby is the most common and least expensive Port and isn't meant to be aged.

Vintage Port is from one particularly favorable vintage. It is meant to be aged in the bottle for many years, then decanted (see entry 306) before drinking. Late-Bottled Vintage (LBV) Ports are made from wines of a single vintage, but they have spent more time aging in barrels than Vintage Port. Where the Vintage Port maintains more of its original big fruity flavors, the LBV Port's time in the barrel tends to move it a bit toward the tawny flavors. More important, the time in the barrel makes the wine mature more quickly so that it is ready to drink when released. LBVs are also less expensive than Vintage Ports.

Tawny ports have some oxidization from being stored in barrels. Unless labeled Colheita or Garrafeira, a tawny Port is a blend of several vintages. The winemaker's goal year after year is consistency of flavor. Tawnies marked with an age (generally ten, twenty, thirty, or forty years old) are blends of vintages that average the age listed. Colheitas and Garrafeiras are tawnies made from a single vintage. Tawny port prices vary from less than $20 for the basic versions up to the $300 range for special vintage tawnies.

White Port is also made but is less common. See also entry 181.

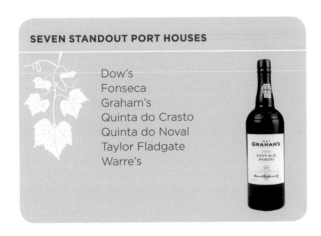

SEVEN STANDOUT PORT HOUSES

Dow's
Fonseca
Graham's
Quinta do Crasto
Quinta do Noval
Taylor Fladgate
Warre's

161 What is Madeira?

Madeira is Portugal's other renowned fortified sweet wine, from the islands of Madeira off the coast of Portugal. The wine making is similar to that of Port, with one major distinction: they actually slowly cook the wine at between 100 and 140 degrees to rush the aging process. The result is a nutty toffee flavor and an incredibly long-lived wine. The best grapes used for Madeira are Sercial, Bual, Verdelho, and Malvasia, but the farmers slowly stopped planting these in favor of Tinta Negra Mole, a bland but inexpensive grape. Recently, Madeira's winegrowers have been going back to the superior grapes hoping to drive their market upscale. See also entry 181.

FOUR DEPENDABLE MADEIRA MAKERS

Blandy's
Broadbent
Cossart Gordon
Leacock's

Atlantic
Ocean

FRANCE

● Bilbao

GALICIA

CORDILLERA
CANTÁBRICA

NAVARRA

SOMONTANO

PYRENEES

RÍAS BAIXAS

BIERZO

SIERRA DE LA
DEMANDA

COSTERS
DEL SEGRE

Barcelona

VALDEORRAS

LA RIOJA

Ebro

CATALUNYA

Minho

TORO

Duero

CARIÑENA

PENEDÈS

VINHO
VERDE

DOURO

RIBERA DEL
DUERO

CALATAYUD

PRIORAT

Douro

RUEDA

VALENCIA

TARRAGONA

Oporto

CASTILLA Y LEÓN

Madrid ◉

DÃO

Mondego

SPAIN

BAIRRADA

Tajo

LA MANCHA

Valencia

Tejo

LA MANCHA

VALENCIA

RIBATEJO

JUMILLA

Lisbon ◎

SETÚBAL

PORTUGAL

VALDEPEÑAS

ALENTEJO

Guadiana

Guadalquivir

MONTILLA-
MORILES

Sevilla

ANDALUCÍA

SIERRA NEVADA

Mediterranean
Sea

MÁLAGA

JEREZ

Málaga

Atlantic
Ocean

ALGERIA

MOROCCO

0   50   100
miles

162 What are the up-and-coming Spanish regions?

Rías Baixas, in the northwest of Spain, was a sleepy wine area until the world developed a taste for Albariño. That one grape now accounts for more than 90 percent of the area's wine production. It resembles a lighter version of Rhône Viognier, all peaches and apricots, and in the hands of a talented winemaker, it has perfect acidity.

The Priorat area is for fans of Sonoma Zinfandel (see entry 108), Amarone (see entry 156), or South Australian Shiraz. The area is rocky, remote, and mountainous. The grapes—mostly Garnacha Tinta (Grenache), Cariñena, and Cabernet Sauvignon—have to struggle to live, and produce powerful flavors and plenty of natural sugar. Drinking a Priorat will leave your teeth stained, your soul warmed, and your wallet a good deal thinner. See also entries 107 and 220.

SIX SPANISH WINERIES TO WATCH

Rías Baixas
Bodegas Martin Codax
Pazo de Señorans

Priorat
Clos Mogador
Costers del Siurana
Melis
Vall Llach

163 What grapes are used for Rioja?

Rioja is Spain's most famous wine-growing area. Here, the Tempranillo grape is king, and in the hands of one of the good Rioja winemakers can make a mesmerizing wine. Besides Tempranillo, the DOCa (see entry 45) standards allow three other red grapes in Rioja: Garnacha Tinta, Mazuelo (aka Cariñena), and Graciano. Ninety percent of the wine from Rioja is red, and most of that is a blend of Tempranillo and Garnacha Tinta. Tempranillo by itself can be light colored, tannic, and acidic, so winemakers often blend in the robust Garnacha Tinta to give it more body. The finished blend creates complex, earthy aromas with traces of leather and red cherries. White and rosé wines account for only 10 percent of Rioja's production. Viura, Malvasia, and Garnacha Blanca are the white grapes, while a terrific dry rosé is made from Garnacha Tinta.

A SECOND SIP *The Ribera del Duero region's main grape is also Tempranillo (or Tinto Fino, as they call it locally), but the authorities also allow grapes such as Cabernet Sauvignon, Merlot, Malbec, or Garnacha to round out the blends, with the result that Ribera del Duero wines are often more robust than Rioja wines. Bodegas Emilio Moro, Condado de Haza, Pesquera, and Pingus are good examples.*

164 How is sherry made?

Sherry is made from three grapes: Palomino, Pedro Ximénez (called PX), and Muscat of Alexandria. Sherry starts as a white wine that is fermented until it is dry. Depending on the style of sherry being made, neutral spirits are then added to bring the alcohol up to between 15 to 22 percent. The wine is then matured in oak barrels using a system called the solera. In the solera system, each year's release of product is bottled from the oldest barrels, then those barrels are topped up with wine from the next oldest barrels, which in turn are topped from the next oldest barrels, and so on until the youngest barrels are topped with the current vintage. The effect of the solera is to blend years' worth of wine together in relatively tiny fractions, giving complicated layers of flavors in the final wine that are consistent from year to year. A bottle of sherry purchased today will contain a fraction of the first wine ever put in the solera, and in some of the older houses, that's well over a hundred years old.

ANNETTE ALVAREZ-PETERS, CWE

Assistant General Merchandise Manager for Wine, Spirits & Beer, Costco

Annette Alvarez-Peters oversees one of the largest wine retail efforts in the United States, which allows her the opportunity to taste an enormous number of wines over the course of a year. She also travels extensively. "I've been blessed to have traveled to so many wine regions around the world—from California, Oregon, and Washington to Bordeaux, Burgundy, the Rhône Valley, Italy, Spain, Australia, Chile, and Argentina—and each region has good, dependable wineries that put out amazing wines year after year," she said. "At home, my wine tastes tend to jump from country to country and varietal to varietal. I like to lay down Bordeaux (mostly from the Médoc), Italian Brunellos, and wines from the Rhône Valley. But for everyday wines, I also like the fruit-forwardness of New World wines. During the warm summer months, I lean toward refreshing rosé wines (I try them all!), or a crisp Sauvignon Blanc or Albariño. People should try something new every time they go out so they can discover a new favorite."

165 What are the different styles of sherry?

Sherry comes in several styles, depending on the initial level of fortification with neutral spirits. Fino and Manzanilla are light, dry, and acidic with nutty aromas. Much of their flavor comes from a thick layer of yeast, called flor, that is allowed to grow on the surface of the wine as it matures in the solera in barrels that are not quite full. The flor protects the wine from oxidation and imparts intricate aromas. Amontillado and oloroso are also dry but progressively darker, more oxidized, and much more complex, with dried fruit and caramel aromas. Cream sherries (which are sweet rather than dry) are made using one of the four wines above with the addition of sweet juice from Pedro Ximénez grapes. Moscatel (aka Muscat) makes a very sweet sherry with the grape's signature floral aromas. Sweetest of all is Pedro Ximénez, one of the world's great dessert wines and criminally cheap for the pleasure it brings.

FIVE EASY-TO-FIND, HIGH-QUALITY SHERRY HOUSES

Domecq
Emilio Lustau
González Byass
Osborne
Sandeman

166 What are Spain's best-known whites?

Macabeo, Xarel-lo, and Parellada are the grapes most Americans have tried, in the form of Cava, the world's best inexpensive sparkling wine, made in the Penedès region. Producers such as Segura Viudas, Cordoníu, Mont Marçal, and the ubiquitous Freixenet all make shockingly good wines for the price.

Albariño is a peachy, aromatic grape grown best in the northwest region of Galicia (see entry 162). Garnacha Blanca is grown across the northeast side of the country and makes heady wine that requires careful growing to avoid overripeness. Other prominent whites include Verdejo, Viognier, Txakoli and Godello. Don't miss sherry, Spain's famous fortified white wine (see entry 181).

what's a wine lover to do?

167 New Zealand: North Island versus South Island

Look at a globe, and New Zealand appears to be so far south that the New Zealanders could reach off their front porches and chip off a piece of Antarctica to ice down their Sauvignon Blanc. Instead, New Zealand's wine-growing areas are at an equivalent latitude to the area from Washington's wine country down to Paso Robles, California. The key to the pleasant climate is the moderating influence of the Tasman Sea on the west side and the Pacific Ocean to the east.

The warmer part of the North Island is home to Chardonnay, Cabernet Sauvignon, Merlot, and Cabernet Franc. Moving farther south toward Hawkes Bay, Sauvignon Blanc, and Pinot Noir take over. The Kiwis' preferred beverage (other than beer) is unoaked Chardonnay, a wine that combines the fruitiness of California versions with the structure of the French. Chardonnay, Sauvignon Blanc, Riesling, and Pinot Noir dominate the cooler vineyards of the south island. The north half of the island is where you'll find the huge, grapefruit-aroma Sauvignon Blancs that have been igniting the world market, but wine connoisseurs are paying the strictest attention to the southern half, in the Central Otago area, which may end up being the second greatest area in the world for Pinot Noir.

wine regions · new zealand

AUSTRALIA

Wellington

NORTH ISLAND

Auckland

Tasman
Sea

HAWKE'S
BAY

GISBORNE
(POVERTY BAY)

WELLINGTON
(MARTINBOROUGH)

Wellington

TASMAN

MARLBOROUGH

SOUTH ISLAND

WAIPARA VALLEY

Christchurch

CANTERBURY

Pacific
Ocean

OTAGO

Dunedin

0   100   200
miles

NEW ZEALAND

SOUTHERN ALPS

A DOZEN OF NEW ZEALAND'S BEST

North Island Wineries

Ata Rangi
Craggy Range Winery
Kim Crawford
Kumeu River Wines
Martinborough Vineyard
Te Mata Estate Winery
Villa Maria

South Island Wineries

Felton Road Wines
Mt. Difficulty
Pegasus Bay Pyramid Valley
    Vineyards
Rippon Vineyard
Two Paddocks

168 South Africa: what is Pinotage?

Pinotage is a grape variety that is a genetic cross between Pinot Noir and Cinsault, developed in South Africa during the 1920s. The goal was to create a variety with the hardiness of Cinsault and the elegance of Pinot Noir, although there is some disagreement as to whether the aesthetics of this goal were achieved. Many South African winemakers have pulled out their Pinotage vines altogether, although there is a sort of national pride movement afoot, with a few wineries making the wine. Most wineries that still use the grape are blending it, usually with Cabernet Sauvignon or Merlot, but Kanonkop and Vilafonté make good varietal versions.

SARA MOULTON
Chef, cookbook author, and television personality

Sara Moulton is a delightful person to share a drink with, open, interested, and very smart. Asked about her favorite wines, she sighs a little wistfully. "If I could afford it, I would be drinking white Burgundies, like any excellent Meursault or Chassagne Montrachet. But if you looked into my refrigerator right now, I'd have this lovely, crisp rosé from Wolffer Estate Winery on Long Island. You'd also find a case of Chateau St. Jean Robert Young Vineyard Chardonnay. It's way more than I would usually spend, but it's wonderful wine, especially as an aperitif."

169 Austria: what are the most common grapes?

Most people new to Austrian wine buy the spicy, pungent white wine grape Grüner Veltliner. The grape has floral aromas, and if you're lucky you'll get an expansive hit of white pepper on the finish. Austria also grows Riesling at every quality level. The best versions come from the Wachau region, where they develop room-filling aromas of green apples and flowers. But Austria's real eye-openers are red wines, especially Blaufränkisch, a grape grown in Mittelburgenland, next to the Hungarian border. It is a stunner, with the fruit power of Syrah or Zinfandel and the tannic elegance of a Bordeaux. See also entry 324.

EIGHT DEPENDABLE AUSTRIAN WINERIES

Familie Nigl
Schloss Gobelsburg
Weingut Bründlmayer
Weingut Ernst Triebaumer
Weingut F.X. Pichler
Weingut Huber
Weingut Kracher
Weingut Prager

what's a wine lover to do?

170 Greece: grapes to look for

Greece is home to more than three hundred grape varieties, most virtually unknown outside of Greece. The vast majority of Greece's wine exports are white wines. Assyrtiko makes a crisp, fresh-tasting wine that works equally well with seafood or as aperitifs. Moscophilero is a pink-skinned variety that is used for aromatic whites and rosés to be enjoyed in the same way. Savatiano is the grape used to make Retsina, the wine with a pine resin aroma that can be a marvelous costar to Greek cuisine. The Greek red grape to look out for is Xynomavro (pictured below), a grape that crosses the earthy subtleties of Pinot Noir and the high-acidity peppery character of a southern Rhône red.

171 Hungary: what is its most famous wine?

Tokaji Aszú is the foundation of Hungary's reputation in the world of fine wine. Although Tokaji has always been considered one of the world's great dessert wines, the Tokaji region was also one of the worst hit by phylloxera (see entry 191), and it has had the unlucky fortune to be right in the pathway of two world wars and a Soviet structure aimed at making oceans of lousy wine instead of attending to Tokaji's royal stature. Today, the industry is coming back, thanks to a huge influx of foreign investment and a more appreciative government. Tokaji is made from Furmint and other grapes in various sweetness levels, starting at dry, but the fame rests on the dessert versions, where the grapes have been hit by botrytis (see entry 182). This is unctuous wine whose sweetness levels are measured in puttonyos, with 3 to 6 puttonyos being the rating most commonly seen on labels.

JERRY SHRIVER

Music and dining critic for *USA Today*

World traveler and wine writer Jerry Shriver mentions Shafer as a perennial favorite for wines, but for everyday drinking, he's far more eclectic. "I never buy more than a few bottles of any particular wine—variety is the wine world's greatest virtue—and a mixed case of low-cost wines is a great educational tool. One fall I needed to get up to speed on Grenache, so I bought a mixed case of Grenache-based wines from Spain, the Rhône, and several other regions and studied them over a series of gatherings. Last summer I did the same thing with rosés, and before that it was Gewürztraminers."

From Grape to Glass

From a farmer staring out at an uncleared field until the bottle hits the shelf is usually a ten-year process. Planting runs over $10,000 an acre. Land can cost over $100,000 an acre in Napa (much less in other places). A new barrel can cost $900. A bottle, label, capsule, and cork run over $1. Wineries cost small fortunes to build. In other words, a bottle of wine is a small miracle, and it's amazing that it costs as little as it does. In this chapter, we explain how it comes to be.

172 How is fine wine made?

1. The grapes have to ripen to perfection.
2. The best grapes are always carefully harvested by hand.
3. The grapes are carried by hand from the vineyard.
4. Pickers drop grapes into vats for transport to the winery.
5. Sorters pull any bad grapes.
6. Grapes are conveyed to be crushed.

7. Winemaker tastes a grape for ripeness.
8. Punching down the cap in an open-top fermenter.
9. Grapes ferment in stainless-steal tanks.
10. Winemaker checks the wine as it matures in oak barrels.
11. The bottling line.
12. Wines rest and mature in the bottle prior to sale.

173 What makes a white wine white?

Almost all grapes have white juice, but white grapes lack the colored pigment in their skins that makes red wine red (see entry 174).

174 What makes a red wine red?

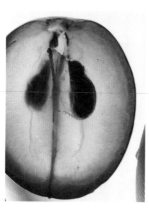

Oddly enough, it is not the grape's juice. More than 99 percent of the world's red wine grapes have white juice. Instead, it is the purple or red pigmentation in the skins that is responsible for the color. The pigments leach out of the skins as the juice and skins soak, or macerate, together after the grapes have been crushed. The winemaker has to achieve a delicate balance between leaving the juice on the skins long enough to get the desired color, but not so long that the juice picks up bitter tannins from the skins and seeds. Modern winemakers are working with a public that equates dark color with quality in red wine. Their solution is to add small amounts of the extremely dark juice from grapes such as Alicante Bouschet or Petit Verdot. See also entry 185.

175   What happens in fermentation?

Yeast metabolizes the grape's sugars, converting them into ethyl alcohol and carbon dioxide. The carbon dioxide is released into the air, and most of the alcohol ends up in the bottle. For details of the fermentation of Champagne and sparkling wines, see entry 178.

176   Rosé and blush wine: what's the difference?

Winemakers use one of two methods for making rosé. For fine rosé wines, the juice of red grapes is allowed to soak with the grape skins for a short time to extract a touch of the skins' color. The winemaker has to get this just right: the skins add not only color, but also body and complex flavors. Part of the winemaker's art is deciding when the color, body, and flavor have hit the perfect combination. Cheaper rosés, sometimes called blush wines, are made by adding red wine or unfermented red juice into the white wine. This generally results in less complexity of flavor, and sometimes a slight sweetness in the wine. White Zinfandel is an example of blush wine.

177 Is there sugar in sweet wines?

Not in the sense of table sugar, which is sucrose (but chaptalization is an exception; see entry 184). The sugars in wine are primarily glucose and fructose, natural sugars that exist in the grapes as a result of the ripening process. Most of these natural sugars are used up by the yeasts during fermentation (see entry 175), unless the wine is intended to be sweet, in which case fermentation stops by itself or is stopped by the winemaker at a point when the desired level of sugar remains unfermented in the wine. See also entry 181.

178 What makes Champagne bubbly?

The traditional method for making Champagne follows six steps.

1. The winemaker creates the base wine, which might be a blend of several vintages, or a single vintage.
2. When the usual fermentation is complete, a second fermentation is started by placing the base wine plus some yeast and sugar into a bottle, then capping it so that the carbon dioxide that results from the second fermentation (see entry 175) occurs under pressure. The carbon dioxide has no place to go, so it remains in the wine as carbonation.
3. The bottles are allowed to rest on their lees (the sediment of the yeast and any other particles floating in the wine) for at least fifteen months, and often much longer.

4. Shortly before the end, the bottles go through riddling (pictured below), a process where the bottles are inverted at a forty-five-degree downward angle and twisted and tapped daily to get the lees to settle slowly into the neck.
5. After the lees have gathered at the neck, an inch or two of the wine in the neck is frozen hard and extracted from the bottle, carrying the lees along with it. A *dosage* (sweet juice that will determine the final sweetness of the wine, such as Brut, Extra Brut, etc.) is added to the bottle and the wine is corked and sealed.
6. The bottle receives further aging.

This is obviously a time-consuming and expensive process. Yet it works so well that winemakers all over the world use the technique, calling it *méthode Champenoise* or *méthode traditionnelle*.

Two other systems exist. The Charmat method uses giant pressurized stainless steel tanks instead of bottles for the wine's second fermentation. It can work very nicely as a faster way of approximating the impact of *méthode Champenoise*. Charmat's best ambassador is Italian Prosecco. Winemakers aiming at the lowest possible price points use the final method, simply injecting carbon dioxide into the wine in the same way a soft drink is carbonated. These wines (especially in the face of excessive partying) are the usual culprits when someone says they can't drink Champagne because "it gives me a headache."

A SECOND SIP *The term Champagne refers only to wine made in the Champagne region of France. Any sparkling wine from outside the Champagne region, even if it is from France, should be called a sparkling wine.*

179 Why do Chablis and Napa Chardonnays differ?

Chablis and most other white Burgundies are made from the Chardonnay grape, and they do taste quite different from most Napa Chardonnays. There are three reasons: terroir, viticulture, and enology. Terroir is the sum of all that is natural that affects a piece of land, including soil, climate, diurnal temperature shifts, and length of growing season (see entry 190). Viticulture (the branch of horticulture dealing with grapes) is the product of tradition and trying to find ways to make the most of a piece of land. Enology covers everything from harvest through the end of bottle aging. It is driven by the winemaker's taste and the marketability of the final product.

All three have a huge impact on the final product. Start with latitude. Chablis is at the cooler latitude of Montreal or Seattle, while Napa is at the same latitude as hotter Athens or Lisbon. Chablis's viticulture is driven by centuries of experience, while Napa's is driven by strong scientific research at UC Davis. Americans prefer a big, buttery, oaky Chardonnay as an aperitif. Europeans buy Chablis because it is a crisp and lively wine ideally suited for a meal. Enologists from both areas make wines that will appeal to their local consumers.

180   How is climate change affecting winegrowers?

Luckily for winemakers, the Old World has kept a good record of ongoing changes for the last thousand years, so it is possible to establish a few correlations. The main areas of influence on grapevines are temperature and rainfall. Warmer weather (within reason) allows grapes to achieve higher sugar levels and additional ripeness, although it also reduces their acidity. These should translate into intense flavors and aromas and the potential for either higher alcohol or more residual sugar. Too steep of a rise in temperature causes shifts in rainfall, making it more difficult for warm, dry areas to support grapevines. The bottom line, with future warming, is that cool areas such as Oregon would be able to make higher-alcohol wines with more intense flavor, while hot dry areas such as Australia's Barossa Valley might become untenable for winemaking.

181   What is fortified wine?

Fortified wine is wine that has had neutral (flavorless) spirits made from grapes added to it either during or after fermentation. The most common examples include Port, Madeira, Sherry, and Marsala, although there are hundreds of fortified wines made worldwide. The most common method of making fortified wine is to halt fermentation by adding spirits (which kills the yeast) while the juice is still very sweet, such as with Port and Madeira. Some of the world's best fortified wines—Banyuls, Muscat de Beaumes de Venises, and Australian stickies (see entry 131)—are made using a method similar to Port. Sherry is fermented until dry, then is fortified with spirits. (Dessert sherries are sweetened after fortification, usually using wine from the Pedro Ximénez grape.) Madeira is made from either of the two methods, depending on the grape it is made from and its level of sweetness. See also entries 161, 162, and 165.

182   What is noble rot?

Botrytis cinerea is the scientific name for a fungus that has a particular affinity for grapes. If it attacks split or damaged grapes, it is called gray rot and destroys part or all of the crop. If it appears on whole, healthy grapes under perfect climatic conditions, it is called noble rot and produces the most honeyed and complex of all dessert wines. Part of its effect is to decrease the water content of the grapes, making the remaining juice considerably sweeter. Noble rot affects the Sémillon grapes of Sauternes, the Chenin Blanc grapes of Vouvray and other Loire Valley wines, Hungary's Tokaji Aszú, German Trockenbeerenauslese Riesling, and several others throughout the world. See also entry 171.

183   Which wines are made from dried grapes?

Virtually all Old World wine-producing countries make a version of dried-grape wine. Drying the grapes can be done on the vine or, more commonly, in large rooms with strong ventilation built for the purpose. Drying brings them to a raisinlike state that sharply intensifies the sugar content by evaporating the water from the berries. Depending on the style of the wine, the high level of sugar can be fermented to dryness for a higher alcohol content, as in the Italian wine Amarone, or the fermentation can be stopped to maintain sweetness. Italy is perhaps the most famous and prolific producer of sweet dried-grape wines, with Recioto di Soave, Recioto della Valpolicella, and Vin Santo. Smaller-production wines, like the French Pacherenc du Vic-Bilh and Commandaria wines of Cyprus, are very hard to find, though worth sampling if you are in situ.

184   What is chaptalization?

Sometimes a winemaker gets stuck with unripe grapes. This happens often in cool climate wine regions, so to increase the level of alcohol in the final wine, the winemaker may add sugar either before or during fermentation (see entry 175). This technique is called chaptalization. See also entries 186 and 187.

185 What is "extended maceration"?

Maceration is when the grape juice soaks together with the red or white grape skins, flesh, seeds, and sometimes stems (known collectively as the pomace) before, during, or after fermentation, extracting color, body, and flavors from it. Some wines gain tremendous character and an amazing enhancement in texture by sitting on the pomace for longer periods of time, which is called extended maceration. It's a bit of a high-wire act, though, because the wine can also become overtannic (see entry 273). "Extraction" is a related term used with red wines. Most of the color, flavor, and aroma of red wine comes from the grape skins during maceration; extraction is the process of obtaining these elements from the grapes. An underextracted wine can taste watery and insipid, while an overextracted one may be highly colored but lack fruit and balance (see entry 276).

186 Where does acidity come from?

The acids in wine are chiefly tartaric acid and malic acid, both of which occur naturally in grapes. Unripe grapes have a high acidity level, and their acidity level falls as the sugar level rises during ripening. Cool-climate white grapes can have so much tart malic acidity (the same kind of acidity in apples) that the winemaker will cause the wine to go through a second fermentation called malolactic fermentation. This converts part of the tart malic acid into softer, smoother lactic acid (the kind in milk products).

Just as winemakers in cool climates have trouble achieving ripeness—and enough sugar in the grapes—winemakers in warm climates sometimes have trouble with overripeness—retaining enough acidity. Their solution is to "acidify" the wine—by literally adding tartaric or citric acid. The earlier this is done, the better, usually before or during fermentation. If the winemaker acidifies later, during blending (see entry 188), the acid may be easy to detect on the palate, once you know what you are tasting for— a disjointed flavor, as if someone added Sweet Tarts to the wine. See also entry 184.

187 What factors determine the alcohol level?

The major factor is the sugar level in the grape juice, but the type of yeast used in fermentation also has an effect. A higher natural level of sugar in the grapes offers an increased potential alcohol level (see entry 175). Because grapes grown in warm climates tend to be riper (having more natural sugars), wines from warm growing regions tend to have higher alcohol and wines from cooler regions tend to have lower alcohol. In some regions, though, the winemaker is allowed to add sugar or concentrated grape must to the grape juice before or during fermentation to increase the potential alcohol level of the wine (see entry 184). In addition, a winemaker's choice of cultured yeasts over natural yeasts—called ambient yeasts—has an effect on alcohol level, with several modern, engineered yeasts producing substantially more alcohol. Finally, the alcohol level of fortified wines is based partly on the addition of neutral grape spirits during the winemaking process (see entry 181).

188 When does blending happen?

Blending specifically refers to combining fermented wines. A famous example is nonvintage Champagne, where the winemaker's principal interest is in creating a cuvée (or blend of wines from different vineyards, vintages, and/or grapes) that maintains consistent flavors within that brand year after year. Bordeaux wines are almost all blends, mainly of Cabernet Sauvignon and Merlot. A winemaker can also blend different grapes in the same vats prior to fermentation, a process called co-fermentation. This process is used for some wines of the Côte Rôtie, where they blend Syrah and Viognier grapes. Winemakers will also utilize field blends, where they harvest from a vineyard that has different grapes growing together. These wines tend to be a bit more rustic, not from practice but because the vineyards were usually planted long ago by farmers more interested in good wine than in varietal purity.

Even varietal wines (wines labeled with a single variety of grape) tend to be blends, though, for two reasons: first, varietal wines are legally required to contain only 75 percent to 85 percent of that variety, with the balance consisting of wine from another grape or grapes blended in; second, even varietal wines that are 100 percent one grape are often blended from different batches of wine made from that specific grape. The wines may be grown in different vineyards, fermented using different techniques, or matured with or without oak, then blended together to add complexity.

189   What role does soil play?

Ideally, soil has three main roles. It provides nutrients and minerals
to the roots of the grapevine; it provides warmth to the grapevine
(absorbing heat either as a virtue of its color or its quantity of surface
rocks and radiating that heat to the plant); and it provides the right
balance between drainage and water retention to feed the roots
without creating conditions favorable to disease. Soil is considered

one of the primary
elements of terroir
(see entry 190) and has an
important impact on the
final flavor of the wine.
For example, the rocky
soil in Priorat (pictured)
helps retain the daytime's
heat against the cooler
evening temperatures.

190   What is terroir?

The French term "terroir" (tare-WAHR) doesn't translate neatly into
English. It means the confluence of weather, soil, elevation, diurnal
temperature swings, topography, and other location-specific criteria.
A French wine lover's feelings about terroir are as close to his heart
as his mother. Over time, smart grape growers came to understand
which grapes work best in their terroir. The Europeans have had a
head start on everyone else with centuries, even millennia, to sort out
the best grapes for their terroir. For instance, they long ago learned
that Pinot Noir grapes like cool, humid climates like Burgundy's,
and that same climate would be intolerable for Syrah, which does
best in the hot climates of southern France. New World viticulturists

from grape to glass

have had to rely on information gleaned over the last 150 years or less. Given that the cycle from raising mature vines to making properly aged wine averages ten years, that's a mere fifteen cycles.

191 What is phylloxera?

Phylloxera is a tiny aphid that kills grapevines through their roots. It was discovered in Europe in 1863 and within ten years had destroyed most of France's vineyards and caused serious damage over most of Europe. There is still no cure for the blight, but resistant rootstocks were developed from American vines in the late nineteenth century—today most grapevines all over the world are grafted onto American root stock to avoid phylloxera.

192 What does "biodynamic" mean?

Biodynamic refers to a cropping system that avoids all man-made chemicals and makes great use of planetary movements as well as the effects of the constellations. It is a modern interpretation of what farmers have known for centuries—that when and how they plant a crop has a profound effect on how the crop performs. Some biodynamic principles drive scientists and skeptics crazy, especially using the movements of the constellations. But several winemakers have become strong proponents, feeling that following biodynamic principles not only produces better grapes but also takes better care of their precious land.

193 Why use oak barrels?

Winemakers can potentially use oak barrels twice during the winemaking cycle—for fermentation and for aging—and both uses are optional, not mandatory. The barrels provide different benefits, depending on which process they are used for. When barrels are used for fermentation, the aromas imparted by the oak (such as vanilla, caramel, coffee) tend to be better integrated into the final wine. Though most wines see time in oak during the maturation process, Chardonnay is the grape most often fermented in the barrel, mostly due to Burgundy winemakers' historical success with the method. After the fermentation phase is finished, oak barrels may also be used to allow the wine to settle and mature. Although the barrels are watertight, they do allow a tiny bit of oxygen in, and alcohol out (by evaporation). These changes take place slowly, and just like any other living thing that has the chance to grow constantly and slowly age, the wine takes on additional complexity, even if it loses some of its fresh vitality. The effects of oak depend on a combination of factors, including the age and size of the barrels, at what stage the barrels are used (fermentation or maturation), for how long they're used, the geographic source of the oak, and to what extent the insides are fire-charred during barrel making. When oak is used for long aging, tannins from the cells of the wood are also contributed to the wine, but when the oak is used for too long, or is too new (see entry 195), the effects of the oak may overpower the wine, which may be referred to in tasting as "over-oaked." See also entry 274.

194 What's the controversy about oak?

With certain grapes and in certain winemaking areas, such as the Chardonnay of Chablis or the Sauvignon Blanc of New Zealand, winemakers have come to believe the use of oak destroys the subtle characteristics of grape and terroir (see entry 190) that make their wine special. There also exists a pendulum effect on how much the wine-drinking consumer wants to taste oak in his wine. As consumers and critics complain about over-oaked wines, some winemakers have responded by quitting oak altogether. Eventually the oak may be missed, and the pendulum will swing back in the other direction.

Economy is another reason to avoid oak. Each barrel costs a small fortune ($350 to $1,000) and each can be used only a few times and makes only twenty-five cases of wine. The use of barrels can add more than $3 to the winemaker's cost per bottle of wine. So what is an oak-loving winemaker to do? So far, the best solutions have been to use the barrels for more than one vintage (see entry 195) or to use a barrel substitute such as oak chips or staves (see entry 196).

A SECOND SIP *The best way to decide how you feel about the use of oak is to compare an unoaked Chardonnay against an oaked one. Once you know what oak tastes like, you can decide how much of it you like in your wine. Choose a reputable winemaker from Burgundy—Jadot, Drouhin, or Latour would be a good choice—and try one of their Chablis and one of their similarly priced non-Chablis Chardonnays from Burgundy. That controls the price, the maker, and the region, so that the major differences you taste between the two will come from the oak.*

195 Why do winemakers use old barrels?

When winemakers choose the right barrels and their effects are smoothly integrated in the wine, new oak barrels add just a hint of vanilla and caramel. But because new oak barrels are so expensive, winemakers frequently reuse barrels for two or three vintages, dividing the wine evenly among one-, two- and three-year-old barrels, then blending the three together at the end. The barrels lose some of their flavor and aroma intensity, but they retain their ability to offer slow oxygenation. In some regions, including Alsace, winemakers use the same barrels for decades because they have zero interest in oak flavors but tremendous interest in its help with maturation.

196 Getting oak flavor without barrels

Winemakers have budgets and time constraints. Given the cost of barrels (see entry 194) and the months or sometimes years that barrel-aging requires, some winemakers look for other ways to add oak character to their wines. One option is to use oak staves (modeled on individual staves from barrel making, like long sticks of oak) which fit into special holders in stainless steel tanks. This is cheaper, but no faster, than using barrels. Oak chips, which can vary in size from shavings to Ping-Pong ball size, work much more quickly and are very cheap. Unfortunately, unless they are applied perfectly, the wine can taste fractured, as if it had oak extract added. When done properly, though, this is an excellent compromise for huge wineries intent on getting a lot of high-quality wine out at a target price. Still, the oak barrel remains the gold standard. See also entry 274.

197 What is "unfiltered" wine?

Most winemakers filter wines to clear them of tiny particles, yeasts, and bacteria before bottling. This is an easy way to ensure that the wines arrive in your glass in good condition, and if the process is done right, it's unnoticeable. But not all winemakers agree that wines should be filtered. In fact, the makers of many expensive wines (as well as inexpensive ones that want to be held in the same company) abhor filtration. They believe it steals the wine's soul, that each particle removed would have added character and color to the wine. They also believe that if the wine is left alone long enough before bottling, most of the undesirable bits will sink to the bottom of the barrels. After weighing the pros (intensity of flavor, aroma, and color) and cons (less stability and the possibility of sediment in the bottle of unfiltered wine), large wineries tend to be fans of filtering because it offers more of a guarantee of problem-free wine. Many smaller or artisanal producers will leave the wine unfiltered, or filter only lightly. You may see "unfiltered" on the label if the producer has decided to market this fact.

198 Have number scores hurt winemakers?

Number scores on wines from the *Wine Spectator, Wine Advocate, Wine Enthusiast,* and other magazines started with the honorable intention of enlightening confused consumers, but scores have also created some unintentional backfires. One of those is that winemakers have come to believe that the magazines' reviewers have preferences for specific flavor profiles, so many winemakers try to make wines that will please the critics in order to get high scores. The difference in pricing and total sales between a wine given a score of 89 and one given a 90 can be mammoth. Consequently, many winemakers, especially those working for the huge companies, are less and less interested in playing to the local and historic tastes of their area and are instead moving toward international flavors. But one of the joys of great wines is that wines from all over the world taste different. As the international style takes over, many of those local flavors are being stamped out.

PATRICK FARRELL, MD, MW
Master of Wine and CEO of BevWizard, Inc.

Patrick Farrell, a physician who loves wine, suggests that a great way to lean about wine is to buy a book on the subject and open up a bottle of whatever you're reading about. "I was reading Kermit Lynch's *Adventures on the Wine Trail*, so I went out and bought a bunch of Kermit's wines and drank them while I read the book. Also, I did my residency in New York City and read the *Windows on the World* wine book by Kevin Zraly and had, thanks to some of my faculty members, some really good Bordeaux wines."

On favorite value wines, he says, "Whitehaven Sauvignon Blanc is a consistent winner. I buy that at Costco for about $12. I've long been a fan of Ridge Montebello, as well as their Zins and Chardonnays. Williams Selyem wines are not cheap, but they are very good quality for the cost. I am a really big fan of wines that get 86 or 87 points in the *Wine Advocate* or *Spectator*. A score like that is like getting kissed by your sister, but I often prefer those wines because they aren't so over-the-top. I also love rosés from all over the globe—especially from Provence, where they are bone-dry and so refreshing. Pinot Blanc, Pinot Gris, and Pinot Noir all work well at the dinner table. Most versions from California are over-oaked, though I love Flowers and Mary Edwards wines."

from grape to glass

Wine and Food

Wine *is* food. Served as a part of the meal for centuries, it enhances the appetite. It cleanses the palate so that each bite of food is tasted fresh and anew. The flavors and aromas in wine pair up with foods, creating new flavor hybrids. Wine aids in digestion. In this chapter, you will learn how to pair wines and foods to get the best flavors possible, and how and why the Europeans have classically paired certain foods with specific wines. The goal here is to give you the information you need to expertly match a wine with its best food.

199 Do I have to follow the "rules"?

No. There is nothing wrong with flying in the face of conventional wisdom and pairing a California Chardonnay with a grilled rib-eye steak or having a bottle of Barossa Shiraz with oysters. If the combination makes you happy, then it works for you. On the other hand, anyone who spends hours fussing over the spices and herbs in a nice dinner will likely care about finding a wine that enhances the food and vice versa. The key is to find a combination that accomplishes two goals. First, neither food nor wine should overpower the flavors or aromas of the other. And second, a bite of one and a sip of the other should make you want to go through the cycle again. As long as you follow those principles, everything should work out fine.

A SECOND SIP *In this section it is necessary to take a generalist's view of the differences between wine-growing regions to help find the right wine-and-food pairing. All wine-growing regions have some winemakers who try to emulate someone else's style, so you might find a Washington wine that tastes like a French wine and vice versa. This is where an informative server or salesperson becomes a valuable commodity. These recommendations pair the classic wines of a grape or region with guaranteed winners for food, but the goal is also to offer ingredient ideas to help you create your own dishes. Don't be afraid to experiment. And if you aren't having a great time, you are taking it too seriously.*

200 White for fish and red for meat?

This rule is easy to remember but grossly inaccurate. Learning to pair food and wine is too complex to be summed up in a simple phrase. A sensory evaluation of food and wine involves aromas, tastes, weight, density, and mouthfeel, and those characteristics can yield hundreds of permutations, some quite unpredictable. White Pinot Gris from Alsace goes well with their local pork stew, while Oregon salmon works well with Oregon's red Pinot Noir. The best rule is to try not only some established combinations but also try nontraditional ones that appeal to you.

201 What is one easy guideline?

Whether you're trying to find a wine for a dish or a recipe for a wine, think of its country and region of origin. What do the local residents eat and drink? Want a Pinot Noir? In Oregon, salmon is the most popular fish, and the most popular wine is Pinot Noir. Try them together.

202 How many calories are in a glass of wine?

The majority of a dry wine's calories come from alcohol. One gram of alcohol is about 7 calories, and a 5-ounce glass of wine is just over 140 grams of liquid. Using the alcohol percentage of the wine, you can figure out how many grams of alcohol are in a standard glass. A German Kabinett Riesling at 8 percent alcohol would be carrying 78 alcohol calories ($140 \times .08 = 11.2$ grams of alcohol in the glass $\times 7$ calories), while a 14 percent Sonoma Zinfandel would have 138 alcohol calories. The wines with the biggest calorie count are sweet fortified wines such as cream sherries or Ports. At 20 percent alcohol, these wines yield 250 alcohol calories, and that's before adding in a significant number of sugar calories. In general:

> **DRY RED WINE** (5 oz.) = 130 calories
> **DRY WHITE WINE** (5 oz.) = 120 calories
> **CHAMPAGNE** (5 oz.) = 100 calories

203 What is an "aperitif wine"?

An aperitif wine is consumed before a meal. Traditionally, in Old World Europe, an aperitif was often a sparkling wine, a liqueur, or a fortified wine meant to stimulate the appetite. Prime examples include Campari, Punt e Mes, Lillet, Dubonnet, various vermouths, and Champagne. With regard to wine, especially in the New World, the term has expanded to include wines that stimulate conversation—that is, high alcohol (about 40 proof) and low acidity wines meant to be pleasant even without food. The prime examples in the United States are any sparkling wine, California Chardonnay, and Italian Pinot Grigio. Soft New World reds such as Pinot Noir or Merlot, or jammy wines such as Zinfandel also do well. See also entry 204.

204 What wines are best for sipping without food?

White wines with moderate acidity, well-balanced alcohol, and light-to-medium body do best, but red wines with soft tannins will also work. Every country makes at least a few wines that fit the criteria.

FRANCE	Champagne and other sparkling wines, Sancerre, Muscadet, Pinot Blanc, rosé, Côtes du Rhône
ITALY	Prosecco, Pinot Grigio, Gavi, Sauvignon, Pinot Bianco, Montepulciano d'Abruzzo
SPAIN	Cava, Albariño, Verdejo, Fino or Manzanilla Sherry, Bobal, Rioja Blanco
PORTUGAL	Alvarinho, dry white Port
NEW WORLD	Sparkling wine, Chardonnay, Pinot Grigio, Sauvignon Blanc, Pinot Noir, Merlot, Zinfandel

wine and food

205 Which wines are best for cooking?

Remember this rule: if the bottle label says "Cooking Wine," don't use it. Wines made expressly for cooking are usually of very low quality. Cook only with wines you would be happy to drink. Beyond that, it's usually best to cook with a wine made from the same grape you will be drinking with your meal, and vice versa—coq au vin made with Pinot Noir deserves a Pinot Noir with dinner.

206 Is wine vegan?

The best answer is: it depends. Most wines use animal products to process the wine so it doesn't look cloudy. The two most common things used are egg whites and Bentonite clay. For a person trying to avoid all animal products, Bentonite is the best way to go. The problem is, hardly any winemakers take the trouble to put something on the label affirming it's vegan-friendly. Kosher wines are always OK for vegans, but good bottles can be hard to find outside major cities, and the best (such as Château Valandraud, from Bordeaux) can be brutally expensive. Newton in California makes three wonderful vegan-friendly wines, a Chardonnay, a Cabernet Sauvignon, and a Merlot, but they all run about $50 a bottle. From Australia, Brown Brothers Liqueur Muscat is a great dessert wine that uses no animal products, and one of the Barossa's superstars, Peter Lehmann, makes almost all of his wines without animal products. Finally, Champagne goes with everything, and both Bollinger NV and Piper-Heidsieck's NV are vegan-friendly. Your retailer may also be able to recommend wines that are produced according to vegan standards.

207 What to bring if I don't know what's on the menu

Almost everyone loves Champagne, and it is a superb food wine that also works well for sipping. Most chefs appreciate Riesling for its vivid acidity and appley aromas. Its fruitiness and acidity make Riesling a good match with almost any food. Look for a dry version such as Trimbach's from Alsace or a Kabinett from Germany. For red wines, the goal should be to find a subtle version that could possibly go with light dishes. Burgundy or a Cru Beaujolais would work nicely. And if the audience is sophisticated enough to appreciate a rosé, a bone-dry version from any New or Old World site would also work well.

208 Why are high-acidity wines good with food?

Rich foods with a lot of cream, butter, or animal fat will throw a fatty blanket over the tastebuds. Wine's acidity comes along and scrubs the tongue clean with every sip, allowing each bite of food to taste like the first. Wines that taste hopelessly austere and acidic on their own come to life around rich foods such as paté, here served with Beaujolais. Acidity can be experienced positively as tartness or liveliness, where the wine almost feels like it is dancing around the tongue. Low-acidity wines don't clean the palate, their intensity can obstruct food's delicate flavors, and they tend to leave simple grape flavors sitting on the palate. In essence, they become another course in the meal.

Champagne is a universally great match with food because of its acidity level, and Riesling is a close second for food-friendliness. Chenin Blanc is not the most versatile food wine, but both New World and Old World dry versions go well with oysters on the half-shell, white fish, butter sauces, and goat cheeses. Of red wines, Nebbiolo and Sangiovese are famously acidic Italians (see entries 153 and 155). Beaujolais is an often overlooked food wine with near perfect acidity. Skip the Beaujolais Nouveau and Villages and buy from one of the ten regions in Beaujolais referred to as crus, which produce stunning wines at ridiculously low prices. Three of them—Fleurie, Morgon, and Moulin-à-Vent—are even better than some of their big brother Burgundies, and at a fraction of the cost.

See also entries 207 and 224.

209 Why are Champagne and oysters a classic match?

Champagne is the most versatile of all wines. It is delightful with raw foods from hamachi sashimi to steak tartare and cooked foods from baked oysters to sautéed foie gras. Champagne has three secret weapons. First, the carbonation acts like millions of tiny scrubbing bubbles to cleanse your palate. Then its refreshing acidity works with the carbonation to make each taste as rousing as the first (see entry 208)—it acts like a spritz of lemon juice on raw oysters. Finally, since Champagne is available in different textures and levels of sweetness, you can even fine-tune the pairing. The most common levels of sweetness made in Champagne, with each consecutively sweeter, are Brut, Extra Dry, and Demi Sec. The next entry features foods that are ideal matches with Champagne and sparkling wines.

210 Sparkling performances

There is no more versatile wine to make a dinner perfect than a well-made sparkling wine. For foods as delicate as oysters all the way to a grilled steak, a perfect sparkling wine awaits the chance to be paired with your cuisine.

IF YOU'RE HAVING . . .	TRY . . .
Brut Blanc de Blancs Champagne (100 percent Chardonnay)	delicate white fish, shellfish, pastas with light sauces
Brut Blanc de Noirs Champagne (100 percent Pinot Noir)	darker poultry, oily fish like eel or tuna belly
Brut Cuvée Champagne (Neither Blanc de Blancs nor Blanc de Noirs, a mixture of grapes)	light poultry, most cheeses that aren't too pungent, lightly smoked white fish, sushi
Brut Rosé Champagne	pink meats such as pork or veal, pink fish such as salmon, rich shellfish, crab omelets
Extra Dry Champagne or sparkling wine	spicy Asian foods
Demi Sec or Sec Champagne or sparkling wine	cheese or unsweetened berries
Prosecco	aperitifs, seafood such as calamari, lighter risotto, and pasta
German Sekt	pork and sauerkraut dishes
Sparkling Shiraz	grilled meat during dinner and chocolate afterward
Spanish Cava	savory tapas such as Pollo al Ajillo (chicken with garlic) or Espárragos Blancos (white asparagus) for dry versions; Manchego y Membrillo (Manchego cheese with quince paste) for sweeter versions

211 Any easy matches for Chardonnay?

Chardonnay is one of the most popular wine grapes in the world, whether in the elegant Burgundy style or the extra-fruity and densely flavorful California version. Many people drink the wine as an aperitif (see entry 203) rather than with a meal because it is a friendly drink without food, and notoriously tough to match with most cuisines. No matter the style, the one ingredient you can count on pairing with Chardonnay is butter. Whether you prefer the cleansing acidity of the French approach or the ripe, high-alcohol American variety, it will make magic with butter. Chardonnay also does well with shellfish, so lobster or crab dipped in butter is as good as it gets. The classic French matchup is snails with butter and parsley. Roasted corn on the cob with butter also works well. Cream is almost as good, whether sour or fresh. Both baked potatoes with sour cream and pasta with shrimp and a pesto cream sauce go well with either the New World style or the Old (see Introduction). See also entries 76 and 213.

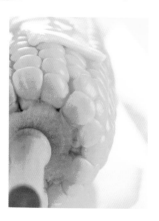

212 What foods go with Gewürztraminer?

The winemakers of Alsace hold their hands over their hearts when they speak of Gewürztraminer. Few wines anywhere can boast such complexity of aromas, with its hint of petrol, paperwhite narcissus, and roses. Styles run the gamut, but most are either regular-harvest and dry, late-picked and unpredictably dry (Vendange Tardive, or what we call Late Harvest), or late-picked and sweet (called Sélection de Grains Nobles). Many Asian foods work well with the dry versions, especially Vietnamese spring rolls, curries, and spicy or gingery Chinese, Thai, or Vietnamese dishes. The dry Vendange Tardive allows you to try the Alsace dish *choucroute garni* the way it was meant to be eaten. This dish is packed with intense flavors from sauerkraut, sausage, and smoked meats, and the floral Gewürztraminer contrasts the food and adds layers of new flavors. The sweet Sélection de Grains Nobles is a rare and wonderful wine that should be drunk by itself, but if you must, a not-too-sweet *panna cotta* works nicely.

While dozens of countries grow Gewürztraminer, the only other place besides Alsace to really master it is the Alto Adige in Italy, where the wines are very much lighter and lower in alcohol. A frittata Granapadano with cheese is a good match, as is any Thai dish with coconut and curry.

213   Pairing wine and cheese

Wines generally pair correctly with cheeses from the same area, but don't fear trying others as well. Here are a few dependable winners:

WINE	IDEAL CHEESE MATCHES
Beaujolais (Cru)	soft cheeses such as Camembert and Brie
Burgundy (red)	Epoisses de Bourgogne
Burgundy (white)	Aisy Cendré or Cîteaux
Cabernet Sauvignon	cheddar (sharp)
Cava (Extra Dry style)	Manchego with quince paste
Champagne (Brut style)	Brie
Chardonnay (New World)	Humboldt Fog goat cheese
Dessert wines	Roquefort, Double Gloucester, aged Gouda, Parmesan, or Epoisses de Bourgogne
Gewürztraminer	Muenster (young cheese with dry Gewürz, aged with sweet)
Malbec	Parmesan
Merlot	Brie
Moscato d'Asti	Robiola di Roccaverano or mild goat cheese with a drop or two of good olive oil
Nebbiolo	truffled cheeses
Pinot Grigio	Grana Padano
Rutherglen Muscats	veined cheeses
Sangiovese	Pecorino
Sauvignion Blanc	fresh goat cheese
Tempranillo	Manchego, Campo de Montalban, Murcia Al Vino, or another goat cheese
Zinfandel	Roquefort

214 Pinot Grigio and Pinot Gris: what's the difference?

Pinot Grigio is the Italian name for the grape the French call Pinot Gris. The two countries produce very different styles of wine, and producers of the grape from around the world have adopted one name or the other to define their own style. Pinot Grigio has become synonymous with the light, refreshing style, no matter where it is made. If the label says Pinot Gris, as in Alsace, the wine will be more complex and intense, with higher alcohol and such intensity of flavor and density in the mouth that it may be too much even for Chardonnay drinkers.

For Pinot Grigio and food pairing, *light* is the catchword. Think of light fish, light soups. The Italians love Pinot Grigio with *zuppa de pesce*. New World Pinot Grigio has a tad less acidity, but enough to work with California cuisine, such as grilled shrimp, mild white fish with a lemon butter sauce, grilled calamari, or pasta with a light cream sauce.

In France, they serve Pinot Gris with meat, especially pork with dill sauce and the Alsace version of sauerkraut. The other great location for the Pinot Gris style is Oregon, where the wine isn't quite so massive and frequently has even better acidity. Steamer clams, raw oysters, and mussels done in a *moules marinière* style work beautifully for a light meal. The Oregon version can also handle sweet shellfish and cream, like crab bisque. Both New World and Old World styles marry with spicy Asian foods—whether Thai, Indian, Malay, Vietnamese, Chinese, or Japanese—so perfectly as to be a no-brainer. See also entry 239.

215   How to try Riesling

Riesling comes in three styles. Germans make it as a light, low-alcohol wine with big aromas and plenty of acidity. Just across the Rhine in Alsace, the Riesling is higher in alcohol and fruitier. In the New World, the wine generally slots neatly between the two Old World versions. In all locations, Riesling can come in any style, from tongue-puckering dry to honey sweet. Its range of flavors and fantastic acidity put it up there with Champagne as one of the world's best food wines. Germans drink Riesling with everything, but that's at least partly due to civic pride rather than culinary creativity. In both Alsace and Germany, they pour Riesling with the myriad versions of pork and sauerkraut because its fruitiness is such a nice contrast with the acidity of the sauerkraut. New World versions love light fish-and-butter sauces such as trout with brown butter. Barely sweet Rieslings from all over the world go well with Indian food and almost all spicy Asian foods. See also entries 207 and 208.

A SECOND SIP *There are two confounding problems with Old World Rieslings that make it difficult to pair them perfectly. The Alsace wines have no indication of sweetness on the label and can range from dry to quite sugary; and German winemakers, who are under a lot of pressure since the world started its love affair with dry wines, are now allowing dry vinification of their wines. In the recent past, the classic German styles of Riesling in order of sweetness were Kabinett, Spätlese, Auslese, Beerenauslese, and Trockenbeerenauslese. Now a few wineries even make high-alcohol, bone-dry Ausleses, and the consumer can no longer rely on these words to reveal the sweetness of the wine in the bottle. Since there's no way to predict the sweetness of either Alsace or German Rieslings, you'll have to rely on a good seller who knows the product.*

216 What foods go with Sauvignon Blanc?

Here again we have three very different versions of wine made from the grape. New Zealand's has such intense grapefruit flavors that you might wonder if the winemaker vinified grapefruit juice instead of grape juice. California wines add other tropical fruit aromas such as pineapple and passion fruit. The Old World's Sancerre and Friulian Sauvignon (the Italians omit the word "Blanc") epitomize the fruit itself. They are much more subtle and multifaceted, with hints of steel, just-mown grass, pineapple, and citrus intermingled.

The New Zealand version needs something to mitigate all that grapefruit, and sweet shellfish such as scallops with a lemon-butter sauce works perfectly. Most New World versions can be stout enough to stand up to trout amandine or even fried chicken. Old World Sauvignon Blanc is more restrained and complex, but its acidity complements fatty fish, butter, and cream, such as poached salmon with béchamel sauce. See also entry 90.

HINT *For a perfect pairing, start with a simple piece of fresh goat cheese, add a drizzle of lemon juice, a few drops of good olive oil, and a sprinkle of white pepper. Grab a loaf of crusty bread and a bottle of Sancerre, and life will look very nice.*

217 What's the rule for Viognier?

Viognier is catching on all across the world as people discover its lush, generous flavors and perfumed peachy aromas. The New World versions (see entry 92) vary from simple wines, some of which are a bit low in acidity, to perfectly rounded, dry, and acidic wines. The Old World version (called Condrieu) reduces the peach aromas while adding steel and mineral plus other stone fruit aromas. But the bottom line is, if it goes with peaches, it will go with Viognier. And, of course, what's more classic with peaches than cream? The Viognier will need to have bracing acidity, so be sure to ask, but cream sauces will work well. Roast pork or ham and sweet potatoes do well with peaches and also with Viognier. New World Viognier also mates well with sweet shellfish such as crab, shrimp, lobster, or scallops. Condrieu has enough mineral flavors to go well with dill, so try salmon with dill butter sauce.

218 What should I serve with rosé?

Rosés come in every level of sweetness, but the best food wines will be dry to off-dry, with good acidity. A good rule of thumb is that pink foods will go with pink wine. So think of salmon, snapper, shrimp, lobster, veal, pork, mild charcuterie, and even rhubarb, as long as it's in a savory dish. Rosés go well with tomatoes and chile peppers. Pasta with crushed tomatoes and basil or Sichuan food are great choices. On the casual side, almost any rosé is a great summertime wine—served chilled with backyard-type foods, including barbecue, rosé does dual duty as both white and red.

219 Why does meat pair so well with Cabernet?

Hang around folks in the wine industry long enough and you'll hear the phrase "Slab and a Cab." While that cogent phrase is meant to be clever, it's also true that nothing works with a Cabernet Sauvignon better than a slab of meat, preferably one that is roasted or broiled at heat sufficient to caramelize the surfaces. This holds true with an austere and elegant Bordeaux as much as with a massively fruity Napa Cab. The meat and wine perform a delicate dance in which the meat's fats and proteins hug the mouth, protecting it from the wine's tannins, until those tannins finally start to strip the fats and refresh the palate. The redder the meat, the better the match, so try things like grilled rib eye or tenderloin steak, prime rib, grilled lamb chops, or rack or roast leg of lamb. For one-pot cooking, braised shoulder meat or beef stew also work. The sticking point will be the sauce. Cabs from New World locations such as California and Chile have plenty of fruit, barrel character, and alcohol, so you can easily use fresh herbs such as basil, thyme, rosemary, or tarragon. With a Bordeaux, the perfect accompaniment is roast beef with a slab of butter. Toss some baby peppers and zucchini with olive oil, then salt and pepper, and broil them until they are lightly caramelized and you'll have the perfect carnivore's banquet. See also entry 221.

220 Is Grenache good with food?

Grenache is one of the dominant grapes in southern Rhône wines and is also widely used in Spain (where it's called Garnacha) and Australia. It's frequently low in acidity and tannin, so it's usually blended with other grapes such as Syrah and Mourvèdre, although we're starting to see it as a single varietal wine. Grenache has two key flavors: blackberries and black pepper. Anything savory that pairs well with these will pair well with Grenache. Grilled or roasted meats, green salads with not-too-acidic dressings, goose or duck liver, sautéed duck breast, and even hamburgers match well with Grenache. But it meets its highest calling with lamb, whether a roasted leg, braised shanks, a grilled rack, or lamb pie. To experience Grenache at its best, find a blend from the areas of Châteauneuf-du-Pape, Gigondas, or Rasteau in France, Priorat in Spain, or South Australia (G-S-M is the local term, which stands for Grenache-Syrah-Mourvèdre). Grenache also contributes some of the world's great rosés, wines ideal for grilled burgers, fried chicken, and starchy vegetables such as peas and corn. See also entry 107.

221 What wines are best for carnivores?

Meat is the perfect use for wines with plenty of tannin—think Cabernet Sauvignon (see entry 219). The big tannins, dark fruit flavors, and plummy aromas of Argentine Malbec make a great wine for the Argentine national dish, the huge servings of various grilled meats called *parillas*. Beef with a good hit of smoke, parsley, basil, thyme, garlic, lemon juice—all these things work with a good Malbec.

Tuscans, too, are great carnivores. In fact, their beloved *bistecca alla fiorentina* is such a massive slab of grilled meat it would cause most Texans to go apoplectic. These are the largest of all cattle, with bulls that stand six feet at the shoulders and weigh up to 3,800 pounds. A well-marbled T-bone is food for four, and nothing goes better with it than a bottle of nicely aged Brunello.

For a braise or a stew, go instead to Piedmont for a Barolo, Barbaresco, or Barbera, or to the Southern Rhone for a Grenache-based blend. A Southern Rhone red will also work with lamb. The Basque are great lovers of lamb, and the reds of Rioja (made from Tempranillo) and rosés made from Garnacha (aka Grenache) are community favorites. The Greeks like Naoussa with lamb, made from the very tannic Xynomavro grape.

For recommendations for pork or barbecue, see entries 218 and 233. See also entries 200, 208, and 219.

222 Pairing wine with wild game

The trick here is to remember that game is gamey. For wild venison or pig, the "wild" flavors call for a similar approach in the wine. Old World wines that have a reputation for wild flavors include Rhône wines from the areas of Crozes-Hermitage, St. Joseph (both made mostly from Syrah), and Gigondas (Grenache, Syrah, and Mourvèdre). All three of these grapes are grown worldwide, and they all have ripe berry and dark fruit flavors. So if blackberries or plums would pair well with the game, so would these wines. California's Rhône Rangers (see entry 118) are still operating at full speed, proselytizing for these Rhône grapes, especially in the Paso Robles area—if you want a New World version, try one of Cline's Ancient Vines wines, the Carignan, Zinfandel, or most especially the Mourvèdre. Italy's Barolo (made from the Nebbiolo grape) and the Pinot Noir of Burgundy and Central Otago in New Zealand can also have gamey aromas and robust fruit flavors, although not as intense. They would work nicely with hare or game birds. See also entry 144.

223 What foods go with Merlot?

Until the movie *Sideways* cast Merlot as a villain, it was one of the world's most popular grapes. The good news, for those who love the grape's velvety mouthfeel and dark fruit flavors, is that many Merlots are now bargains for the quality. For the Old World versions— Bordeaux from the areas around St. Emilion and Pomerol, and all over Italy—expect more tannins and a bit more austerity, but also more nuanced aromas. Dishes with savory tomato sauces and rich proteins are right for these wines—a meat loaf with a light tomato sauce or a lasagne. New World Merlots, especially those from the Americas, have more generous fruit and softer tannins and work well with any meat. They also have enough fruit to stand up to a pan-sautéed duck breast with a tart blackberry sauce, or pork chops in a mustard cream sauce.

224　How to try Nebbiolo

Nebbiolo is one of the world's best food wines (see entry 208). It is the grape of Barolo, Barbaresco, Gattinara, Ghemme, and Roero, all areas in Piedmont. Nebbiolo by itself is so tannic it might remind you of sucking on yesterday's tea bag, but the second you add a big protein to the equation, the fruit flavors pop out. The Piemontese people provide the best tip on what to match with Nebbiolo. *Tonno di coniglio* is a classic dish whose main flavors are rabbit, a hearty vegetable broth, and sage. Or you can get these flavors with grilled pork tenderloin with cubes of cooked butternut squash sautéed with butter and sage. The local beef is as good as Argentine beef, so if you want a grilled steak, go high quality. Finally, for vegetarians, remember that Piedmont is home of the white truffle, and what's better than pasta with butter and a drizzle of white truffle oil? See also entry 153.

225 What foods go with Pinot Noir?

Just as the movie *Sideways* buried the Merlot business, it gave Pinot Noir growers all over the world the best years of their lives, though a newcomer who tastes a Pinot from each of Oregon, California, France, New Zealand, and Australia won't think they're tasting the same grape. Pinot Noirs range from delicate and perfumed Burgundies to Zinfandel-like versions from California, so matching them with food can be a challenge. The heartier California wines from the Russian River Valley, Carneros, and the Central Coast do nicely with braised lamb shanks or a roasted pork shoulder. For vegans, try mushroom-barley soup or a grilled portabello and a side of bitter greens such as mustard or kale. The wine's fruitiness will play off the greens beautifully. See also entry 102. One ingredient works with all: mushrooms, especially when combined with meat. Salmon with a mushroom sauce is a perfect foil for any of the drier versions, such as the wines of Burgundy, the Adelaide Hills of Australia, and the Willamette Valley in Oregon. Central Otago in New Zealand is one of the most exciting Pinot areas in the world right now because of its juxtaposition of Old World complexity and New World fruitiness. Try Kim Crawford's Central Otago "Rise-and-Shine" Creek Pinot Noir along with mushroom crostini.

226 Does tomato sauce work with Chianti?

Yes. Pasta with a fresh tomato sauce brings out the fruitiness of the Sangiovese grape used in Chianti, and its famous acidity can stand up to that in tomatoes. Sangiovese is the workhorse grape of Italy—it shows up in Tuscany's Chianti and Brunello as well as in wine from dozens of other areas throughout the country, any of which pair beautifully with tomato-based dishes. See also entry 155.

227 What do the Aussies eat with Shiraz?

New World Shiraz (such as from Australia, California, or Washington) has a colossal fruitiness that is fun for the drinker, but tough on the cook. You want food that is texturally as dense yet that contrasts with the fruitiness of the wine. One ingredient that works with all Shiraz is smoke. Any country's version of barbecue works (dry-rubbed—no sauce!), whether pork, beef, lamb or mutton, chicken, or a fatty fish such as salmon. The Aussies eat lamb with their Shiraz. One wine choice that would cover all the bases is a wine made by several companies that the Australians call G-S-M (Grenache-Syrah-Mourvèdre). For carnivores and vegetarians alike, pizza margarita works well. Another vegetarian dish with broad appeal requires a loaf of good, crusty bread, some top-flight olive oil, smoked salt (available in gourmet shops), a few heirloom tomatoes, a handful of fresh basil leaves, and some fresh mozzarella: layer the tomatoes, basil, and cheese, and drizzle with oil for a nice Caprese salad. Lightly season it with the smoked salt and use the bread to soak up the tomato juices and olive oil. See also entry 233.

228 What wine goes best with Spanish tapas?

This one's simple: stay local with Tempranillo. Spanish Tempranillo is grown across Spain, but Rioja wines are probably the best-known version. Tempranillo really needs food, but it needn't be complicated. A wedge of either Manchego or Campo de Montalban cheese and a loaf of bread would be fine. The Spanish love *patatas a la riojana,* a combo of potatoes, sausage, onions, garlic, and peppers. The fat in most any type of sausage works with the cleansing acidity of Tempranillo, and if the sausage is mildly picante, like chorizo, all the better. Paella is a work of art that changes with every making, but the constants are rice, stock, saffron, and olive oil. As a featured ingredient, most any nonleafy vegetable and any animal is fair game. For lighter seafood and vegetarian tapas, try a white wine from the Spanish Albariño grape, or a Portuguese Vinho Verde, from the same grape, called Alvarinho in Portugal—or a light, nutty fino sherry. See also entries 162, 163, and 166.

229 What foods go with Zinfandel?

This is America's wine. Big, brash, powerful, occasionally too aggressive, but always beckoning. The grape was popular with early Italian immigrants in California, and it works well with all the Italian-American hybrid dishes that are so popular in America, such as pizza-parlor pizza, spaghetti and meatballs, or any of the myriad tomato-based pasta sauces. In fact, anything with tomato sauce works well with Zinfandel by bringing out its sweetness. Zin even pairs nicely with the San Francisco fish dish cioppino.

Grilled meats or sausages also work, and Zinfandel is the only wine to drink with fajitas. And if you want a red quaffing wine, Zinfandel is one of the best because of its exuberant fruitiness (but watch out for the typically high alcohol). See also entry 108.

230 How do sauces affect a pairing?

We use sauces to impart additional flavors, pleasing aromas, moistness, and a silky mouthfeel to food. But because many sauces contain acidity and fats, they can make for a tricky wine pairing. There are combinations that might sound good but taste bad. Sauvignon Blanc and sea bass normally work well together, but put a citrus-based sauce on the fish and it falls flat because the acids in the wine and the sauce fight each other. A wine such as Riesling, with a bit of sweetness to balance its acidity, goes well with pork, but add a sweet fruit sauce and the wine will taste purely acidic, because the sweet sauce overwhelms the sugars in the wine. Most sauces contain ingredients, such as herbs, spices, or mustard, that are just as strongly flavored as the main ingredient of the dish, so care is required. It's best to look back to the Old World cuisine the grape originally came from to see if that culture uses in its own foods the main flavor ingredients that are in the sauce you have in mind. For instance, Germans cook with dill, so you can count on it working with Riesling. Herbes de Provence contains thyme, savory, rosemary, basil, bay leaf, and marjoram—all of which work with the Mourvèdre, Syrah, and Grenache of the Bandol region of Provence. See also entry 208.

231 What goes with spicy foods?

Every person has a different number of taste buds. Folks with the most taste buds have the most trouble with chiles and other spicy foods. It is also much harder to find a beverage to put the fire out. There are dozens of myths about what puts out the fire in your mouth (note: eat some bread). As for wines, the semisweet wines of Alsace, Austria, and Germany in the Old World, and Mendocino and Washington in the New World, work with spicy foods from India, China, Korea, Japan, and Southeast Asia. Grapes that work include Riesling, Grüner Veltliner, Gewürztraminer (see entry 212), Pinot Gris, and Muscat. Picante Mexican foods, especially with tomato sauces, are much harder to match. The best choice is what the Mexicans drink—an *horchata,* a fruit juice, or a beer—or go with nice iced sangria made from Zinfandel or Syrah.

232 Are sweet wines inferior?

You may have heard a rumor that sweet wines are unsophisticated. Its origins likely lie in the fact that, traditionally, terrible wines have hidden their dreadfulness with sugar. Whether it's your granny's $3 bottle of cooking sherry or a $2 bottle of white Zinfandel, sugar hides all ills. But it's the quality of the wine that gave rise to this myth, not the sweetness. Some of the world's greatest wines are sweet and some are dry. The important question is not "Is it sweet?" but "Is it good?"

233 What wines go with barbecue?

There are three styles of barbecue: without sauce (dry-rubbed), with a vinegar sauce, and with a sweet sauce. For dry versions, virtually any red wine will work, but barbecue is a food of the Americas, so go with an American grape such as Zinfandel or Petite Sirah (there's nothing petite about it). Vinegar sauces are very hard to match, because the vinegar is highly acidic, and when you combine the two, the wine will taste dead. Break down and have a beer. A big, brooding red wine is the way to go for the sweet sauces. Use the sweet sauce very sparingly and have a Shiraz (see entry 227), Zinfandel, Petite Sirah, a French Rhône wine (northern or southern), a Spanish Priorat or a Barbera from Piedmont. This is also one of the few places where the notoriously un-food-friendly White Zinfandel works—especially with spicy barbecue. See also entry 231.

234 What pairs well with chicken?

The old axiom "white wine with white meats, red wine with red meats" has some limited value, but not when it comes to chicken—one of the culinary world's great inventions is coq au vin, and the "vin" is red Burgundy from Pinot Noir. Pinot does go with almost any chicken dish, as long as a pungent sauce doesn't dominate the flavor. Chicken is also one of the few meats that goes well with a buttery California Chardonnay. Riesling goes with everything, chicken included. And then there's cru Beaujolais, the bargain basement wine of Burgundy. Made from the Gamay grape, it makes magic with the juicier and more flavorful dark meat of a chicken. Look for wines from the Fleurie, Morgon, and Moulin-à-Vent areas of Beaujolais. Chicken salad comes in hundreds of variations, and a wine pairing depends entirely on the ingredients used to make it, although Rieslings generally work. For fried chicken, try a sparkling wine similar to the quality of the fried chicken. Fast food? Have a cheap Cava. Painstakingly made at home with your great-grandmother's recipe? Have a nice Champagne.

MAYNARD JAMES KEENAN

Winemaker (Caduceus Cellars) and singer

Maynard James Keenan—lead singer for Tool and A Perfect Circle—has had fourteen Top 40 singles and sold more than 15 million albums. With all his success in the world of rock and roll, what really lights his rockets is making wine. Asked how he made the transition, he laughs. "Wine, women, and song. Seems simple enough." He says his concept of wine has changed from big bruisers to more elegant wines over the last few years. "I am from the U.S., so sugar was a portion of my diet," he said. "So when I started with wines, I wanted super-rich, super-oaked-out wines like Silver Oak and Grange. But as my palate developed, I got into the more subtle and restrained wines."

His recommendations for learning are all about contrast. "[When it comes to] pairing wines with food, develop a relationship with a good wine guy and have him recommend a wine that goes with a dish, but also one that doesn't go at all. It's important to catch the failure as much as the success. Once you've found a great food/wine pairing, drink a Coke and have a Snickers bar, and see how they completely destroy the experience. Or go for extremes, like have a bottle of Conundrum followed by a big buttery Chardonnay from California. Or get a Penfolds Bin 389 Cab Shiraz and then go the opposite with a French Pinot. That's how you learn."

what's a wine lover to do?

235 What to pour with Thanksgiving dinner

When it comes to turkey, there are two model choices: a cru Beaujolais from the Juliénas or Morgon area or an acidic American Merlot such as Chappellet from California or Chateau Ste. Michelle's Cold Creek Vineyard from Washington. The wine for a big banquet should have plenty of acidity. High-acidity wine isn't so good as an aperitif, but it is perfect for a huge meal. Both the Beaujolais and the Merlot are magic with turkey and just as good with ham, but it is vital to avoid serving sweet foods with these wines, or the wines will taste sour. Tart cranberries are fine, but the less sugar the better. If your ham has a sweet brown-sugar glaze (or if southern-style sweet potato casserole tops your menu), opt for a white with a hint of sweetness. A fruity German Riesling in the Spätlese style would be ideal. From the United States, choose a Riesling from New York, Michigan, Washington, or Mendocino County, California. See also entry 82.

236 What wines go with fried foods?

It depends on what's being fried and what sauces you might use. Light tempura fish with a delicate soy-based sauce goes nicely with Blanc de Blancs Champagne (which is also amazing with French fries), Chablis, New Zealand Chardonnay, Sancerre, or dry to off-dry Riesling. At the other extreme, a chicken-fried steak with cream gravy would need New World Cabernet or Shiraz. The key for any pairing with fried foods is mouth-cleansing acidity in the wine, to laser through the frying fat. After determining acidity, pick a wine that would go with whatever is being fried. See also entry 237.

237 Good wines for fast foods

Fast food doesn't have to be bad food, and every meal deserves wine. Here are some options for pairing some everyday foods with a compatible wine.

IF YOU'RE HAVING . . .	TRY . . .
burgers (with cheese; with bacon)	Zinfandel, southern Rhône, Australian G-S-M
hot dogs/corn dogs	Washington Merlot
pizza	Zinfandel or Chianti Classico
fried chicken	Spanish Cava or California sparkling wine
tacos	Sangria
French fries	Cava, Champagne, or Prosecco
popcorn shrimp	Chablis or Chilean Sauvignon Blanc
Buffalo wings	Riesling
ribs	Syrah or Shiraz
Philly cheesesteak	Australian Merlot or Argentine Malbec
subs	Alsace Riesling or Oregon Pinot Noir
sushi (see entry 240)	Champagne or Riesling
eggrolls	New Zealand Sauvignon Blanc

238 What to consider when pairing wine with fish

Fish come in varying levels of fat and intensity of flavor. Fish at its lightest, such as flounder, matches perfectly with a crisp, young white wine, one whose flavors and aromas won't overpower it. France offers several candidates, including Chablis, Muscadet, Sancerre, Champagne, and either white Graves or Entre-Deux-Mers from the Bordeaux region. Italian Gavi, Soave, or Pinot Grigio and Spanish White Rioja also work well. From the New World, either a Chilean Sauvignon Blanc or a dry Washington Riesling are mild enough to work with lightly flavored fish.

At the other end of the spectrum are the fatty fish, such as sea bass, salmon, mackerel, herring, and sardines, plus steak fish, such as tuna and swordfish. These have enough flavor to pair with a lighter red wine. Old World wines that match up include Burgundy, a cru Beaujolais, Nero d'Avola, or a rosé from Rioja or Bandol.

One other type of seafood (not really a fish) is squid. While most commonly served battered and fried as "calamari" with tomato sauce, many California restaurants serve squid steaks made from huge squid. The steaks are usually sautéed and served with lemon and butter, and butter equals Chardonnay. This is one dish where a great California Chardonnay like Mount Eden Vineyards really works. Mediterranean-style sautéed squid of the type served in rings can be paired with any of the whites for light fish (above) or shellfish (see entries 239 and 240).

How to pair wine with shellfish

Bivalves (oysters, clams, mussels, and scallops) require a very light, unoaked wine. Some of the best wines for bivalves come from Friuli and the Alto Adige, both in Italy. These are white wines from grapes such as Sauvignon Blanc, Pinot Bianco, Friulano, Sylvaner, Müller-Thurgau, Pinot Grigio, and Chardonnay. The traditional wine for oysters is the French Muscadet, but it's a wine that has a good deal more charm consumed on the French coast than sitting in your dining room. Oregon Pinot Gris and dry versions of Washington Riesling also work well, and any unoaked Sauvignon Blanc. For fried oysters or clams, see entry 236.

Crustaceans (shrimp, crab, lobster) are sweeter and have more flavor, so they can stand up to bigger wines. A classic combination with crustaceans, especially with a butter sauce for dipping, is Chardonnay. Whether an unoaked, acidic wine like Chablis or an oaky, big-boned version from Sonoma, Chardonnay will always do well with butter. For crustaceans served without butter, say chilled shrimp or crab cakes, go for a Burgundy or a light Viognier.

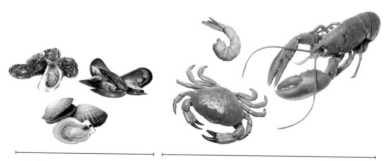

LIGHTER, UNOAKED WINE   HEAVIER OAKY WINE

240 What goes with sushi or sashimi?

Following the "do what the natives do" philosophy, the best wine is rice wine—sake. When matching sushi with grape wine, the trick is to remember that the rice has vinegar and sugar in it, both of which can impact wine negatively. A great way to match sweet rice with an off-dry wine is to pour a wine from Alsace, especially a Riesling or a Pinot Gris. Another grape that works well with sushi is Chenin Blanc. Vouvray is the place for Chenin, and an ideal example is Domaine des Aubuisières Vouvray Cuvée de Silex. Remember to go light on the soy sauce—its umami flavor (the meaty, savory flavors) will drown most wines.

Sashimi, since there's no rice involved, can go with wines from all over the world. Lightness is one key, but many of the fish, and especially the roe, are rich enough to stand up to Chardonnay, as long as it is unoaked. A premier cru (or "1er cru") Chablis offers most of the flavor of a Grand Cru at a much lower price. These Chardonnays are 180 degrees from the California versions. Their fragrance comes from terroir and the grapes and nothing else. Chablis is cool enough to keep the acidity high, which gives the wine both buttery and lemony character, just right for sashimi. An even better choice is a Blanc de Blancs Champagne, the picture-perfect marriage of Chardonnay, lively acidity, and tongue-scrubbing bubbles. Try Ruinart or, for an American sparkling wine, Schramsberg. See also entry 76.

241 What to drink with salad

The potential spoiler here is acidity, especially from vinegar. Too much can spoil almost any wine. A salad without vinegar, such as a simple *caprese,* will go beautifully with a light white wine such as Soave or Pinot Grigio. For green salads, take a taste before you decide on a wine. Something with a lot of fat to its acidity, like a caesar salad or potato salad, will work well with Chianti. For a Niçoise salad, take a hint from its origin and pair it with dry rosé. For spinach salads, especially with bacon and/or mushrooms, Pinot Noir works well. Most bottled salad dressings are rather sweet, so look to off-dry whites (see entry 270) if you want to pair them with wine.

242 What wine goes with fresh fruit?

Matching wine with fresh fruit is easy as long as you don't allow the sugar in the fruit to dominate that in the wine. The best approach is to serve a wine that is slightly sweeter than the fruit. Watermelon would make a New Zealand Sauvignon Blanc taste like the skin of an unripe grapefruit, because New Zealand Sauvignon Blanc is completely dry. But a sweet wine such as Moscato d'Asti would be perfect. The acidity and relatively low sugar in citrus mean a dry wine will work, perhaps a Chardonnay or Gewürztraminer, but be sure to avoid any wine that has a citrus flavor, especially New Zealand Sauvignon Blanc. For something as sugary as ripe figs, the big sweet wines like an Australian sticky or a Spanish Pedro Ximénez will work well.

In general, avoid serving a wine with a fruit that is used to describe the wine's aroma. Combos such as Viognier and peaches, California Sauvignon Blanc and pineapple, Riesling and apples, Zinfandel and plums, are guaranteed to conflict. One wine that will work with most fresh fruits is a good quality Asti Spumante. Forteto della Luja and Marco Tintero are both delicious and inexpensive. For pairing wine with fruit desserts, see entry 243.

SHERI SAUTER MORANO, MW
Master of Wine

"I was on a trip to Italy with my high school Latin teacher and my parents had given permission for me to have wine with meals." Sheri Sauter Morano is laughing, trying to decide whether she wants this whole story in print. "Even though it was just cheap table wine, I was fascinated that it was so much a part of the pleasures of the table. Back to the States, I just paid more attention to wine. The day I turned twenty-one, I went into a store and said, 'I want to know what Cabernet tastes like and what Merlot tastes like.'"

She started taking classes at the International Wine Center and eventually sat for the brutal Master of Wine exams. Today, she is a wine educator who tastes wines from all over the world. I asked about wines under $30. "I am a big fan of Austrian whites, especially Hirsch's Trinkvergnügen, which like most Grüner Veltliners is a delicious and food-friendly wine. There are also a lot of nice wines coming out of Spain, like wines from the Toro appellation, especially Spanish Sons Tempranillo by the Farina family. In my wine cooler right now, there are a ton of Ridge Zinfandels. I always have a bottle of Moscato di Asti on hand because it is a great summertime drink. Also, Trimbach and Hugel are two great wines from Alsace. Finally, I always have Lucien Albrecht Cremant d'Alsace Brut Rosé chilled and ready to drink."

243 How to pair wine with dessert

In general, it's a good idea to have the wine be sweeter than the dessert, but this rule is only somewhat helpful: the temperature and fat content of the food make a difference, and chocolate is famously difficult to match. If the dessert is creamy and cold, such as cheesecake or ice cream, the wine must be much sweeter. In chocolate, the higher-cacao versions match up nicely with a variety of fruity but dry red wines. Lower levels of cacao (meaning higher levels of sugar) require sweeter wines.

Most every country that makes wine makes dessert wines, and winemakers use every grape imaginable. France makes the most sweet wines, chief among them Sauternes, Sélection de Grains Nobles, Vouvray Moelleux, and Muscat de Beaumes de Venises. But Germany's Riesling Trockenbeerenauslese, Portugal's Port wines (see entry 160), Spain's Pedro Ximénez, and Canada's ice wine (see entry 133) can all lay claim to greatness. Australia's stickies (see entry 131)—such as R. L. Buller Premium Fine Muscat—have one more benefit: value.

IF THE DESSERT IS . . .	TRY . . .
High-cacao chocolate (less sweet)	Cabernet, Malbec, Merlot, Port, Zinfandel
Creamy and cold	Pedro Ximénez sherry, or Muscat de Beaumes de Venises
Fruity	Moscato d'Asti
Nutty	Cream sherry or Madeira
Caramel	Vouvray Moelleux, Banyuls, Australian sticky

A SECOND SIP *A cheese course can be a perfect time to serve sweet wine (see entry 213), and sautéed foie gras is classic with Sauternes, but it's just as happy with many of the great sweet wines. The fact is that many "dessert wines," despite their sweetness, are best not matched with desserts. The best match often is with a single ingredient with complex flavors and substantial fat (to offset the acidity typical of sweet wines).*

244   How to pair older wines

The older the wine, the less intense and complex should be the food and sauces or condiments paired with it (unless the wine you're working with is massively sweet, in which case follow the rule for pairing wine with dessert, entry 243). Otherwise, older wines pair with the same foods you would pair with their younger counterparts.

245   How to clean wine stains

First of all, always blot, never scrub. If possible, start by getting all of the excess wine blotted up. Then put a generous amount of either white wine or club soda (not seltzer) on the spot and blot until the stain goes away. If it is still visible, there are two final options. A product called Wine Away really works, or you can try a solution of mild detergent and hydrogen peroxide. Either *can* discolor the fabric or carpet, so test on an out-of-sight place. Remember, move quickly.

How to Taste

It is not necessary to learn how to critically taste to enjoy wine. But for those who are curious about why they like a wine, or interested in knowing more about varietals, learning the routine can help enormously. We start with the process of tasting, then cover faults and strengths, styles and procedures. You'll also learn how to keep records and how to set up a dozen formal tastings, including recommendations for appropriate wines. This chapter will reward working through in order.

246　Why taste wine?

The enjoyment of wine is just like any other pursuit. A person doesn't have to be a graduate of the Actors Studio to enjoy watching Meryl Streep. On the other hand, occasionally watching *Inside the Actors Studio* makes watching Ms. Streep even more impressive. So keep delving deeper and deeper into the world of wine as long as it remains fun. Once it becomes a chore, drop back a level or two. Occasionally, though, a wine's charms will grab you so hard that tasting the wine shifts from a procedure to an epiphany. That sudden leap of perception doesn't happen very often, but it takes only a few times to hook you. From that moment, tasting wine will be like playing a slot machine: lots of running through the various steps of tasting hoping for the ka-ching of victory.

247　Will I look silly?

TV and movie directors love to make fun of the rituals of tasting. All the sniffing, swishing, and spitting can look absurd in the hands of a gifted comic. Luckily, frequent practice of the more ceremonial parts of tasting allows a person to get through them without attracting too much attention. This is a pursuit where practice does make perfect. In the beginning, it might take time to remember the steps of looking, sniffing, and tasting (see entry 257), but after a little experience, you'll be able to do it quickly and casually.

248 Why keep records?

"Hey, honey, what was that terrific wine we had last month at Nobu?" Oops. This happens to everyone. They find a super wine, intend to remember it, and then can't. Was it Château La Tour Haut-Brion or Château Latour à Pomerol? Was it a Robert Sinskey wine or a Robert Biale wine? Whether you use a tiny voice recorder or an unobtrusive notebook, try as soon as possible to at least get the wine name, producer, vintage, appellation, grape, cost, and some sort of note as to whether you would like to buy it again. It takes less than thirty seconds to write "2008 MacMurray Ranch Sonoma Coast Pinot Noir, $18 and worth buying by the case at that price." If you want, add a few aroma or taste words that have meaning to you. Keeping a small notebook or creating a smart phone file with this information allows you to remember good wines and avoid bad ones, but it is also great information for the restaurant waitstaff and the wine shop salespeople. If you can show them a few wines that you've enjoyed in the past, they can confidently recommend something new. See also entry 10.

249 How to describe a wine to friends?

The point here is to communicate. Did you like it? Was it worth the money? Here are ten really useful and quick bits of information to share.

1. Which company made the wine
2. What grape it's made from
3. What country and appellation it is from
4. Where you bought it (store or restaurant)
5. Where you drank it (at a restaurant, or at home with a great meal, on the patio with popcorn, etc.)
6. A general descriptor ("delicious," "wonderful," "lousy," etc.)
7. Something about the intensity ("huge" or "light" or "just right with the food")
8. A comparative judgment ("It tastes almost as good as X," or "It was even better than that wine we had at the Strip House.")
9. How much it cost
10. Something about its price versus quality (like "a bargain," "great value," or "expensive but worth it")

250 What's the easiest way to learn wine?

Taste as much and as often as possible. The only way to learn about wine is to taste it. Absolute beginners should go to a store that's convenient (but see entries 1 and 2), ask for whoever their best wine person is, and tell them you are a beginner but are starting to learn about wine. Ask for a case of mixed bottles of wine (buying a case usually gets you a discount), set a price limit (anywhere above $100 for all twelve will be fine), and tell them you want the best wines they can fit into that price range. (If twelve bottles is too many at once, try a bottle a week.) Be casual about drinking the wines, but keep notes (see entry 248) and read about the grapes and locations in this book and some of the other books recommended in entry 331. If both the wines and the salesperson pleased you, once you've worked your way through the twelve bottles, go back and candidly explain what was good and bad about each wine, and ask for another six. If neither the wine not the person pleased you, go to another store and try again. Before long, a trustworthy seller will emerge and a few grapes and places will start to stand out as favorites. At that point, you'll know more about wine than 95 percent of the population, and you'll have a trusted guide for future explorations. See also entries 10, 252, and Tasting 1, page 279.

251 Learning about the various wine-growing areas

Once you have a good grip on the different ways several grape varieties can taste in different locations, it's time to study specific places by trying several wines from the area. The goal here is to try to tease out any overarching tastes or aromas. It is also a great time to do a bit of reading about the area, information that is easy to glean from this book or Karen MacNeil's *Wine Bible* and Web sites such as the ones in entry 354. Open a bottle each night and read about the winery and the area while tasting the wine. It might fuel your interest in traveling to wine-growing areas, which, of course, is the best way of all to understand them. Here are a few topics to delve into that will enrich your understanding of a place: local cuisine, types of wine made, history of wine production, effect of geography and climate on grape growing, amount of wine made, specialties of the region, up-and-coming winemakers. Keep delving as long as you are interested, and if it gets boring, stop the studying and just finish the wine! See also Tasting 9, page 289.

252 How to taste in order

The problem with tasting or serving more than one wine at a time is that red wines have more texture than white, big wines choke out delicate wines, and sweet wine makes dry wines taste astringent. The rules to remember are:

1. white before red—Sauvignon Blanc before a dry rosé before a Shiraz
2. delicate before strong—Pinot Noir before Merlot before Zinfandel
3. dry before sweet—Chardonnay before an Auslese Riesling before Sauternes
4. old before young

If no one in the group is familiar enough with the wines to know which order to serve in, keep in mind that food will help cleanse your palate of a wine's aftertaste. Which food? Remember the adage "Buy with bread, sell with cheese." That means cheese masks flavors and bread doesn't. Both will remove the aftertaste of the prior wine from your palate, but the cheese will interfere with the flavors of the next wine—a slice of crispy French bread won't. See also entry 253.

253 How to cleanse your palate

Wine leaves flavors in your mouth that will change the flavors of whatever wine follows. Whether it causes a clash or enhances your experience, you won't get a proper idea of each wine's flavor without refreshing your palate. A bland bread or cracker will absorb any remaining wine and create a blank slate, ready to taste the next wine.

254 Avoiding the buzz

This is a challenge when you're tasting several wines. In general, women start getting tipsy after two 5-ounce glasses, and men after three. If you are at a wine tasting with multiple wines, the first solution is to taste smaller quantities, 1 or 2 ounces, and only finish a wine that you really love and dump out the rest. Second, drink a similar amount of water between each group (or "flight") of wines. Third, and this is most important, spit (see entry 255).

255 How to spit

We're all taught that it is indelicate to spit in another person's presence. The problem is, it can also be indelicate to get drunk in another person's presence. When a critical tasting encompasses dozens of wines, sometimes hundreds, you are stuck with making a choice between looking bad or acting badly. And this problem doesn't arise just in a formal tasting. It takes only a couple of days of tasting up and down Highway 29 in Napa to understand the importance of making the choice to spit.

Learning the art of spitting takes a bit of practice. Usually at tastings there will be a dump bucket so that several people can have a place to spit cleanly. Dump buckets have one serious problem: splash-back. Getting hit by recoiling droplets from a bucket that's been used by the crowds is not very sanitary. And when there are hundreds of other wine drinkers involved, it's sometimes impossible even to get to the dump bucket. The best solution is to carry a cup or glass to spit into, then dump it occasionally. Nothing works better than a coffee mug. It's opaque, so no one has to see its contents, and it holds quite a bit of wine. Put your lips just over the rim and gently spit your wine. It's unobtrusive, polite, and clean. At a sit-down multibottle tasting, it's an especially good idea to have an empty coffee mug at each seat so people can inconspicuously spit instead of having to get to a dump bucket after every sip.

The purpose of spitting is to be able to accurately judge the wines you're tasting without becoming intoxicated. Spitting is a matter of individual stamina.

256   What glassware to use?

Any time you critically taste multiple wines of the same grape variety, it is important to use identical glasses. This is also important for tasting multiple wines blind (see entry 282). For more advice on buying glasses, see entries 288 and 289. If your household doesn't have enough glasses for a large tasting party, the best option is to rent them. That way, you'll be sure to have identical glasses and you won't have to wash them.

257   What's the procedure for tasting?

Years ago, some unknown soul developed a great mnemonic device built on the letter *S*, which wine lovers have used ever since. In its most basic form, it is just three words: *See, Sniff,* and *Sip.* Then someone added two more *S* words: *See, Swirl, Sniff, Sip, Savor.* I would change that total to six: *See, Sniff, Swirl, Sniff, Sip, Savor.*

258 What should I see in a glass of wine?

If possible, look at the wine against a white surface, which will allow you to see the wine better. Use a tablecloth, a napkin, or a menu. Tilt the glass so the wine is about a half inch from the lip and look at it against that white background. First, check the clarity. White wines should be transparent and reds somewhat translucent, unless the wine is purposely unfiltered (see entry 197). Then check the color, which should be appropriate to the grape and the age of the wine. Different types of grapes have different amounts of pigment (largely from anthocyanins in the skins) and therefore make wines of slightly different colors. Young red wines have vivid colors in shades of red or purple. As the wine ages, the color changes from red to brick to brown. White wines start somewhere between clear and straw colored, then age into shades of gold and finally light brown. Nebbiolo, for instance, the grape of the Piedmont wines Barolo and Barbaresco, begins its life ruby colored and progresses to brickish, whereas a Zinfandel from Sonoma starts off deep purple and progresses to a cigar box brown. See also entry 260.

259 How and why to swirl wine

Swirling is important because it allows you to take in aromas that don't otherwise float out of the glass. Start with a glass that is at most one-quarter full to keep the wine from sloshing up the sides during the swirling. Between your thumb and first two fingers, hold the stem just above the base. Keeping the base snug to the table, move it quickly three or four times in a circle (either clockwise or counterclockwise) about twice the size of the base. Sniff the wine. If aromas start to appear, swirl vigorously and sniff again. The agitation allows any scents that aren't yet airborne to volatilize (change from the liquid state to a gaseous one) and gives each wine the chance to reveal as many aromas as possible. See also entries 261 and 262.

260   Deciphering legs, or tears

Legs or tears are a phenomenon seen mostly with strong, alcoholic wines. After the wine is swirled, the side of the glass retains a film of liquid that slowly drips back into the wine. Classically, these drips have been called legs, although "tears" better describes what they look like. For decades, new drinkers were taught that these legs indicated a top-quality wine. Despite the fact that the "legs = quality" equation was easily refuted by demonstrating the perfect legs on a jug wine, the myth hung on. A more recent myth is that the legs mean only that the wine has high alcohol, which is easy to disprove with any number of low-alcohol wines. The truth is that the cause of legs is complicated, having to do with the differing evaporation rates of alcohol and water, along with different innate surface and interfacial tensions. So there is a basic correlation between legs and alcohol, but none between legs and quality.

261 How do I sniff wine?

Sniffing is one of two places where people worry about looking silly (the other is swishing wine in their mouths while searching for flavors; see entry 266), but it's really simple enough to do unobtrusively. After you swirl the wine, the aromas will be floating in the air inside the glass and all that's required is to tilt the glass about forty-five degrees and maneuver it so that the tip of your nose is just inside the glass, then inhale twice, quietly and slowly. That's it. Remember that the aromas that get stirred up by swirling disappear within a few seconds, so it's important to go ahead and sniff. Also, wine has its own aroma and flavor when it is still, which may change after the wine is swirled. It is important to sniff both before and after swirling.

There is one common and embarrassing error that happens to everyone at least once. At some point, everyone makes the mistake of tilting the glass too much. That leads to the awkward moment where they inhale the wine, which leads to paroxysm by both drinker (choking) and friends (laughing).

262 What to sniff for

The majority of our experience of wine comes from the olfactory system. Our ability to perceive taste with our tongue is limited to salt, sweet, sour, bitter, and umami. In contrast, our olfactory system can recognize thousands of aromas, even when they include complex combinations at infinitesimal strengths. When a person talks about the flavor of a wine, they are really judging two things—taste and smell—and of the two, the aromatic part is much more powerful.

It's not important to spend a long time sniffing. Professionals do it because they are looking for every last adjective they can find. What's important is what *you* are trying to accomplish. The top level on the pyramid in the next entry can be accomplished with one quick whiff. The second and third levels might take a few seconds of concentration. Teasing out all the aromas at the base of the pyramid can take several minutes. Think of the top level as the approach to take at a party steeped in conversation, level two at an intimate dinner, and level three if an aroma is immediately recognizable. The information in level four is needed only in a formal tasting, at a dinner with other wine enthusiasts, or when trying to compare and contrast varieties from different wineries or growing areas as a learning experience. See also entry 264.

263 Four levels to sniffing a Sauvignon Blanc

You could choose to spend time relishing your wine, attending to its every nuance. Or you could take a quick sniff to make sure it's to your taste. In fact anything is correct, as long as it gives you the information you want. The pyramid below shows four different responses to a glass of New Zealand Sauvignon Blanc.

"Nice."

"It smells a little like pineapple."

"That's a powerful grapefruit aroma. It must be from New Zealand."

"I smell strong honeysuckle, petroleum, and pears with hints of hazlenuts, honeydew, mown grass, and gunflint."

264 How to identify smells and flavors in wine

The easiest way is to break down the aromas into categories. Start with fruit aromas. For red wines, slot the wine into either red fruit (strawberry, raspberry, red currant) or black fruit (black plum, blackberry, black cherry). For whites, choose tropical fruits (passion fruit, pineapple), citrus (grapefruit, lemon), or pome fruits (apple, pear). In addition, most wines will have other aromas, such as vanilla, caramel, black pepper, minerals, herbs, or flowers—anything that strikes you. Think of spices, vegetables, or even unpleasant aromas. Some of France's most prized wines smell like a barnyard after a summer rain; Barolo is said to smell of tar and roses. The important thing is to keep your mind open and look for both the striking and the subtle. If you have trouble with this procedure, don't worry. The aromas can be very delicate, and it can require practice to attach names to them. The good news is you enjoy wine just by putting it in your mouth and swallowing it.

265 Where do the terms for aromas come from?

It's not uncommon to open a wine magazine and read something like: "The X Chardonnay is buttery with a tiny bit of flint and green apples, while the butterscotch flavors are well tamed for a Central Coast wine." People often wonder why wine lovers don't just say, "This wine tastes like a Chardonnay." The intent of all the nonobvious (and non–grape-related) terms is to help transfer information. Otherwise, faced with a wild variety of Chardonnays from Napa, Burgundy, Friuli, and the Adelaide Hills, there would be no way to distinguish among different Chardonnays. The vocabulary helps hone in on specific flavors as well as on the subtleties of a winemaker's art or of a particular vintage.

Over the centuries, wine aficionados have invented a language of common terms to describe the aromas and flavors of a wine. In order to make sure people understood one another, the terms referred to things most people had experienced, like the aroma or flavor of fruits, spices, or flowers. Two famous wine people have helped codify these terms, and both cover their topics in easily understandable prose.

Ann Noble is a past professor at the University of California, Davis who specializes in sensory chemistry. She put together many of the terms used for wine and developed a brilliant tool, the Wine Aroma Wheel. This breaks down aromas into categories: caramelized, chemical, earthy, floral, fruity, microbiological, nutty, oxidized, pungent, spicy, vegetative, and woody. Each category holds as many as twenty-five descriptors. It is a marvelous aid for focusing on the aromas commonly found in wine, and well worth the low price (www.winearomawheel.com).

For readers who really want the full monty, Frenchman Emile Peynaud (1912–2004) wrote the 368-page *Le goût du vin* (*The Taste of Wine*), which covers far more than most people would ever want to know about tasting terms. For students of wine flavors, it is a modern Rosetta Stone.

266 Why do wine pros slurp the wine?

When you draw air through the wine by slurping the wine in your mouth, it volatilizes the aromas in the wine (transforms them from a liquid to a gaseous state), making them easier to smell. The result is a better idea of what it will taste like by the end of the evening. See also entry 268.

267 What is retronasal tasting?

The olfactory system doesn't shut down after sniffing. After a wine or food is in your mouth, you can get additional aromas via the retronasal passage as airborne aroma molecules travel up the back passage from your throat to your nasal cavity. As an experiment, while holding your nose, take a small sip of an aromatic wine and swallow it. Notice how simple the wine tastes. All the nuances are gone because you have stopped retronasal aromas from traveling into your nasal cavity.

We usually fail to differentiate between "aromas" and "tastes" and instead compound the two into "flavor." Because of the anatomical connection between our oral and nasal cavities, it's important to try to tease out the difference between an aroma and a taste. The tongue picks up degrees of sweet, sour, salt, bitter, and umami (savory or brothy). The olfactory system is more complete. Take a strawberry: the tongue senses sweet and sour, but the olfactory system picks up an avalanche of aromas and synthesizes them into one word, *strawberry.* Neither the olfactory system nor the tongue can get the whole picture. After you swallow a sip of wine, inhale and exhale again through your nose to experience the retronasal aromas.

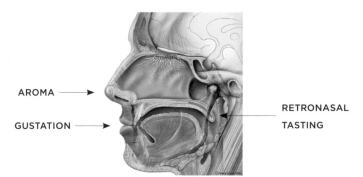

AROMA ⟶

GUSTATION ⟶

RETRONASAL TASTING

268 What should I notice when I sip?

Pay attention to four sensations: retronasal aromas, tastes, mouthfeel, and density. Foremost is the retronasal information. That is like opening an encyclopedia of your sensory history. Spend a little time delving around in those sensations. Some aromas will be so subtle as to almost vanish, but others will be recognizable. Think of fruits, flowers, vegetables, plants, animals. Remember, this sipping should be fun, so just say whatever comes to mind. Then pay attention to the five flavors (sweet, sour, bitter, salty, and umami, although the last two are very rare in wine). Next is how the wine feels in the mouth. Sparkling wines tend to tickle the tongue. Big New World wines sometimes have enough alcohol to burn the palate. Red Burgundies can feel velvety. Young Riojas can suck all the moisture out of your mouth. Finally, how dense or thick is the wine? This is its body. As an example, Monterey Chardonnay is much closer to the density of apple juice, while an Italian Pinot Grigio is more like water. See also entries 263 and 264.

	WHITE	RED
LIGHTER BODY		Beaujolais
	Muscadet	Dolcetto
	dry Riesling	most Pinot Noir
	Pinot Grigio	Sangiovese
	Chablis	Merlot
	Sauvignon Blanc	Grenache
	Grüner Veltliner	red Bordeaux
	white Burgundy	California Cabernet
	California Chardonnay	Sauvignon
	Viognier	Australian Shiraz
	sweet Riesling	Zinfandel
FULLER BODY ▼		Port

269 How do I savor a wine?

Savoring a wine is nothing more than integrating all of the sensory data from the *See, Sniff, Swirl, Sniff, Sip, Savor* procedure. A tasting in the midst of conversation or one with a lot of wine and a limited amount of time won't leave much room for savoring, but a critical tasting demands at least a moment to make a final evaluation. The time will be well spent, whether you use a behavioral assessment (Is the wine worth buying? By the case? Is it good enough to give as a gift?) or a numerical score or letter grade. The 100-point scale is popular because it gives readers a fast, shorthand evaluation of a reviewer's moments spent savoring a wine. Should you always trust these scores? You can when they are your own. That's why it is so important to keep notes (see entry 248). Try using a score sheet like the one in entry 283.

270 What's a "dry" wine?

A dry wine is one with very little or no sugar left in the juice after fermentation (see entry 175). In tasting, there will be no impression of sweetness in a dry wine. A wine with a very slight sweetness is referred to as "off-dry."

BONE DRY   DRY   OFF-DRY   MEDIUM-DRY   MEDIUM-SWEET   SWEET

271 How do sweetness and fruitiness differ?

In the world of wine, sweetness means one thing only: the amount of residual sugar that remains unfermented when the wine is made (see entry 175). Fruitiness is the tendency of wine to taste and smell of fruit, and when the fruit is a sweet one, such as pineapple, plum, or berries, people occasionally mistake the fruitiness for sweetness. One way to tell the difference is to hold your nose while tasting the wine. Sweetness will still be there, but fruitiness won't. See also entry 270.

A SECOND SIP *The effect of residual sugar on your palate is enhanced by alcohol level and subdued by acidity, so a highly acidic Riesling with 7 percent alcohol and 2 percent residual sugar will taste less sweet than a low-acidity Napa Chardonnay with 15 percent alcohol and only 1 percent residual sugar.*

272 What does acidity taste like?

The main acids in wine (tartaric, malic, and lactic) add zing to a wine—a little sourness, and a bright, clean feeling. Without them, a wine tastes flabby and uninteresting. For a continuum, start by imagining the taste of a very ripe plum compared to a fresh-picked grapefruit. Very "plummy" red wines, such as poorly made Zinfandels, lack the acidity that helps strip and clean the palate

how to taste

to prepare it afresh for its next food or drink, a basic task of all "food wines" (see entry 208). A wine with a greater resemblance to grapefruit juice, like some of the most aggressive New Zealand Sauvignon Blancs, will have so much acidity that it tastes sour and leaves the mouth puckered and unable, at least immediately, to taste at all. In between are hundreds of shades of acidity that add beautiful, bright, fresh, and slightly tart flavors. In general, if you like Champagne, Riesling, or Chablis (whites) or Sangiovese or Beaujolais (reds), you might prefer high-acidity wines.

273   What's tannin?

LEAST TANNIN

white wine

rosé

Beaujolais

Dolcetto

Grenache

Merlot

Pinot Noir

Tempranillo/Rioja

Sangiovese/Chianti

Shiraz/Syrah

Cabernet Sauvignon/ Bordeaux

Nebbiolo/Barolo

▼ **MOST**

Tannins are a group of astringent and sometimes aggressively distasteful substances called polyphenols that show up in red wine. They are a by-product of the seeds, stems, and skins of the grapes used to make the wine, and sometimes the barrels used to age it. When tasting wine, search for the mouth-puckering effect that you get from tasting strong black tea that has sat on the leaves too long. That astringency and slight bitterness is tannin. Tannins come either "ripe" or "unripe," depending on the ripeness of the grapes at harvest. Ripe tannins can give a soft, velvety mouthfeel that wine drinkers love, but unripe tannins create bitterness and a drying feeling. In small quantities, tannins can make wine taste more structured and give it the feel of gripping your mouth as you taste it. See also entry 221.

274 What does oak taste like?

Used properly, oak barrels impart spicy flavor (like cinnamon or cloves), an aroma of slightly burnt toast, and an additional level of character to wine. But when a wine has too much oak (from maturing too long in oak barrels, or barrels that are brand-new), it adds unfriendly tannins and intense coconut or caramel flavors that overpower the wine. The winemaker's task is to pick the right barrels for each wine to get just the right amount of "oak influence."

French oak (*Quercus sessiles*) offers an aroma profile that's very different from American oak (*Quercus alba*). While both offer some degree of toast, vanilla, and caramel aroma, the barrel-making process has evolved to match the personality of the wine the barrel is used for. French oak has a toasty aroma; it's subtle and elegant, and is easily integrated into wines that can be described the same way. American oak is more intense (with more powerful vanilla and sometimes with a coconut, clove, or even dill aroma) and easily recognizable in the wine, and the more "American" the wine (like Zinfandel or Petite Sirah), the better the American oak works. Oak is also sourced in Slovenia, Hungary, and other countries, and each has its own slightly different flavor profile. For more on oak, see entries 193 to 196.

275 Intensity versus complexity

Intense wines have huge amounts of one or two aromas; complex wines have many aromas that are balanced in a way that allows all of them to be smelled. Wine lovers used to be able to make the generalization—still mostly true—that those who prefer intensity will prefer New World wines, while those who prefer complexity will prefer Old World wines. Now, winemakers on both sides are gradually changing camps to conform to their desired market. See also Introduction.

276 Determining balance

A wine is said to be balanced if several elements—acidity, residual sugar, fruitiness, tannins, body, and alcohol—are all present without drawing any undue attention. A well-balanced wine that allows a person the freedom to contemplate all of these characteristics is one of the grails of winemaking. Certain types of imbalance are so common they even have names. For instance, a wine that is low in acidity and tannin while high in fruitiness, body, and alcohol is called a fruit bomb. A wine that is high in alcohol is termed "hot." A wine that is low in acidity is called flabby, while one with too much acidity is called lean.

277 What is a "long finish"? Is it good?

"Finish" denotes how long the flavors of a wine linger after you swallow it. It's hard to predict which wines will have a long finish, but it can be said that the intensity of the aromas and density of the wine have something to do with it. The reason critics and experienced tasters prefer a long finish has more to do with the fact that many wines with a short finish are substandard. On the other hand, a long finish doesn't necessarily mean the wine is exceptional—the finish is just one indicator of quality.

278 Why might a wine smell bad?

Bad smells come mainly from two sources: poor winery hygiene and tainted corks. The bad hygiene is not dangerous; it simply allows the bacteria that creates "off" aromas to grow in various places in the winery. These smells will be like a wet and wooly dog, rotten eggs, skunks, well-used sweat socks, the smell from striking a match, or even an unshoveled barnyard after a rain. Certain of these smells will dissipate a few minutes after the bottle is opened or decanted (see entry 304) and others indicate more serious flaws that entitle you to return the bottle to the store. For more information on specific flaws in wine, see entry 34. See also entry 280.

279 What is "corked"?

An "off" aroma or flavor in wine may be due to a tainted cork; in this case the wine is referred to as "corked" and sent back (in a restaurant) or returned to the store. Cork taint occurs when one or more of eight known chemicals forms in the cork. The main culprit is 2,4,6-trichloroanisole (TCA). TCA is the nightmare of all winemakers who use cork because no matter how artfully they make their wines and how carefully they ship them to market, bad cork can ruin the product.

Corked wine is usually said to smell (and taste) of wet cardboard or mildewed newspaper, and the problem can be very obvious, or very slight. A very slight cork taint is probably worse than a bad taint from the point of view of the winemaker; these wines will just be tired and uninteresting rather than smelly, and consumers can mistake the taint for bad winemaking and decide to stop buying the wine without ever realizing the problem lay with the cork.

Cork taint affects one in twelve bottles, but unfortunately for winemakers, the statistic doesn't describe the reality. TCA runs in batches, and one bad shipment of corks can ruin a winery's reputation. This is one reason for the recent development of alternative closures for wine bottles, such as screw tops (see entry 280).

280 Overcoming the screw-top stigma

Screw tops had a bad reputation because they were associated with cheap convenience-store wines, but the fact is that screw tops' failure rate is close to zero—meaning they create an effective oxygen barrier for the wine and aren't susceptible to cork taint. Cork's main benefit is for wines that are meant to be aged, and since hardly anyone ages wines anymore, screw tops are the better choice. Granted, there is something celebratory about pulling a cork, but the celebration evaporates when the wine smells like old sweat socks. Consequently, screw tops are gaining fans even among such top winemakers as Bonny Doon, Plumpjack Estates, and Sonoma-Cutrer.

281 What is blind tasting?

An experiment done in Texas gave a group of people three glasses of Cabernet Sauvignon. The wines weren't identified in any way except on the coasters beneath the glasses, one of which said France, one California, and one Texas. The people were asked to taste the wines and rate which was the best. The French won, followed by California, with Texas finishing last. The trick was, all three glasses contained the exact same Cabernet. That is the power of knowing anything about a bottle of wine while trying to evaluate it.

The alternative is to taste "blind," where the taster knows nothing about the wine in the glass. Inevitably, the label and the

size, shape, and color of a bottle will influence any taster—beginner and expert alike—and thousands of psychology experiments have proven that a person's expectations will always cloud his or her evaluations. In wine tasting, keeping those expectations under wraps is simple: offer the wine already in the glass, or seal each bottle in a brown paper bag. When the pourer or host knows what is being poured, it is called a single-blind tasting (that is, only the taster is "blind"). But psychologists know that if the scientists are with the subjects during an experiment, the results will be skewed. The scientists inevitably watch for their subjects' reactions, and the subjects just as inevitably try to get clues from the scientists. Under the strictest conditions, when the pourer or host pours and then leaves the room before the tasters arrive, it is called a double-blind tasting (both the host and the taster are "blind").

282 How to set up a blind tasting

One simple and casual way to do this is to have each person attending the tasting bring one bottle of wine and, without revealing it to the others, uncork the bottle and slip it into one of a number of identical paper bags, sealing the top. When all wines are packaged this way, each person may know what he or she brought but won't know any of the other wines. The bagged wines are then shuffled and numbered on the outside of the bag, then poured into glasses in numbered order. At the end of the tasting, the bottles are revealed. For further tips on running a tasting, see entry 283.

DENMAN MOODY
Wine writer
www.denmanswineblog.com

I once saw Denman Moody identify a bottle—blind—of 1982 Château Palmer, a feat not many in the wine industry could replicate. Over his career writing for the *International Wine Review* and the *Revue du Vin de France,* not to mention his own *Moody's Wine Review,* Mr. Moody has had an incredible number of opportunities to taste rare and expensive wines, far more than most people in the wine business. Ask him about a favorite, and he'll wax poetic about an 1870 Château Lafite Rothschild that had been stored since new at the Glamis Castle cellar in Scotland. Or he'll talk about tasting verticals of Domaine de la Romanée-Conti's flagship wine, "Romanée-Conti" (current vintage going for about $10,000 a bottle). So what does a man like this drink at home? "We choose our house whites and reds based on value," he said. "Columbia Crest Grand Estates Chardonnay and Merlot from Washington State are wonderful, and for around ten dollars a bottle, inexpensive enough to serve nightly."

283 How to host a tasting

Here is a system that works for any size group from two to twenty-four. Tastings work better when everyone is seated at a table, so each person has room for multiple glasses and a place to write. If this is a club where people share expenses, have just one person buy the wine to ensure the theme is followed and the bottle temperatures are all the same (see entry 285), and have everyone else chip in their share at the end of the night. You will need:

1. A tasting sheet (see opposite) and a pen for each person.
2. Identical glasses for each person to match the number of wines being tasted. If you are tasting more than four wines in a session, the same four glasses can be reused for successive rounds. The glasses must be identical because different shapes yield slightly different flavors (see entry 288); we're trying to control variables.
3. One dump bucket for every four people, and coffee mugs or opaque cups for spitting (see entry 255). Champagne ice buckets work well as dump buckets, as do the cheap paper buckets sold at paint shops.
4. If you want to taste blind, you'll need an identical bag for each bottle and tape or rubber bands to close the top, plus a marker to number the bags with the bottles in them. See entry 282 for further tips on blind tastings.
5. Serve some food, but make it simply a palate cleanser, such as bread (see entry 253), or a bland protein such as roast beef or boiled shrimp.

As you pour the first four wines, control the portions so you can taste the maximum number of different wines. One-ounce pours will allow everyone to try a dozen wines and still consume only 2.4 standard glasses of wine (see entry 254), which should be fine for most people.

Tasting Sheet

	COMMENTS	MY SCORE	GROUP SCORE	VINTAGE	WINE	PRICE
1						
2						
3						
4						
5						
6						
7						
8						
9						
10						
11						
12						

284 What are vertical and horizontal tastings?

Rather than comparing wines selected at random from all over the world, or even from a specific region, a horizontal tasting narrows the variables by focusing on wines of the same vintage, grape variety, and village, but from different wineries. For example, the theme might be a number of different 2006 Zinfandels from Paso Robles, or it could be a dozen 1994 Ports. A horizontal tasting vividly demonstrates the impact the winery has on the wine—both in its vineyards and in its winemaking methods. Be sure to do horizontal tastings at least single blind, preferably double blind. By contrast, a vertical tasting is a tasting of the same wine from the same producer, where the only difference in the wines is the vintage. See also entry 44 and Tasting 12, page 291.

TWELVE ORGANIZED WINE TASTINGS

Whether you prefer an intimate gathering for four or a good-sized revelry, a wine tasting offers memories, learning and—with moderation, of course—a pleasant amount of social lubrication. Here are several tips on how to make it perfect. While two friends enjoying a nice bottle could be a great wine tasting, here, the goals will be something a bit larger and more ordered. These tastings can be one-off affairs, or monthly get-togethers, or, best of all, the foundation for a regular structured tasting group. Tasting with a group of people allows everyone to try several wines at once and focus their thoughts by discussing their findings. Most of the wines should be easy to find or order. And if you can't find the recommended wines, ask a trusted wine seller to recommend something from the same area with similar flavors.

Tasting 1: Getting to Know the Standard Grapes (Level one)

This tasting will allow the guests to try twelve different grapes—or choose just four or six if you'd rather have a smaller tasting. This doesn't have to be blind, since the goal is simply to experience the grape. No matter how many wines you serve, serve them in the order in which they are listed here (see entry 252). The grape variety is listed in **boldface**.

THE $100 CASE

Cristalino Brut Rosé **Cava** (rosé)

Veramonte **Sauvignon Blanc** (white)
Chateau Ste. Michelle **Riesling** (white)
Columbia Crest Two Vines **Chardonnay** (white)
Santa Julia **Viognier** (white)

Pepperwood Grove **Pinot Noir** (red)
Banfi Chianti Classico **Sangiovese** (red)
Gallo Sonoma **Merlot** (red)
Concha y Toro **Cabernet Sauvignon** (red)
Trumpeter **Malbec** (red)
Columbia Crest Two Vines **Syrah** (red)
Rancho Zabaco Dancing Bull **Zinfandel** (red)

Tasting 2: The Standard Grapes
(Level two)

Again, the goal is to get an idea about the appearance, aromas, and flavors of these wines. While these wines come in at an average of just over $20 each, this is the price range in which a producer can hire a great winemaker and provide the tools he or she needs to make exceptional wine. Serve the wines in the order in which they are listed here (see entry 252). The grape variety is listed in **boldface**. There is no need for tasting blind.

THE $250 CASE

Trimbach Reserve **Pinot Gris** (white)
Chateau St. Jean Fumé Blanc **Sauvignon Blanc** (white)
Eroica **Riesling** (white)
Chateau St. Jean Robert Young Vineyard **Chardonnay** (white)
Yalumba **Viognier** (white)

Siduri Russian River **Pinot Noir** (red)
Badia a Coltibuono Cultus Boni Chianti Classico
   Sangiovese (red)
Mollydooker The Scooter **Merlot** (red)
Catena Alta **Cabernet Sauvignon** (red)
Don Miguel Gascón President's Blend **Malbec** (red)
d'Arenberg Laughing Magpie **Shiraz** (red)
Rosenblum Paso Robles **Zinfandel** (red)

Tasting 3: The Standard Grapes
(Level three)

It's possible to spend ridiculous amounts of money on wine, but in this case, averaging a bit less than $42 a bottle gives 99 percent of the quality available at any price. Serve the wines in the order in which they are listed here (see entry 252). The grape variety is listed in **boldface**. There is no need for tasting blind.

THE $500 CASE

Michael Redde Sancerre **Sauvignon Blanc** (white)
Domaine Zind Humbrecht Clos Windsbuhl **Pinot Gris** (white)
Gunderloch Nackenheimer Rothenberg Spätlese
    Riesling (white)
Newton Unfiltered **Chardonnay** (white)
Guigal La Doriane Condrieu **Viognier** (white)

Louis Jadot Beaune les Theurons **Pinot Noir** (red)
Banfi Poggio alle Mura Brunello **Sangiovese** (red)
Pepper Bridge **Merlot** (red)
Dehlinger **Cabernet Sauvignon** Reserve (red)
Catena Alta **Malbec** (red)
Guigal Crozes-Hermitage **Syrah** (red)
St. Francis Pagani Ranch **Zinfandel** (red)

Tasting 4: Less-Common Grapes
(Level one)

The goal here is to expand your knowledge of some of the world's less-known grapes. Serve the wines in the order in which they are listed here (see entry 252). The grape variety is listed in **boldface**. There is no need for tasting blind.

THE **$150** CASE

Zardetto **Prosecco** Brut (white sparkling)
Banfi Perlante Gavi **Cortese** (white)
Tablas Creek **Grenache Blanc** (white)
Berger **Grüner Veltliner** (white)
Columbia Winery **Gewürztraminer** (white)

Les Jamelles Rosé **Cinsault** (rosé)
Condesa de Leganza **Tempranillo** Rosé La Mancha (rosé)

Mano a Mano La Mancha **Tempranillo** (red)
Catherine & Pierre Breton Bourgueil Trinch
 Cabernet Franc (red)
MandraRossa **Nero d'Avola** (red)
Cline Ancient Vines **Mourvèdre** (red)
Rosenblum Heritage Clones **Petite Sirah** (red)

Tasting 5: Less-Common Grapes
(Level two)

Here are sixteen grape varieties matched with some of their finest proponents. This case averages $25 a bottle, so these aren't cheap wines, but the ratio between cost and quality makes this a case of bargains. Some of these wines will be impossible to find on local shelves, but a browse of the Internet or a willing shopkeeper should help you get any of them readily. Two wines that will surprise many tasters are the bone-dry Domecq Manzanilla Sherry and the honey-sweet Blandy's fifteen-year-old Rich Malmsey Madeira, both wines that are priced dramatically below their quality level. Serve the wines in the order in which they are listed here (see entry 252). The grape variety is listed in **boldface**.

THE $300 CASE

Segura Viudas Brut Reserva Heredad **Macabeo, Parellada**
(white sparkling)

Domaine des Baumard Savennières **Chenin Blanc** (white)
Pazo de Señorans **Albariño** (white)
Feudi di San Gregorio Cutizzi **Greco di Tufo** (white)
L'Ecole No 41 Seven Hills Vineyard Estate **Sémillon** (white)
Domecq Manzanilla Sherry mostly **Palomino** (white)

Joseph Drouhin Moulin-à-Vent **Gamay** (red)
Bruno Giacosa **Dolcetto** d'Alba Falletto (red)
Prieler **Blaufränkisch** Ried Johanneshöhe (red)
Quinta do Vallado **Touriga Nacional** (red)
Vietti **Barbera** d'Asti Tre Vigne (red)

Blandy's 15-Year-Old Rich **Malmsey** (white)

Tasting 6: Old World Versus New World

Being able to peg Old World and New World styles (see Introduction) is one of the most important skills a wine lover can learn. It allows you to communicate a whole set of variables quickly, including flavor, concentration, and impact of terroir (see entry 190). This tasting is intended to make the differences easy to see, smell, and taste. This group of wines is widely available and inexpensive. Taste by the pair, paying close attention to color, intensity of aroma, flavor, and mouthfeel. For this group, taste in the order in which the wines are listed (see entry 252) and don't worry about tasting blind. It is more important to focus on the differences, and knowing which wine is which can be helpful.

THE $200 CASE

Sauvignon Blanc
Domaine des Corbillières Touraine (France) *versus*
Kim Crawford Sauvignon Blanc (New Zealand)

Chardonnay
Louis Jadot Pernand-Vergelesses Blanc (France) *versus*
Chateau St. Jean Belle Terre Vineyard (USA)

Riesling
Gunderloch Riesling Trocken (Germany) *versus*
d'Arenberg The Dry Dam (Australia)

Pinot Noir
Joseph Drouhin Vero Pinot Noir (France) *versus*
Cono Sur 20 Barrels Pinot Noir (Chile)

Sangiovese:
Banfi Chianti Classico Riserva (Italy) *versus*
Bonny Doon Ca' del Solo Sangiovese (USA)

Cabernet Sauvignon
Torres Gran Coronas Cabernet Sauvignon (Spain) *versus*
Chateau Ste. Michelle Indian Wells Cabernet Sauvignon (USA)

SERENA SUTCLIFFE, MW

Master of Wine, senior director of Sotheby's, and head of Sotheby's Worldwide Wine Department

Serena Sutcliffe has been a Master of Wine since 1976. Absolutely no one on earth gets to try a wider range of rare and outrageously expensive wines than she does.

Of course, there's more to wine than rare and expensive bottles. "I don't always drink the great classics, even though that is what I do for a living. At the moment I am absolutely passionate about both reds and whites from Austria and Greece. In Greece, George Skouras's wines are absolutely fantastic; he is the king of Greek wine. I'm also very interested in some of the Austrian wines from Burgenland, where they are producing stunning red wines from Blaufränkisch. At the moment Weingut Familie Prieler is the one I find really super."

How did she get started? "Well, I came in through France, which I still think is the greatest starting point and I still recommend it as the best first step. The country has so many different climates and grapes, and most of what you learn from France will serve you for the rest of your life. Start from north to south, Alsace down to Spain."

how to taste

Should you be lucky enough to be able to afford this world-class tasting, this would be the ultimate taste-off, the best of the best. Be aware that at this level, experts disagree about these wines, sometimes violently. However, these wines are consistently among both the best and the most expensive wines on earth. Just as in sports, on any given day a champion might be knocked off by a pretender, but these wines will always get back up again. At the time of writing, the cost of this three-case tasting would be around $50,000—by any standards, this would be a party to remember. Set this up as a double-blind tasting (see entry 281)—for these prices, you could hire a few servers to keep the tasters in high suspense.

THE **$50,000** TASTING

The Chardonnay Fight
Domaine Leroy Corton Charlemagne (France)
Domaine de la Romanée-Conti Montrachet (France)
Louis Jadot Montrachet (France)
versus
Kumeu River Mate's Vineyard (New Zealand)
Rochioli Rachel's Vineyard (USA)
Kistler Cuvee Cathleen (USA)

The Pinot Noir Conflict
Domaine de la Romanée-Conti Romanée-Conti (France)
Domaine Dugat-Py Chambertin (France)
Joseph Drouhin Musigny (France)
versus
Rochioli West Block (USA)
Kistler Bodega Headlands Cuvee Elizabeth (USA)
Domaine Drouhin Cuvee Louise (USA)

The Bordeaux-blend Battle

Château Ausone (France)
Château Petrus (France)
Château Lafite-Rothschild (France)
versus
Quilceda Creek (USA)
Shafer Vineyards Hillside Select (USA)
Two Hands Aphrodite (Australia)

The Italian Varietal Confrontation

Angelo Gaja Sori Tilden (Italy)
Antinori Tignanello (Italy)
Bruno Giacosa Barolo Le Rocche del Falletto Riserva (Italy)
versus
Pride Mountain Sangiovese (USA)
Penfolds Sangiovese Cellar Reserve (Australia)
Leonetti Cellar Sangiovese (USA)

The Rhône Varietal Shoot-Out

Guigal Côte-Rôtie La Mouline (France)
Chave Hermitage (France)
Clos Erasmus (Spain)
versus
Mollydooker The Velvet Glove Shiraz (Australia)
Torbreck Les Amis (Australia)
Saxum James Berry Vineyard (USA)

The Dessert Wine Competition

Château d'Yquem Sauternes (France)
Domaine Trimbach Gewürztraminer Sélection de Grains
    Nobles Hors Choix (France)
Kracher Muscat Ottonel Trockenbeerenauslese ZdS (Austria)
versus
R.L. Buller Calliope Rare Tokay (Australia)
d'Arenberg Daddy Long Legs (Australia)
Sine Qua Non Mr K The Strawman Vin de Paille (USA)

how to taste

MADELINE TRIFFON, MS

Master Sommelier and wine director for the Matt Prentice
Restaurant Group, Detroit

Madeline Triffon spent some time thinking about her answers to
the question of how to learn about wine and came up with these
eight little pearls of wine wisdom:

1. Keep a little tasting notebook. It doesn't have to be fancy.
   No tasting notes, just the date, where you had it, and what it
   is. Write down everything you see on the label, whether you
   understand it or not. And only write down wines you love.
2. As soon as possible after having a great wine, get a book and
   read a bit about the wine region, then go to the winery's Web
   site and read just a little about the winery. If you do this for a
   year, you will know much more than most.
3. Shove your boat away from the shore of comfort labels and
   always try something new.
4. You don't have to read a book about Moroccan food to order
   Moroccan food. If you go to restaurants that have a wine
   program that they are proud of, look for the most obscure wines
   and just try them.
5. Evan Goldstein's book *Perfect Pairings* is a great place to start
   because it is about food with wine as an addendum. Kevin
   Zraly's *Windows on the World Complete Wine Course* and Karen
   MacNeil's *Wine Bible* are the best entry-level wine books,
6. Regarding retailers, if you get to trust someone, give them
   your money, tell them what you like, and ask them to pick out
   a mixed case, or six bottles. They will trip over themselves to
   help. Also, take a look at the clubs, like Costco or Sam's—no
   one can beat those prices.
7. Form or join a dining group. If you want to taste expensive
   wines, you will be able to taste several by bringing just one.
8. *Ignore ratings!*

Tasting 8: One Variety from Many Places

Only a relatively few grape varieties are both easy to grow and popular enough to have spread around the world. Chardonnay, Sauvignon Blanc, Cabernet, Merlot, and Syrah are the best bets. A Chardonnay tasting could hit various areas in California, Washington, Australia, New Zealand, and France, as well as Italy, Chile, and almost anywhere else people grow grapes. Ditto for Syrah. Tasting a single variety from all these areas really hammers home the point of how terroir and local custom drive the final flavors of wines.

Tasting 9: The Wines of a Single Place

This tasting allows you to get an idea of the subtle impact of the micro-terroir (see entry 190) within a single appellation. The goal is to taste enough versions of the appellation's wine to get past the influence of the winemaker and down to an idea of what the terroir contributes. Old World wines are easier for this tasting because the varieties grown tend to be consistent, even within an entire region. If your group has a favorite appellation, spend a session tasting wine from only that area: Chardonnays from the Côte de Beaune. Rieslings from the Mosel Valley. Pinot Noirs from Central Otago. Nebbiolos from Barbaresco. Cabernets from Napa. Syrahs from Crozes-Hermitage. Merlots from Walla Walla. Tempranillos from Priorat. Zinfandels from Dry Creek. Knowledgeable tasters who want to drill down to the influences of place can try tasting multiple wines from a single famous vineyard, such as Clos de Vougeot, Dutton Ranch, or Doctorberg.

Tasting 10: Comparing Two Great Places, for Advanced Tasters

This tasting requires as many examples as possible—twelve from each place is the minimum—because the goal is to taste past the winemaker's interventions to find the similarities that point to the impact of terroir (see entry 190). For the greatest impact, the tasting should be conducted double-blind (see entry 281). Tasting a dozen bottles of Barossa G-S-M (Grenache-Syrah-Mourvèdre) versus a dozen like bottles from Paso Robles grants enough breadth to see beyond the winemaker's skills. It is a bit more difficult with six from each place. The tasting could compare regions, such as Chablis versus Mâconnais (Chardonnay), Mosel versus Alsace (Riesling), Pomerol versus Columbia Valley (Merlot), or Hermitage versus the Barossa (Syrah/Shiraz). Or it could be more specific and compare vineyards, such as Pagani Ranch versus Rockpile or La Romanée versus La Tâche.

Tasting 11: Several Wines from One Winemaker

For this tasting, participants should already have extensive experience with tastings 9 and 10 so that they really understand the impact of specific areas' terroir (see entry 190). That way, when you taste the work of a specific winemaker, you will be able to identify how it is different from the norm. While most winemakers claim that their total focus is on letting the terroir speak for itself, the truth is that every one of them approaches that goal differently. An experienced wine lover can deduce a winemaker's stamp, whether it's a similar aroma from a barrel choice or a level of richness from a certain time of harvest. This type of tasting works best with willful winemakers who have strong opinions on winemaking, like Italy's Giuseppe Quintarelli, France's Olivier Humbrecht, or Spain's Alvaro Palacios. Unfortunately, this precludes most inexpensive wines. Someone like Ray Einberger, winemaker at Columbia Crest, must be considered one of the world's best winemakers simply because he can produce rivers of exceptional wine for less than $15 a bottle. But at his market level, he must concentrate on consistency. Farther up the cost ladder, winemakers usually focus on demonstrating the individuality that works best for this tasting.

Tasting 12: The Vertical Tasting

The vertical tasting is the gold standard for people who are deeply committed to learning about wine. Here, the group tastes a single wine (of identical producer and bottling) through multiple vintages. Vertical tastings are generally possible only through the largesse of a winery or a collector, so they aren't very common. As rare as they are, they offer a phenomenal opportunity to see how a winemaker copes with the many year-to-year changes in the vineyard. Wine experts will always make time for a vertical tasting, even if the wine being tasted is not one of their favorites. Don't ever miss the opportunity to attend one! See also entry 44.

ROBERT MARK KAMEN, PH.D.
Screenwriter and winery owner (Kamen Estate Wines)

Robert Mark Kamen sold his first screenplay and used the money to buy Sonoma property so he could plant a vineyard. There, he makes what he calls a "fantastic, big, mountain-grown, organically farmed seventy-five-dollar Cabernet." As befits a man whose films (*The Karate Kid, The Transporter, Taken, The Fifth Element,* and many more) have made well more than $1 billion, he politely scoffed at the question of what his inexpensive house wines are. "All the wine I drink is expensive," he noted with a laugh. "I mostly drink European. Châteauneuf-du-Papes from Domaine de la Solitude and Domaine du Pegau; upper-end Spanish wines like Pingus, Clos Erasmus, and Clos Mogador; Côte Rôties like Guigal's La Landonne, La Mouline, and La Turque. And I love white Burgundies. Any high-end white Burgundy that comes along, especially a Bâtard-Montrachet or a Le Montrachet."

It's always nice to know what to drink should you ever come into serious money.

Serving Wine

Not everyone needs to be a Master Sommelier. Simply getting the bottle open and a bit of wine poured into a glass without too much spillage is all most people need, and that is covered in this chapter. Your enjoyment of wine can be further enhanced by understanding types of glassware, serving temperatures, qualities of corkscrews, decanting, and breathing. For the resolute reader, we even cover the centuries-old way of opening a bottle of Champagne with a saber.

285 What is the best serving temperature?

Ninety-eight percent of the homes and restaurants in America serve their white wines too cold and their red wines too warm. This wastes the wine's potential. If a wine is too cold, it won't release its aromas and the acidity will gain an advantage over the sugar, making the wine seem out of balance (see entry 276). This is one of the reasons people who drink inexpensive, low-acidity Chardonnays tend to prefer them very cold—the frigid temperature makes the wine taste like it has more acidity. A higher serving temperature for whites makes the aromatics jump out of the glass and makes dry wines taste a touch fruitier, useful when the wine seems too austere.

The idea of serving red wine at room temperature is left over from ye olde days, prior to the advent of air-conditioning. The wine would come up from the cellar at about 58°F and slowly warm up to room temperature—which at the time, before central heating, was the low sixties. Today, even an air-conditioned room is generally in the 70°–75°F range, which is just too warm. Even worse, many consumers and even restaurants store their red wine in the hottest room, the kitchen. At home, chill a red wine in the refrigerator for about fifteen minutes to cool it off. If your red is too warm in a restaurant, ask the server to chill it for you for five or ten minutes in an ice-water bath, and it should be good for the whole meal.

Remember that cool and warm are relative terms—as wine sits in the glass it will eventually come to room temperature, so start a bit cool. Use the numbers below as a guide, and don't worry about being a few degrees off on either side. After you've used a wine thermometer a few times, you should be able to just feel the bottle and get a good idea of its temperature. See also entry 38.

TYPE OF WINE	EXAMPLES	TEMPERATURE (°F)
NV sparkling wine	Prosecco, Cava, Asti Spumante, Moscato d'Asti, most American and Australian sparkling wines	37°
Complex sparkling wines	Champagne, vintage American sparkling wines	45°
Light-bodied or inexpensive whites	Pinot Grigio, Riesling, Sauvignon Blanc, Sancerre, most Spanish white wines, Fino Sherry	45°
Complex white wines	Chardonnay, Burgundy, Alsace wines, Rhône wines, high-end German Rieslings, Grüner Veltliner, Australian stickies, white dessert wines	52°
Light-bodied or inexpensive reds	Pinot Noir, Beaujolais, young Sangiovese and Tempranillo, Cabernet Franc, rosé	52°
Dense red wines	Zinfandel, Petit Sirah, Shiraz, Rhône wines	57°
Complex, tannic red wines	Bordeaux, Barolo, Brunello, Chianti Classico Riserva, Cabernet Sauvignon	60°

286 How to cool wine quickly?

Two things make wine cool quickly. The most important is a slurry of ice and water. The ice-only approach is very slow, but adding water enables contact with every part of the bottle surface, thereby speeding the process. Another trick that helps wine cool down is circulating the wine in the bottle so the warmer liquid comes in contact with the glass. The closer the wine is to the ice water outside the bottle, the faster it cools. The wine in the center of the bottle cools more slowly. Agitation helps equalize the wine's temperature. To accomplish this—but don't do this with old, rare, or otherwise valuable wines—spin the bottle by holding the neck between your two hands and spinning vigorously two or three times every few minutes while the bottle is in the ice water. Ten minutes in a freezer usually works as well.

287 How many servings in a bottle?

A 750 milliliter (standard) bottle of wine equals 25.4 ounces—or five 5-ounce servings, the same as the standard restaurant serving. As for alcohol, a 5-ounce pour of wine equals one shot of spirits or a 12-ounce serving of beer.

HINT *It may be interesting to note the following breakdowns.*

> *1 barrel = 25 cases of wine*
> *1 barrel = 300 bottles*
> *1 barrel = 1,500 five-ounce glasses*

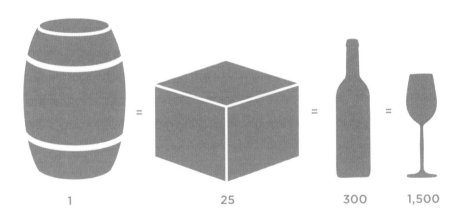

1   =   25   =   300   =   1,500

288 What should I look for in a wineglass?

There are essential features to look for in a glass, and then there are extras. First, the essentials. A wineglass should have a tulip-shaped bowl on a stem with a foot—straight-sided tumblers and the like should not be used for wine tasting. This is because the tulip-shaped bowl of a wineglass collects the aromas of the wine inside the glass, allowing you to smell them better, and the stem allows you to hold the glass without warming the wine with your hand.

After these essentials, there are some important additional factors to consider, depending on how serious you are about wine. It is possible to buy a single size and shape of glass that will suffice for all wine types, but it is known that certain bowl shapes are most suitable for collecting the aromas of certain wines. At the most basic level, wineglasses for white wine tend to have smaller bowls than wineglasses for red wine, so it makes sense to buy two types of glasses, one for whites and one for reds. Take this a step farther, and it is possible to buy a specialized size and shape of glass that is made specifically for each different type of wine—so, one glass for red Burgundy, one for Rhône wines, one for Bordeaux reds, one for Port, and so on. It is up to you how far you go. Another important feature of top-quality wineglasses is a cut rim rather than a rolled rim. A rounded lip on the rim of a glass causes a subtle upward arc of the wine as it flows into your mouth, kind of like the stream of water from a fountain, allowing some of the wine to bypass a very important part of your tongue. Cut rims solve the problem. The best way to test a glass in the store is to put your thumb on the outside of the glass and press your index finger's nail against the inside. Pull up so that your nail drags across the rim. It should feel flat, as if the glass has been cut. See also entry 289.

A SECOND SIP *The research and care that Georg Riedel devotes to his stemware is remarkable enough to keep the company at the top of the marketplace. The strongest evidence of this is the number of winemakers who pour their wines into Riedel glasses—and these aren't just expensive wines. Back in the late 1980s, wine luminary Angelo Gaja was sipping some great Barolo with the California winemaker Robert Mondavi. Gaja raved about Riedel glasses, and after trying them out, Mondavi called the head of all his tasting rooms and told him to throw away all the glasses and replace them with Riedels, even for their least expensive wines. That's a serious endorsement.*

GREAT GLASSES

For the Beginner ($10 and less/glass)

Riedel's Wine Series or Riedel's line for Target
Schott Zwiesel's Tritan Forte
Spiegelau's Vino Grande

For the Collector (more than $10/glass)

Riedel Vinum or Sommelier series
Schott Zweisel Enoteca

The Riedel Vinum Collection (from left to right): Bordeaux, Pinot Noir, Riesling Grand Cru, Shiraz/Syrah, Sauvignon Blanc, Champagne, Montrachet/Chardonnay.

serving wine

289   Any glasses to avoid?

Yes, there are three types of glasses you really should avoid for wine tasting. The least offensive is the mass-produced tulip-shaped glass that has a lip so thick you can feel it with *your* lips. Many budget glass companies put this bead around the rim to help strengthen the glass, but the thick lip causes the wine to leap from the glass instead of roll from it into your mouth. The second type of glass to avoid, even if it is luxurious in an anachronistic sense, is cut crystal. Being able to examine the wine is an important part of tasting, and it's difficult to see the wine through the prism of the carvings. The third type of glass to avoid, and the worst case, is one with a colored bowl through which you'll have no way of seeing your wine. Is it old or young? Is it oxidized? Unfiltered? With a colored glass, you won't know the answer to any of these questions until you take a sip, and by then you might get an unpleasant surprise. See also entries 288 and 290.

A SECOND SIP *If you're worried about the lead content in crystal, be aware that, although it is true that acids cause lead to leach, and wine is highly acidic, wine doesn't stay in your glass long enough for lead to leach into it. Lead crystal decanters can be a bigger problem, but again, only if you use a decanter to store Port or other fortified wines for days at a time, which also allows the wine to lose all its youthful vigor. If you would rather not worry about it at all, many glass companies offer lead-free product lines.*

290 Are stemless glasses any good?

The famous stemless "O" glass was designed by Maximilian Riedel to appeal to younger wine drinkers and those who like to use dishwashers. There are two reasons the glass with a stem is a better design for wine tasting. First, the wineglass stem keeps the warmth of your hands from affecting the temperature of the wine, and second, it keeps the oils from your hands off the bowl, so you can see the wine more clearly. Furthermore, you should never put a wineglass in the dishwasher because of the possibility of pitting or breaking. The "O" glass is a fun concept—if you end up with a collection, they work great with iced tea.

291 How to wash a wineglass

The process is quick and easy, once you've done it a couple of times.

1. Run your hot water until it is as hot as it will get.
2. Hold the glass under the water, and use the pressure of the water like a brushless car wash all over the glass.
3. If there are stubborn lip marks, use a soft linen towel to rub them off, then hit the area with the stream of hot water again.
4. The best drying method depends on your water. If you have hard water, dry the glass as soon as possible to avoid spotting, which means you'll have to do it by hand. If your water's not too hard, you can turn the glass upside down on a drying towel and let it drip-dry.

HINT *The one complication is lipstick stains. These just won't come off without elbow grease, and sometimes detergent. If you have to use detergent, when the glass is clean, keep rinsing it until you can't smell the soap.*

serving wine

292 What to do about musty-smelling glasses

If you keep your glasses upright, your cabinets clean, and you cycle through all your glasses weekly, you won't be familiar with this phenomenon, but sometimes an unused wineglass ran smell like a mildewed dish towel. The cause is a combination of paint, still air, and dust. Add those up and your wine barely has a chance to express its own aromas. The best solution is to buy a stemware rack, install it away from the kitchen's oils, and hang your glasses upside down so they can breathe. (Unfortunately, most of us want our wineglasses close to the kitchen.) If you sniff an empty glass and it smells funky, sacrifice a tablespoon of the wine and roll it around in the glass until every part of the bowl has been rinsed. Then throw that rinsing wine down the drain and start over. Works like a charm.

RANDALL GRAHM
The original Rhône Ranger, author of *Been Doon So Long,* owner of Bonny Doon and Pacific Rim wineries

Randall Grahm is one of those lucky people who is both phenomenally successful and really happy with what he does, which is to gently terrorize the complacent. His knowledge of wines, even those he doesn't make, is encyclopedic. We asked him about some of his favorite European wines. "It is relatively easy to make wines in a consistent manner if one experiences the very dependable weather we enjoy in the New World. What is utterly breathtaking is to observe winemakers produce, over and over again, enjoyable wine in vintages that are utterly loopy—rather like Roberto Clemente hitting base hits from balls that were pitched to him in the dirt. In Germany, the master is unquestionably Helmut Donnhoff, who produces consistently great wine every vintage without fail. In Burgundy, one thinks of

the late master Henri Jayer, and in more recent times, it would
be Bernard Dugat and certainly Bize-Leroy. For consistent Rhône
wines, I have lately been really knocked out by Cuilleron, and for
the out-of-the-park experience, it has to be Thierry Allemand,
whose Cornas Cuvée Sans Soufre is my standard for great Syrah.
But at home, especially in warm weather, it is generally a crisp
Mosel Spätlese, ideally one that has at least ten (better fifteen)
years of age. I generally love all of them, but am especially keen on
the wines of von Schubert."

293 What is the capsule for?

The capsule of a wine bottle is the tin or plastic hood that covers the
cork and opening of the bottle. In the early days of wine bottles, after
the bottle was corked, it would be dipped in hard wax. That way,
the royalty could tell if the help was taking a tipple. The rise of the
mercantile class in Europe created a desire to imitate the royals, and
the capsule as we know it today was the outcome. Over the years,
it's been made from lead, tin, and plastic. Why are we still using
something that was made to keep you out of a bottle? The capsule
makers will tell you that it helps keep light from the cork, or it helps
keep the cork in the bottle. The truth is, we're just used to the idea.

A SECOND SIP *For a young wine without sediment
in the bottle (see entry 306), the simplest way to rid yourself
of the capsule is to turn the bottle sideways, grab the capsule
with your dominant hand and the middle of the bottle with
your other hand, and twist off the capsule in one piece. Many
capsules are loose enough that they will come off with a few
twists. These very casual methods are quick and effective but
are not suitable for restaurant service.*

serving wine

294 How to open a wine bottle

1. Remove the capsule: sommeliers use the small blade of their corkscrew to circle around the bottle neck beneath the lip, then cut firmly upward from the ring just created to make a flap under which you can insert the tip of the blade. Lift and peel off the top cap of the foil, leaving the lower part intact on the neck of the bottle. The easier way (shown) is to insert the blade at the bottom of the capsule, rip unward, grab the flap, and pull it off.

2. Open the bottle: insert the worm of the corkscrew in the cork and twist slowly, keeping the worm vertical. Stop before the worm comes through the bottom of the cork inside the bottle.

3. Brace the lever of the corkscrew on the lip of the bottle and use it to help you pull the cork slowly and gently, to avoid breaking it. (If the cork breaks, see entry 297.)

4. If any residue or cork dust is on the bottle lip, wipe it off with a towel or napkin, then pour the wine.

295 What kinds of corkscrews are there?

The Basic Tool

The Pulltaps waiter's corkscrew is a masterpiece of smart design that includes a never-dull serrated knife, a strong, Teflon-coated worm (the part that penetrates the cork), and a two-part, hinged lever (the stroke of genius). This design allows you to keep the angle of the pull as vertical as possible, which means no more broken corks. Corks are easily broken using cheaper, older designs with a single leverage point that bends the cork during the final pull. The final benefit of the Pulltaps is for folks with tender hands. Instead of going the cheap way and having sharp edges, the Pulltaps is contoured, rounded, and comfortable. As with most good ideas, there are many knockoffs of the Pulltaps corkscrew. The Pulltaps costs about $9.

Screwpull makes several openers that do exactly what the name implies—you screw, it pulls. Until the Pulltaps came out, the Screwpull opener was the easiest on the market. A thin Teflon worm enters the cork with minimal force, and all you have to do is keep turning until the cork comes out. For anyone who finds pulling a cork to be a physical challenge, the Screwpull opener is easy to use. Problems can arise with recalcitrant corks, because the pull pressure can force the Screwpull's arms off the bottle lip; also, the arms are strong but not unbreakable, and the glue holding the screw to its fulcrum wears out over time. Still, this easy-to-use opener costs less than $20.

The Luxury Tool

As fast and nimble as the Pulltaps is, some people prefer a little more pomp and luxury in their wine implements. Wine lovers will usually end up with a Rabbit-style device sometime in their lives. They pull the cork straight out of the bottle, which means fewer broken corks, and are very fast to use because of the method of locking the bottle with your left hand and using leverage with your right. Their main drawback is that the lever allows so much pressure on the worm that it has been known to stretch. The Metrokane Rabbit is the most common of this type of product. The Original runs about $40; different versions can cost as much as $150, but you're paying for glitz rather than function.

The estate opener, as these are sometimes called, is a big, heavy brass apparatus that attaches permanently to your counter. That gives you good stability but restricts you to one location to open your wine. The main problem with them is that the gears inside tend to get rough over time, so expect to buy a new one every few years. And depending on how vigorous you are, you may have to replace the worm as often as annually. This device costs about $100.

The Laguiole waiter's corkscrew costs up to $295. For your money, you get a handmade instrument with a sharp blade and a strong worm—and the satisfaction of knowing you have one of the more expensive wine openers in the world. The sides will be clad in one of a dozen special materials, from translucent acrylic to wood from a 223-year-old *Tulipier de Virginie* tree from the garden of the Château de Versailles.

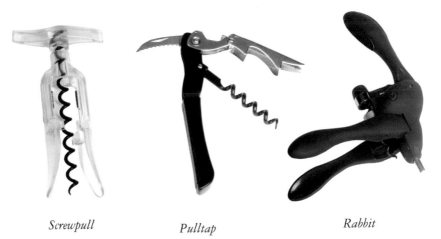

Screwpull   *Pulltap*   *Rabbit*

296 Any wine openers to avoid?

Avoid any T-shaped corkscrew that requires you to screw the worm in and simply pull the handle to extract the cork by brute force. These provide no leverage, so they require the most strength of any opener, and the suction in a tightly corked bottle can cause wine to splatter when the cork comes out. The worst are the little $1 plastic openers where you insert the worm protector in a hole to make it into a T-shaped torture device.

Another popular but less-than-ideal corkscrew is the wing-style opener. Looking at it, it seems like a good idea. It's made of metal, the "arms" that rise as you insert the worm look substantial, and the screw has big, dense threads. But it's difficult to get the large stainless steel worm into a cork, and because of the design, you have to screw and pull, then take the time to screw still deeper and pull again.

297 How to remove a broken cork

Both wet and dry corks (see entry 37) will break, and it always seems to happen when you are having a party. If the cork breaks but it is dry inside, there's a good chance the wine in the bottle will be sound. Slowly push the part of the cork that is stuck in the neck down into the bottle. (If you press too hard or fast, wine will come out like a rocket, splattering you and your ceiling.) Next, you'll need a strainer and, unless the mesh is very fine, several layers of cheesecloth or a single layer of clean panty hose to line the strainer. Sacrifice a little of the wine to rinse any detergent aroma out of the piece of panty hose, then pour through the strainer into your glass.

If the broken cork is wet, return the bottle and ask for a refund. Usually the wine inside will be spoiled, so there's no reason to try to get into the bottle. If it is an old bottle, or one you can't return, follow the dry-cork method and beware of potential spoilage (see entry 34).

298   How to minimize dribbles when pouring

When Master Sommelier candidates take their exams, one of the tests is on pouring and service. It may seem simple, but it is a complex dance to keep the bottle from dripping on the table without agitating the wine. Master Sommeliers give the bottle a slight twist and then lift it to stop drips, but they also keep a small towel on hand for any dribbles. Aside from this technique, there's a device that ranks with the Pulltaps Waiter's Corkscrew (see entry 295) for greatest wine invention of the twentieth century: the Drop Stop wine pourer. The pourer is a flexible metalized Mylar disc that is thin enough to curl into a tube shape and fit in the mouth of a bottle. The thin, curved edge of the Mylar stops the flow of wine without drips. These things are ridiculously cheap, usually a dollar or two each.

299 How to open sparkling wine

We've all seen folks who grab the bottle with both hands and use their thumbs to force the cork out with a huge POP! There are two problems with that approach. First, it is dangerous. The pressure in a bottle of Champagne typically reaches 80 pounds per square inch. To put that in perspective, a car's tires have about 30 pounds per square inch of pressure. Second, the all-thumbs method causes the Champagne to spew out of the bottle, wasting some of the precious wine and much of its fizz. The only benefit to this method is the festive pop, but Champagne is an elegant wine—it prefers a whisper. Follow these steps to open any bottle of bubbly.

1. Start with a very cold bottle, which minimizes the explosive pressure of the bubbles. Search the foil for a little tab that will help make a clean rip around the lip. Remove the foil cap.
2. Next, untwist the wire cage. One in a hundred corks will pop before you even try to get it out, so try to get the cage off as quickly as possible, then use your thumb to hold the cork down.
3. Drape a dish towel over the cork both to get a better grip and to slow down the rocketing cork if it comes out harder than expected (when you're more used to the process it's fine to do this without the towel). Next, hold the bottom of the bottle with your right (or dominant) hand, and hold the cloth-covered cork in your other hand with your thumb and middle finger wrapped around the cork.
4. Now remember: NO POPS! The goal is to hear a gentle whisper, a quiet hissssss sound. Holding the cork still, gently twist the bottle with your right hand. Go slow. When you feel the pressure pushing the cork out, try to let it out as slowly as possible. Remember, quiet is the key.

300 What is sabrage and can I do it at home?

Sabrage is one of the world's great party tricks, left to us by the dashing soldiers of the Napoleonic era. Using a saber and a very cold bottle of Champagne, with one vigorous hit you remove the bottle's lip and the cork. A good saber runs $250, but the spine of a stout chef's knife works just as well. Chill the bottle in the refrigerator, then put it in the freezer for about half an hour before opening it. Feel the bottle to locate the two tiny seams in the glass, on opposite sides of the bottle, running from top to bottom. The goal is to hit the bottle precisely where one of those seams meets the lip. Remove the foil and wire basket. With the back of your hand facing the floor, put your thumb in the dimple (called the punt) on the bottom of the bottle and use your fingers to hold the bottle, aiming it away from yourself (and everyone else) in the two o'clock position. Make sure one of the top-to-bottom seams is facing straight up. Place the saber on the seam at the halfway point between top and bottom. Run the saber to and fro along the seam a few times to get used to the feel, then, in one strong move, draw the saber tight against the bottle and run it up the seam away from you to strike the lip. The top will fly ten feet, a shower of bubbles will remove any glass shards, and the guests will be very impressed. If any of your guests ask if the process is potentially dangerous, the answer is "maybe." But it's also fun.

301 How long is an open bottle good?

It depends on what you want from a bottle of wine. Oxygen destroys wine, and it starts affecting the wine as soon as you open the bottle. The juice in a day-old bottle stored in the fridge won't taste terrible or be harmful to your health; it just won't have the bright freshness of a new bottle. A good bottle of wine should evolve from the beginning of the meal to the end. See also entry 304.

302 How to preserve an open bottle

If you do want to save an open bottle of wine, the goal is to protect it from oxygen, or at least slow down oxygen's effects. The plunger devices that suck the air out of the bottle are meant to create a vacuum, and if you pump them until all of the air is out, they might work. Unfortunately, the device can also suck some of the life out of the wine. Sniff while pumping and you'll smell fragrances evaporating into the air.

Most fine wine shops sell cans of inert argon gas that you can inject into a bottle to protect the wine from oxygen. These do a fine job, although the price can add up and some claim they can taste argon. Another good strategy is to get an empty half-bottle, fill it with the leftover wine, and recork it so there is hardly any air in the bottle. At the most casual level, stick the cork back in the bottle and store the bottle in the refrigerator, whether the wine is white or red. Just as cold helps preserve vegetables and fruits, it will help preserve the wine, at least over a single night.

303 What to do about particles in wine

Americans like their wines to be clear and clean, but some of the greatest wines in the world have stuff floating around in them. White wines that get too cold somewhere along the journey to the glass can develop tartrate crystals (which may look like sea salt flakes or crystals in the bottom of your glass) and either rustically made, unfiltered (see entry 197), or very fine red wines will throw a sediment, meaning there will be a black powdery or flaky substance on the bottom or side of the bottle. Neither kind of particle will hurt you or the wine, although you will want to avoid pouring sediment in your glass. If the wine bottle sits upright overnight and you handle it carefully, most of the sediment should stay at the bottom. Either decant the wine (see entry 306) or pour slowly and avoid pouring the last ounce or two. See also entries 297 and 305.

304 Does wine need to "breathe"?

Most wine does not need to undergo the transformative effects of contact with oxygen—it is ready to drink when you open it, and like all wine, will develop different aromas and flavors over time as it sits in the glass. The issue of exposing a wine to oxygen can be controversial. Whether the wine is young or old, red or white, sweet or dry, there's an expert somewhere who will get angry over letting wine come into contact with air or giving it a generous amount of time to air in a decanter. Most say that the younger the wine, the more air it needs. But a vocal minority believes old wines also benefit from air. If the wine has a rich, thick feel in the mouth, but there's not much aroma or flavor, it's likely a good candidate for getting some air in a decanter.

Another reason to let wine breathe is if there are any unpleasant aromas when you sniff the first pour. If so, the contact with air will change the wine and it *might* help—emphasis on *might,* because there is no way for a normal consumer to tell if allowing the wine to breathe will create a positive change. In some cases, it actually deadens a wine. The best way to go about deciding is to either decant the wine or go ahead and pour it into the glasses and then taste again before serving. Older wines are more delicate—pour a tiny taste and let it sit in the glass for five or ten minutes, then taste again before deciding to decant. If the wine loses its aromas in the glass, don't let it breathe—serve it straight from the bottle and be prepared to drink fast.

A SECOND SIP *For young red wines that have good texture but not much flavor or aroma, aggressive decanting can sometimes make all the difference. These wines aren't defective, but they usually improve after given some contact with oxygen. It sounds overly dramatic, but decanting the wine and shaking it so hard that the wine develops a foam on top can hurry the process of breathing.*

305 How to know if a wine needs decanting

There are two reasons to use a decanter: to allow the wine to breathe (see entry 304), or to allow you to separate the wine from its sediment. All old red wines, as well as a few young ones, will have a flaky black sediment in the bottle that not only feels unpleasant on the palate, but also tastes awful. It is easy to judge whether an old red wine needs to be decanted off its sediment. All older red wines should be stored on their side. Pick up the bottle gently to avoid disturbing any possible sediment and, before you open it, check for a dark, grainy stain of sediment on the underside of the bottle, inside. (It is gravity that causes sediment to collect there.) You may have to shine a flashlight on the bottle to get a clear view. If you see any sediment at all, the wine should be decanted, and it's best to stand the bottle upright for a day or two, if you have the time, to allow the sediment to fall to the bottom. See also entry 306.

306 How to decant

1. If the wine has sediment in the bottle, handle it carefully and/or let it sit upright for as long as possible (up to a day or two) before decanting it, to allow the sediment to settle. When you open the bottle, remove the entire foil from the neck.
2. Place a lit candle (or ask someone to hold a flashlight) on the counter such that you will be able to see its light through the shoulder of the bottle.
3. Slowly start pouring the wine into the decanter. The goal is to make it a single, slow, continuous pour.
4. The moment you see any sediment come to the shoulder of the bottle, stop pouring. You will need to sacrifice an ounce or two of wine to avoid the sediment.

Storing and Aging

Most everywhere in the world, people drink wine within hours of buying it, so, for them, the whole subject of storing, aging, and keeping track of their wine bears little significance. That is unless you fall deeply in love with a specific wine and want to be able to drink it for the foreseeable future, or if you develop a love for the beauty of older wines' elegant and mellow maturity. This section also covers ways of keeping track of your collection, both what you currently have and what you've tasted before.

307   Why age wine?

In prior centuries, farmers had trouble getting grapes to the level of ripeness today's consumers prefer. The wines were lean and tough, and the only way to make them drinkable was to let them sit in the cellar for a few years, where they would soften up. Today, most wine is consumed within twenty-four hours of purchase. Still, there are some wines—mostly renowned Old World wines—that deserve time to age. The goal of aging is that, over time, red wines tend to taste less tannic and acidic (although the actual amount of acidity in the wine stays the same), and the aromas of both red and white wines become more complex and better balanced. The color also changes— from its original purple or ruby to brick and then to leather for reds, and from almost colorless or straw colored to amber and then brown for whites.

308   Which wines are worth aging?

This is one of the most unpredictable questions in wine. Mediocre or bad wines generally get worse, so there's no point in aging them, and it's important to note that the vast majority of inexpensive wines, say under $20, need no aging whatsoever. The winemakers know they will be drunk almost as soon as they're purchased, so they make the wines for immediate consumption. Great wines can show gorgeous changes over time (see entry 307), but knowing which ones are great is tricky. If a wine has well-balanced fruit flavors, but it's too tannic (see entry 273), age will improve the tannins, making them softer and more palatable. Great vintages of Burgundy, Bordeaux, Rioja, Barolo, and Brunello only achieve their best performance after several years in the bottle. Some expensive New World wines, principally

from Napa and South Australia, aim to emulate this Old World age-worthiness. Certain white wines also age nicely, adding depth of character, including the best German and Alsace Rieslings, top white Burgundies, and many dessert wines. The best strategy for gauging the timing is, when you fall in love with a fairly high-quality wine, buy a case of it and drink one bottle each year. In this way, you'll have the opportunity to taste the wine evolving. When it starts to get "tired"—the fruit aromas are disappearing, nutty or earthy aromas develop, or the color changes to brick (for reds) or amber (for whites)—then it's time to finish up whatever is left. See also entry 309.

309 How long should I age it?

If you have wine that you want to age, store it in a dark place with a stable temperature of 55 to 60°F and more than 50 percent humidity, where the wine will not be agitated. The best way to get an estimate of a wine's aging ability is to ask the winemaker or a smart wine dealer. While they may not be exactly right, at least you'll have an idea. Sometimes this information can be found on the winery Web site. Barring that, you'll have to use your own judgment. In general, Old World wines can age longer than New World ones because of the difference in winemaking styles (see Introduction). No wine under $20 a bottle is really meant to be saved for a long period. Still, Old World whites will generally be good for three to five years and reds for five to ten years. New World whites should be consumed within a year or two of the vintage, and reds within three to five years. For more expensive or collectible bottles, age-ability depends on the particular wine, its vintage, and the conditions in which it is stored. The most reliable way to experience a wine at its peak is to buy a case and start drinking a bottle a year a few years before you estimate the wine will be at its peak.

310 What's the best way to store wine?

Just like most foods, wine keeps better at cooler temperatures and ages faster at warmer ones. The worst place to keep wine is in a hot kitchen or near the radiator. Whether in a root cellar, a specialized wine cave, or a wine refrigerator, wine is happier in a cool, humid environment. Gary Farrell, who is winemaker at Gary Farrell Wines in Sonoma, believes the single most important issue for preserving wine is consistent temperature. As long as the wine rests at a reasonable temperature (50 to 65°F), consistency is the key.

White and sparkling wines can be stored in the refrigerator. Red wines should be stored in the coolest (above 50°F) and darkest possible place, as long as the temperature is consistent. Racks are a matter of taste and willingness to spend. There's nothing wrong with using the cardboard cases the wines come in, just remember to store the wines on their side to keep the corks wet. For a stackable solution, plastic milk crates work fine. From there, there is a full continuum, and it's quite possible to spend more money on the racks than on the wines they hold—the sky is the limit. Companies like IWA and the Wine Enthusiast carry nice selections of racks in every price range. For serious collectors without a place for climate-controlled storage, most cities have refrigerated storage facilities just for wine where collectors can rent space.

311 How can I keep track of my wines?

Two problems arise when folks try to keep track of their wine. The main concern is trying to recollect: Have I had that before? Did I like it? How much did I pay for it? Is it worth buying again? (See entry 248.) The second problem is correctly remembering what you have at home, and the more wine you have, the more difficult it is. A three-ring notebook is a handy tool for both of these tasks. Keep the tasting notes in the front and the inventory in the back. Keep it either close to your wine or where you drink it. The beauty of this system is that you can carry the notebook to the store. Using a standardized tasting note format (see entry 283) allows the notes to stay in some kind of order, which is incredibly valuable in a store. Even if you don't want to buy the same wines, the information will help the salesperson guide you better.

To organize the actual bottles in your collection, try sorting by grape, country, or drink-by date, according to your personal preference. You also might consider writeable hang tags, which allow you to see what the wines are without moving the bottles. For larger wine collections (say, more than twenty cases), use the notebook solely for tasting notes and use a database program such as Filemaker or Access for inventory, which gives a sortable, searchable system that's also printable.

Of course the easiest way to handle all of this data is to use a smart phone app or a portable solution like a netbook or laptop.

Wine Travel and Learning

For anyone even remotely interested in the joys of wine, nothing beats visiting the world's winemaking regions. For each region, we have recommended wineries that provide an outstanding opportunity to taste and learn. Outside of Napa and Sonoma, you should set up an appointment. Wineries that are small and in great demand will require an appointment, as will most wineries outside of the USA.

No matter what region you're in, be sure to check the winery's Web site, under "Visiting," "Cellar Door," or "Tours," for hours, what is included in the tour, and any fees for the tour or tastings. Many wineries require reservations, and all appreciate a call.

UNITED STATES

316 How to do Napa

Napa's strengths and weaknesses are one and the same. All the wineries are on or just slightly off Highway 29. That makes everything easy to find, but it also makes the traffic hellacious. The road is so loaded with wineries that you can pull out of one and into the next without ever getting back on the road. Also, many Napa wineries charge high prices—up to $30—for tours and tastings. Its number of wineries is stunning. Ditto for the restaurants. It's possible to have one of the most sublime meals of your life, and spend a lot of money.

The wineries below are arranged from south to north. Even though the two most distant wineries are less than two hours apart, the easiest solution is to stay in St. Helena, which places you in the center of the action. You can cover these twelve wineries comfortably in three days, as long as none of the three are a Friday, Saturday, or Sunday. If you are there over a weekend, plan on hitting just three wineries per day.

RECOMMENDED WINERIES

Acacia (Carneros, www.acaciawinery.com)
Domaine Carneros (Carneros, www.domainecarneros.com)
Stag's Leap Winery (Napa, www.stagsleap.com)
Domaine Chandon (Yountville, with a fantastic restaurant, www.chandon.com)
Robert Mondavi (Oakville, www.robertmondaviwinery.com)
Flora Springs (St. Helena, www.florasprings.com)
Newton (St. Helena, www.newtonvineyard.com)
Beringer (St. Helena, www.beringer.com)
Duckhorn Winery (St. Helena, www.duckhorn.com)
Rombauer Vineyards (St. Helena, www.rombauervineyards.com)
Clos Pegase (Calistoga, www.clospegase.com)
Chateau Montelena (Calistoga, www.montelena.com)

317 Making sense of Sonoma

Sonoma is much more of a pleasant, laid-back experience than Napa—the restaurants, wineries, and lodgings all have a homier, more welcoming feel—but it is also more spread out and burdened with twisty roads and angry police. The wines don't yet have Napa's reputation, but that means they are still closer to fiscal earth. Plus, many people prefer their more generous flavors. Sonoma rewards the wine lover willing to ferret out the small glories. Remember to ask the tasting room folks about which small wineries are their personal favorites, the ones they visit on their days off. Here are two one- or two-day tours.

LINDA MURPHY

West Coast correspondent for *Decanter* magazine and West Coast editor at Jancisrobinson.com

Linda Murphy is a popular figure among wine journalists. She's jovial, knowledgeable, the winner of two James Beard Awards, and a wine populist in the best sense. She has tasted thousands of wines, but asked for a single favorite, she demurred and offered two: "I was able to taste Domaine de la Romanée-Conti wines from the 2005 vintage in a reverential setting. That was certainly a highlight, yet I got just as much pleasure drinking a modest Savigny-lès-Beaune red Burgundy from a plastic cup, served with microwaved lasagne and shared with a dear friend on a train from Beaune to Florence."

Her favorite house wines are simple but reliable. "It would have to be Sauvignon Blanc, a varietal I enjoy drinking in all seasons," she says. "Kim Crawford's from Marlborough, New Zealand, has been in my fridge frequently since 1999, and the Kenwood Sonoma County Sauvignon Blanc comes at a great price. If I get a second choice, it would be Pinot Noir, as it goes with so many dishes and is delicious to sip on its own. Pinot can be quite pricey, but Siduri offers several different Pinots from California and Oregon at affordable prices."

RECOMMENDED WINERIES

The Russian River Valley Area

J Vineyards & Winery (www.jwine.com)
Rochioli Vineyards (www.rochioliwinery.com)
Gary Farrell Winery (www.garyfarrellwines.com)
Williams Selyem (www.williamsselyem.com)
Iron Horse Vineyards (www.ironhorsevineyards.com)

Close into Sonoma

Chateau St. Jean (www.chateaustjean.com)
Cline Cellars (www.clinecellars.com)
Kenwood Vineyards (www.kenwoodvineyards.com)
Sebastiani Vineyards (www.sebastiani.com)
St. Francis Winery (www.stfranciswinery.com)

wine travel and learning

318 How to taste Paso Robles

This is cowboy country. The residents revel in the fact that Jesse and Frank James hid out in the town then called El Paso de Robles. That town is still a good place to hide out while tasting wine in the area. There is a lot of great wine being made in the region, especially by the Rhône Ranger contingent, a group of winemakers intent on bringing the grapes of France's Rhône Valley to the U.S. (see entry 118). Wineries are popping up in the Paso Robles area faster than anywhere in California, so this is also a great place to ask the tasting room staff about new places to go. One logistical note: don't try to make a day trip from L.A. to Paso—it's about a four-hour drive with no traffic. Instead, find a place to stay in or close to Paso Robles itself, and rent a car. Your trip will be much more leisurely and enjoyable.

RECOMMENDED WINERIES

Dark Star Cellars (www.darkstarcellars.com)
Eberle Winery (www.eberlewinery.com)
J. Lohr Vineyards (www.jlohr.com)
Justin Vineyards (www.justinwine.com)
Meridian Vineyards (www.meridianvineyards.com)
Peachy Canyon Winery (www.peachycanyon.com)
Tablas Creek Vineyard (www.tablascreek.com)
Wild Horse Vineyards (www.wildhorsewinery.com)

319 Finding bargains in Mendocino County

Mendocino County wines (from Mendocino or Anderson Valley) are bargains compared to those of its neighbors in Sonoma and Napa; in fact, Mendocino is very much like Sonoma was twenty years ago. Folks here are very close to the earth—the wine producers are mostly farmers, aiming at a better crop every year, and Mendocino County is the hotbed of organic farming in the U.S. wine business. Locals joke—a little—that cannabis is the big cash crop, although grapes are catching up. When the growers and winemakers get together, a wonderful camaraderie comes from an industry that knows it is doing good work, and just waiting for the world to catch up. Make the city of Mendocino your home base for wine travel because of its artsy atmosphere and pleasant coastal weather.

RECOMMENDED WINERIES

Bonterra Vineyards (www.bonterra.com)
Brutocao Cellars (www.brutocaocellars.com)
Handley Cellars (www.handleycellars.com)
Husch Vineyards (www.huschvineyards.com)
Londer Vineyards (www.londervineyards.com)
Navarro Vineyards (www.navarrowine.com)
Parducci Winery (www.parducci.com)
Roederer Estate (www.roedererestate.com)

320 Experiencing Willamette Valley Pinot Noir

Oregon is synonymous with Pinot Noir, ever since the movie *Sideways* catapulted the grape into the pricing stratosphere, and prices have gone up everywhere, including restaurants, hotels, and wineries. The prices of mediocre wines have gotten sucked up the price chain along with the great ones. The best advice in Oregon is to go to a few well-known wineries that have had some years of success and taste through their wines, then ask about which of the new wineries are making the best wines. Any of the places below would be a good starting point. A few are brutally expensive, but they have a history of giving quality for cost. Despite the rise in prices, there are still some spectacular restaurants with perfectly fair prices. Like the wineries, they are the ones that have been there for a while, through good times and bad, proving their value. A good choice for a stay in the Willamette Valley is at the Hotel Oregon in the town of McMinnville. As for dining, Tina's, Dundee Bistro, and Red Hills Provincial Dining are all dependably excellent, fairly priced, and in the town of Dundee just fifteen minutes from McMinnville.

RECOMMENDED WINERIES

Adelsheim Vineyard (www.adelsheim.com)
Argyle Winery (www.argylewinery.com)
Beaux Frères (www.beauxfreres.com)
Carlton Winemakers' Studio (www.winemakersstudio.com)
Chehalem (www.chehalemwines.com)
Domaine Drouhin (www.domainedrouhin.com)
Domaine Serene (www.domaineserene.com)
Penner-Ash Winery (www.pennerash.com)
Ponzi (www.ponziwines.com)
Soter Vineyards (www.sotervineyards.com)

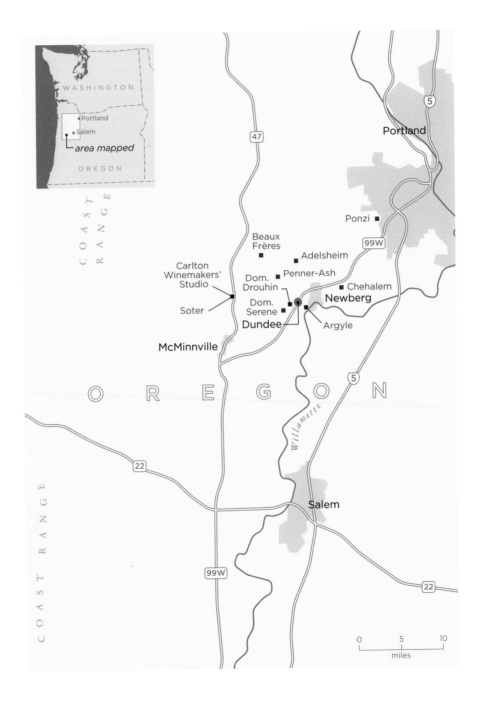

321 What's the best home base in Washington?

Washington is the most exciting wine state in the country (see entry 122), and, unbelievably, it's still not drawing many tourists. As word continues to get out, that will change. Try to get there before it becomes Napa 2. Most of the Washington wine country spreads over the eastern part of the state, and getting around can take a while. The best home base is Walla Walla, a town with several good restaurants and tolerable lodgings. If you fly into Seattle, stop at Betz and Chateau Ste. Michelle on your drive to Walla Walla. Once there, you are within ninety minutes of the rest. Three top-flight restaurants to check out in Walla Walla are 26 Brix, Whitehouse-Crawford, and Saffron, but once in, don't be afraid to ask about good new wineries and other worthwhile restaurants.

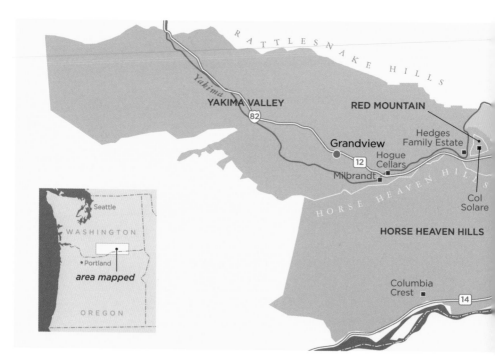

RECOMMENDED WINERIES

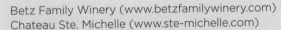

Betz Family Winery (www.betzfamilywinery.com)
Chateau Ste. Michelle (www.ste-michelle.com)
Abeja (www.abeja.net)
Col Solare (www.colsolare.com)
Columbia Crest (an amazing tour; www.columbia-crest.com)
Forgeron Cellars (www.forgeroncellars.com)
Hedges Family Estate (www.hedgescellars.com)
Hogue Cellars (www.hoguecellars.com)
K Vintners (www.kvintners.com)
L'Ecole No 41 (www.lecole.com)
Milbrandt Vineyards (www.milbrandtvineyards.com)
Pepper Bridge Winery (www.pepperbridge.com)
Three Rivers Winery (www.threeriverswinery.com)

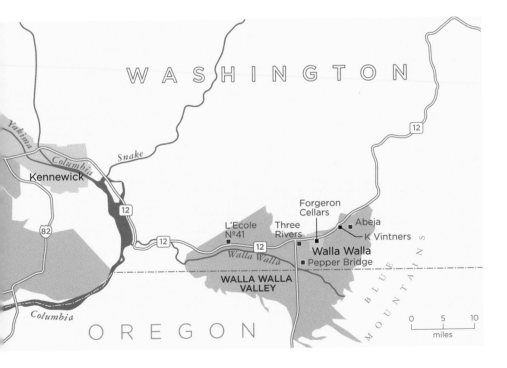

322 Where to go in Argentina

Most Argentinean wineries that make wine good enough to export are good-size operations with beautiful tasting rooms and plenty of English-speaking servers. Your home base should be Mendoza, in the northwest of the country, a lively and delightful town with lodging and food from budget to world-class. Some of the wineries are quite a drive from the main city of Mendoza and offer accommodations, and all will treat visitors with great appreciation. Experienced international drivers might want to consider the stunning drive over the Andes mountains, which drops you smack into Chile's wine country.

Anyone traveling as far as South America should communicate with the winery to coordinate visiting times and to let them know what you hope to gain from the visit, for instance, you would like to meet with the winemaker, or see the vineyards, or tour the winery. Some wineries charge for tastes, but not many, and the wines are some of the world's least discovered. See also entry 125.

ALPANA SINGH, MS

Master Sommelier, author of *Alpana Pours,* and director of
wine and spirits for Lettuce Entertain You Enterprises

Alpana Singh was the youngest woman to become a Master
Sommelier when she passed the notoriously difficult exam at age
twenty-seven. She has also been named Best Sommelier in America
by *Wine & Spirits* magazine. Clearly, she knows her wine, and she's
willing to share her opinions. "As far as white wines are concerned,
I drink a lot of Sauvignon Blanc," she told me. "It's racy, has a
crisp mouthfeel, and goes with salads or starters, or it works great
to sip while you are cooking. I usually buy from California, New
Zealand, and Sancerre. Whitehaven from New Zealand, Wild
Creek and Bernardus from California are all great, and I also love
François Cotat's Sancerre. I also love sparkling wine and one that
gets overlooked a lot: Lucien Albrecht's Cremant d'Alsace.

"For red wines, Malbec from Argentina is very friendly," she
said. "It is the best style for folks who like big red wines, but it's
still soft without too much tannin. Argentina over-delivers for all
their wines in the quality-versus-cost arena, and it always offers
easy-to-drink wines. I like everything from the Catena family,
Crios from Susanna Balbo, and the Terrazas wines are always solid
and easy to find."

wine travel and learning

323   Australia is huge: where should I focus?

Australians have long been keen visitors to their own wine regions, so the system is well established. Most wineries charge for tastings. The best single home base is the wonderful town of Adelaide, South Australia. Adelaide has every price level of lodging and restaurant imaginable and, with the possible exception of Tokyo's Tsukiji, the world's finest artisanal food market, which is right downtown. In terms of wine, the Barossa, McLaren Vale, and Adelaide Hills are all short drives. The wine scene on nearby Kangaroo Island is just budding, and the island is also the home of the buttery-sweet freshwater crayfish called Marron. The unfortunate fact about Australia's winemaking districts is that they are all in beautiful, fascinating places, full of natural splendor, great food, and friendly people, but they are also hundreds, sometimes thousands, of miles from one another. In any case, here are a dozen guaranteed crowd-pleasers from all over. See also entries 126 and 127, and map on page 133.

RECOMMENDED WINERIES

Ashton Hills Vineyard (Adelaide Hills, www.adhills.com.au)
Cape d'Estaing (Kangaroo Island, www.capedestaingwines .com.au)
D'Arenberg (also home to one of Australia's great restaurants, d'Arry's Verdan, www.darenberg.com.au)
Margan (Hunter Valley, www.margan.com.au)
Penfolds (Barossa, www.penfolds.com)
Petaluma (Adelaide Hills, www.petaluma.com.au)
Peter Lehmann (Barossa, www.peterlehmann.com.au)
R. L. Buller & Son (Rutherglen, www.buller.com.au)
The Willows Vineyard (Barossa, www.thewillowsvineyard.com.au)
Torbreck (Barossa, www.torbreck.com)
Tyrrell's Wines (Hunter Valley, www.tyrrells.com)
Yalumba (Barossa, www.yalumba.com)

JAMES HALLIDAY
Wine writer

James Halliday is the reigning expert on Australian wine, and his *Wine Atlas of Australia* is the definitive work on the subject. We asked him to help us sift through the thousands of wineries for the best available wines under $30. "Chardonnay is dominant here, accounting for fifty percent of all white grapes produced, and hence wines. Its best regions are Margaret River, Yarra Valley, Adelaide Hills, and Mornington Peninsula. A pleasing Chardonnay, such as De Bortoli Sacred Hill Chardonnay, costs as little as seven dollars and fifty cents, but the high-quality wines to look for are Hay Shed Hill, Sharmans, Brookland Valley, Long Gully Estate, Uplands, and West Cape Howe.

"Sémillon is the second-largest variety, and the most outstanding wines, unique on a world scale, are Hunter Valley Sémillons. With the advent of screwcap, these wines will age gracefully for twenty years or more, moving from crisp, minerally flavors with touches of citrus, herb, and grass to a glowing green-gold with touches of honey and lightly browned toast, giving the impression they have been aged in oak, whereas in fact they have been fermented in stainless steel, and bottled almost immediately after the end of vintage. There are many producers making wonderful wine for less than twenty-five dollars, led by Brokenwood, Keith Tulloch, McWilliam's, and Tyrrell's.

"Sauvignon Blanc's leading regions are Adelaide Hills and Margaret River with Shaw + Smith, Wirra Wirra, Geoff Weaver, Ashbrook Estate, Leeuwin Estate Art Series, Stella Bella, Watershed, and Were Estate among the best producers. Riesling is best in Clare Valley/Eden Valley, the Great Southern Region of Western Australia (with its five subregions), and there is a paradise of choice for wines under twenty-five dollars a bottle, including Bloodwood Estate, Duke's Vineyard Great Southern, Larry Cherubino 'The Yard Whispering Hill,' Leasingham Bin 7 Clare Valley, and Frogmore Creek."

For Mr. Halliday's red wines picks, check his Web site www.winecompanion.com.au.

324 Exploring Austria

For centuries, Austrian wine was consumed within Austria, but the world is catching on to these wines' unique flavors and perfumed aromas. All of the wine-making regions are within three hours' drive of Vienna. Anyone who is a fan of both wine and classical music could hardly do better than an Austrian wine trip. The downside is that agritourism is still in the adolescent stage, so it pays to communicate in advance of your trip. The benefit of this is that Austrian producers are still excited that people are coming from around the world to taste their wines, so you will likely be treated with *Gemütlichkeit*.

A wonderful itinerary would be to fly into Vienna, rent a car, then travel the Wachau (staying in Spitz) and drive seventy miles to the Weinviertel (overnighting in Laa an der Thaya). That would allow you to visit some of Austria's best Riesling and Grüner Veltliner wineries and also introduce you to some of the better red wines. See also entry 169.

RECOMMENDED WINERIES

Kracher (www.kracher.at)
Weingut Bründlmayer (www.bruendlmayer.com)
Weingut Ernst Triebaumer (www.triebaumer.com)
Weingut Huber (www.weingut-huber.at)
Weingut Rudolf Kaiser (www.weingut-kaiser.at)
Weingut Schloss Gobelsburg (www.gobelsburg.com)
Weingut Wohlmuth (www.wohlmuth.at)

325 Getting around Chile

As in Argentina, Chilean wineries that export to North America are sizeable, elegantly appointed, and have English-speaking staff in the tasting rooms. Chile is rapidly emerging as a world-class wine producer, so now is a great time to go. Also as in Argentina, the Chileans are so pleased to see international visitors that they treat everyone royally. The best place from which to decamp is Santiago, where you can rent a car and head out of the city's terrible traffic and into wine country. Of the wineries listed below, those in Maipo and Colchague are south of Santiago, and those in Casablanca and Aconcagua are north. See also entries 134 and 135.

RECOMMENDED WINERIES

Casa Lapostolle (Colchagua Valley, www.lapostolle.com)
Cousiño Macul (Maipo Valley, www.cousinomacul.cl)
Errazuriz (Aconcagua Valley, www.errazuriz.com)
Los Vascos (Colchagua Valley, www.vinalosvascos.com)
Montes (Colchagua Valley, www.monteswines.com)
Veramonte (Casablanca Valley, www.veramonte.com)

326 Understanding the French system

It is possible to approach winery visits in France in two ways. The casual way means driving around searching for the many signs offering tastings at tiny wineries. Expect a homey greeting, a comfortable place to sit, and very good wines. The more formal way is to visit larger wineries that have established tasting rooms. The wineries of Bordeaux, Champagne, and Alsace in particular are a bit more like the Napa-style wineries, with tours, tastings, and souvenirs, but many require appointments. It goes without saying that, no matter whether in a tiny town or a huge metropolis, glorious food is around every corner. As you drive, beware of the gendarmes, who have become the most vigilant police of the wine-producing countries in Europe. The wineries recommended here all have tasting facilities. For maps, see pages 142, 144, and 147.

CLIVE COATES, MW
Author, Master of Wine, and Chevalier de l'Ordre du Mérite Agricole
www.clive-coates.com

Clive Coates's book, *The Wines of Burgundy,* is a masterful explanation of the area. Unfortunately, the best Burgundies are beyond most people's means. I asked Mr. Coates how to start learning about Burgundy. "Actually, I think red Burgundies are very easy to pick," he said. "Pinot Noir is very forgiving in a poor vintage, certainly more so than something like Cabernet Sauvignon. The most important thing for folks who would like to learn about Burgundy is to find a friendly neighborhood wine merchant. Then, forget scores. Just tell them what you would like and ask for an excellent wine from a lesser vintage, which will cost less and be ready to drink sooner. But trust your wine merchant.

They will be so excited you ask their opinion because no one does that anymore. They all walk in asking for a '90.'"

Whether Burgundy or not, Coates has a steadfast rule: "Never be afraid to pull a cork. Always get two different bottles—perhaps two wines from the village of Rully or two different wines from one producer—and try them together. That is the best way to learn."

RECOMMENDED WINERIES

M. Chapoutier (northern Rhône, www.chapoutier.com)
Château de Beaucastel (southern Rhône, www.beaucastel.com)
Château de Chamirey (Burgundy, www.chamirey.com)
Château Mouton-Rothschild (Bordeaux, www.bpdr.com)
Domaine Bott-Geyl (Alsace, www.bott-geyl.com)
Domaine des Baumard (Loire, www.baumard.fr)
Domaine Canet-Valette (Languedoc, www.canetvalette.com)
Domaine Jean Chartron (Burgundy, www.bourgogne-chartron.com)
Domaine des Temps Perdus (Chablis, http://clotildedavenne.free.fr)
Domaine Tempier (Provence, www.domainetempier.com)
Dopff & Irion (Alsace, www.dopff-irion.com)
La Soufrandière (Burgundy, www.bretbrothers.com)
Maison Joseph Drouhin (Burgundy, www.drouhin.com)
Maison Louis Jadot (Burgundy, www.louisjadot.com)
Maison Trimbach (Alsace, www.maison-trimbach.com)
Veuve Clicquot (Champagne, www.veuve-clicquot.com)

327 How to see Germany's wineries

Driving or boating up the rivers, you will find many tiny wineries offering tastings, sometimes free and sometimes not. A trip on the Mosel River can't be beat for the quaintness of the villages, the historic power of the amazingly small castles, and the long stretches of tourist-free areas. Stop into a few small and charming tasting rooms along the way and you'll also get the sense that this once great wine-making country is struggling with its own identity. Producers are living the dry-or-sweet debate (see entry 149), and not very comfortably. Still, the very best in Germany rank with the very best in the world, and they know who one another are—so, once you've gotten into a winery that ranks high on your list, ask for referrals to smaller wineries in the area. All the wineries below are exceptional examples of Germany's best. See also entry 148.

RECOMMENDED WINERIES

Dr. Bürklin-Wolf (www.buerklin-wolf.de)
Dr. H. Thanisch (www.dr-thanisch.de)
Dr. Loosen (www.drloosen.com)
Egon Müller Scharzhof (www.scharzhof.de)
Georg Breuer (www.georg-breuer.com)
Joh. Jos. Prüm (aka J J Prüm, www.jjpruem.com)
S. A. Prüm (www.sapruem.com)
Weingut Dönnhoff (www.doennhoff.com)
Weingut Emrich-Schönleber (www.emrich-schoenleber.com)
Weingut Gunderloch (www.gunderloch.de)
Weingut Robert Weil (www.weingut-robert-weil.com)

328 Italy: Where to focus?

Unless the winery has a worldwide reputation and bottles sell for three or four figures each, most Italian tasting rooms are likely to be informal, friendly affairs. There will be fewer English speakers than in other European countries, but few places on earth reward the slow-moving traveler more than Italy. Go to a good wine area, have a cup of coffee, and ask the proprietor for directions to a good winery. Try it, and if you like it, ask them to forward you to another. Tasty, well-spiced food is everywhere, and most reputable restaurants will have perfectly quaffable wines in carafes. Don't expect any Disneyland-style wineries.

Four good areas (with hub cities) to tour would be Piedmont (Neive), Tuscany (Siena), Friuli (Dolegna del Collio), and Veneto (Garda). Only the largest wineries will be available to you unless you have a car, so plan on either renting one or hiring a driver. See also entries 153, 155, and 156. and map on page 160.

RECOMMENDED WINERIES

Altesino (Tuscany, www.altesino.it)
Badia a Coltibuono (Tuscany, www.coltibuono.com)
Banfi (which also has a luxurious hotel and Michelin-starred
    restaurant; Tuscany, www.banfi.com)
Bastianich (Friuli, www.bastianich.com)
Bruno Giacosa (Piedmont, www.brunogiacosa.it)
Ceretto (Piedmont, www.ceretto.com)
Dal Forah Romano (Veneto, no Web site. Contact importer at
    www.viaswine.com)
i Clivi (Friuli, www.clivi.it)
La Contea (Piedmont, www.la-contea.it)
L'Arco (Veneto, www.terraverus.com/arco.htm)
Marchesi Antinori (Tuscany, www.antinori.it)
Mario Schiopetto (Friuli, www schiopetto.it)
Masi (Veneto, www.masi.it)
Pieropan (Veneto, www.pieropan.it)
Poggio Antico (Tuscany, www.poggioantico.com)
Ruffino (Tuscany, www.ruffino.com)
Sassicaia (Tuscany, www.sassicaia.com)
Tenuta Il Poggione (Tuscany, www.tenutailpoggione.it)
Venica e Venica (Friuli, www.venica.it)

329 How to visit the Port producers of Portugal

Visiting the main Port houses of Portugal couldn't be easier, as almost all Port is shipped to the port city of Oporto for blending and aging, and that is where the big Port lodges are located. Most tasting rooms will have an English speaker or two. The big English houses offer on-site tours and tastings, but the best bet for tasting through a wide range of Port wines (dry and sweet) is at the Solar do Vinho do Porto at the Instituto dos Vinhos do Douro e do Porto, the state-operated tasting room. You will have to pay for the tastes, but no other place has the selection. Many of the big companies are moving into the dry table wine business out of necessity, since the world seems to have lost its taste for sweet wines. For the more adventurous traveler, many producers have tasting rooms along the Douro River and throughout northern Portugal. Most prefer an appointment. If driving, be aware that traffic does not move very quickly in rural Portugal, so allow plenty of time. All of the recommendations here have tasting rooms in Oporto. See also entries 160 and 161.

RECOMMENDED WINERIES

Croft (www.croftport.com)
Fonseca (www.fonseca.pt)
Graham's (www.grahams-port.com)
Offley (http://eng.sograpevinhos.eu/marcus)
Quinta do Noval (www.quintadonoval.com)
Sandeman (www.sandeman.com)
Taylor Fladgate (www.taylorfladgate.com)

wine travel and learning

330 How to explore Spain

Spain's wineries are well spread out and require a lot of travel. Just driving the triangle of Spain's main wine-growing regions—from Penedès to Jerez to Rías Baixas—would take about forty hours. It is best to pick an area and concentrate your energies there. Some of the most massive wineries anywhere in the world are in the south around Jerez. This is the home of sherry (see entry 165), until recently a most popular style of wine. The most popular regions currently are the Ribera del Duero and Rioja, with many tourist-friendly facilities and several very large, high-quality wineries and internationally renowned cuisine. The Catalunya area is home to the wine-making areas of Priorat and Penedès and the magic of Barcelona. It should also be high on anyone's list. See also entries 163, 164, and 166.

RECOMMENDED WINERIES

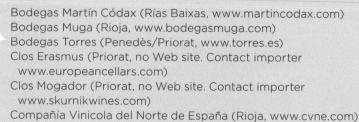

Bodegas Martín Códax (Rías Baixas, www.martincodax.com)
Bodegas Muga (Rioja, www.bodegasmuga.com)
Bodegas Torres (Penedès/Priorat, www.torres.es)
Clos Erasmus (Priorat, no Web site. Contact importer www.europeancellars.com)
Clos Mogador (Priorat, no Web site. Contact importer www.skurnikwines.com)
Compañía Vinicola del Norte de España (Rioja, www.cvne.com)
Cordorníu (Penedès, www.cordoniu.es)
Emilio Lustau (Jerez, www.emilio-lustau.com)
Freixenet (Penedès, www.freixenet.com)
Hacienda Monasterio (Ribera del Duero, www.haciendamonasterio.com)
Osborne (Jerez, www.orborne.es)
Vall Llach (Priorat, www.vallllach.com)

MICHAEL BONADIES

President/CEO of 21c Museum Hotels and noted wine author and speaker

Michael Bonadies is a big, soft-spoken man who has worn many hats over the years, all of which have allowed him to taste the best wines in the world. He often speaks to wine neophytes and is fearless about making recommendations. "In the search for consistently excellent wines, my first stop right now is always Spain," he stated assertively. "For whites there is tremendous quality and value to be found in crisply focused Albariños from such Rías Baixas producers as Fillaboa, Burgans, and Vionta as well as the richer Verdejos from producers in Rueda such as Aura and Villa Narcisa. For reds, I don't think there are two more exciting new regions than Bierzo and Toro in Spain. These are two regions whose reds couldn't be more different in style. The reds of Bierzo, made from the Mencia grapes, are lush and velvety, full of charm, elegance, and grace. My favorite producers are Tilenus, Dominio de Tares, and Castro Ventosa. Bigger and decidedly more fierce, Toro's reds are made from Tinto de Toro, a thicker-skinned clone of Tempranillo that has adapted to Toro's high, wind-swept plateau. Toros are great with anything grilled, and several of the top producers are Numanthia, San Roman, and Finca Sobreno."

331 What else should I read?

The Oxford Companion to Wine, edited by Jancis Robinson (Oxford University Press), is to wine as the *Oxford English Dictionary* is to the English language—the single definitive work on the subject. The contributors to this wine encyclopedia avoid the trendy and time-bound (no wine scores or recommendations) and cut straight to the heart of every wine-related subject imaginable. Way too much information for most, but just right for the obsessive.

Parker's Wine Buyer's Guide by Robert Parker (Simon & Schuster). Every few years, Parker releases a new compilation of short reviews from his magazine, the *Wine Advocate.* Some readers may be opposed to the widespread lazy shorthand of the numeric wine score, but we're now stuck with it. Agree with him or not, Parker's great strength is his consistency, so at least you can predict where you and he differ—which makes his reviews useful, even if you love quiet, elegant wines and he loves barn burners.

Perfect Pairings: A Master Sommelier's Practical Advice for Partnering Wine with Food, by Evan Goldstein (University of California Press), takes the subject of pairing food and wine to its essential elements, teaching us how to make the best possible choices based on ingredients and wines.

The Simple & Savvy Wine Guide: Buying, Pairing, and Sharing for All by Leslie Sbrocco (William Morrow). A lively, even sexy, book on wine by the most entertaining speaker on the fine wine circuit. Never miss an opportunity to see her in action.

Sip by Sip, by Michael Bonadies (Doubleday), is a good book for casual reading while sipping a great wine. Humorous, kind-natured, and knowledgeable.

The Wine Bible by Karen MacNeil (Workman). If the *Oxford Companion to Wine* is the definitive work for the wine student, then *The Wine Bible* is the reference for the wine drinker.

The World Atlas of Wine, by Hugh Johnson and Jancis Robinson, (Mitchell Beazley) belongs on the same (sturdy) shelf as the *Oxford Companion to Wine.* Unequaled.

332 What are the best regional wine guides?

Wine Spectator's California Wines by James Laube (Running Press)

Christie's World Encyclopedia of Champagne and Sparkling Wine by Tom Stevenson (Wine Appreciation Guild)

French Wines by Robert Joseph (DK)

The New Spain: A Complete Guide to Contemporary Spanish Wine by John Radford (Mitchell Beazley)

Vino Italiano by Joseph Bastianich and David Lynch (Potter)

Washington Wines & Wineries by Paul Gregutt (University of California Press)

Wine Atlas of Australia by James Halliday (University of California Press)

The Wines of Burgundy by Clive Coates, MW (University of California Press)

333 What are MS, MW, and CWE?

MS means Master Sommelier, an award conferred by the Court of Master Sommeliers. The program trains very high-end restaurant server/managers, people who know how to stock a profitable wine collection for a high-end restaurant as well as how to properly decant and pour a bottle of wine, all very practical information. MW means Master of Wine, an award from the Institute of Masters of Wine. Most people who study under this program are in the production and distribution sectors of the wine industry or are published wine critics. The goal of both programs is to push the entire industry to a higher degree of perfection. Both MS and MW tests cost more to study for and are more difficult to pass than many graduate school programs. CWE stands for Certified Wine Educator, and is a wine-teaching certificate administered by the Society of Wine Educators.

334 Which are the best Web sites for wine?

www.decanter.com covers the world of wine with some of the most expert writers in the English language. The site is Eurocentric in terms of commerce, but chock-full of global information.

www.erobertparker.com has some free information, but the good stuff costs money. Parker's staff have done an excellent job of improving this site to a very high standard.

www.italianmade.com is the Web portal for the Italian Trade Commission. As such, don't expect favoritism, rankings, or scores, but for a primer on the regional wines and foods of Italy, there's none better.

www.jancisrobinson.com is a free Web site with plenty of helpful information. Join her premium membership to get an online, searchable version (and what a huge help it is) of her two books mentioned above, the *Oxford Companion to Wine* and the *World Atlas of Wine*.

www.wine-searcher.com checks the inventory of 10,000 wine shops to help you find that special bottle you've been hunting for, and then tells you where you can find the best price. Works best for Internet buyers, not so well for in vivo purchasing.

www.wineaccess.com Stephen Tanzer runs the *International Wine Cellar*, a widely read tipsheet that covers a remarkable number of wines in direct language that works for all education levels. His scores are widely respected for being dependable.

www.wineanswers.com has a novel food/wine pairing system that might help jump-start your creativity.

www.winemag.com is the Web site for the *Wine Enthusiast* and, unlike the *Wine Spectator* or *Wine Advocate* sites, this one is free.

www.winepage.de is opinionated and tough (love it!) and a great way to learn about German wines.

www.winepros.org Don't let the amateurish site design put you off, because there is a lot of good information here, as well as links to other good sites.

www.wines.com, a retail site, offers the occasional jaw-dropping bargain.

www.winespectator.com, along with the *Wine Advocate,* is the home of the grammar-school wine grading system. Both also charge to get into their better information. Still, it offers an enormous amount of useful information and unmatched access to wine's holiest places.

See also entry 3.

wine travel and learning

Glossary

Albariño (al-buh-REE-nyo): A grape that resembles a lighter version of Rhône Viognier, all peaches and apricots; in the hands of a talented winemaker, it has perfect acidity.

Alvarinho (al-var-EEN-ho): The Portuguese name for Albariño.

atmosphere: The bubbliness of sparkling wine, based on the pressure of the carbon dioxide in the bottle; one atmosphere measures approximately 14.7 pounds per square inch.

AVA: American Viticultural Area, a specific geographical designation of grape growing areas established by the Alcohol and Tobacco Tax and Trade Bureau.

Cabernet Franc (kab-er-NAY FRANK): Tends to be earlier ripening, lighter in tannin, and somewhat more aromatic than Cabernet Sauvignon (itself a genetic offspring of Cabernet Franc and Sauvignon Blanc) and is often blended with other red grapes.

Carignan (care-in-YAN): A high-yielding grape that can often be overly tannic and acidic. It is widely used in less expensive wines from France and Spain. When blended, it can provide structure.

Carmenère (car-men-YARE): A tart red grape originally from Bordeaux, but now principally from Chile.

Chardonnay (shar-duh-NAY): The world's most popular white wine, it comes in a range of flavors from dry and tart to oaky and buttery, depending on where it's grown and the clientele to which producers are trying to appeal.

Chenin Blanc (SHEH-nin blawnk): A white grape that in cool areas—such as the Loire's Anjou, Vouvray, Savennières, and Saumur regions (the regions you'll see on the label)—has a refreshingly high acidity; wines may have apple, mineral, honey, and forest undergrowth aromas. In warmer areas, the grape tends to grow in huge quantities, increasing the potential for mediocre wines.

Cinsault (sin-SO): A delicate red grape that the southern French have found to be ideal for rosé.

Cru Beaujolais (CRU bo-sha-LAY): The ten delineated areas that are home to the finest wines in Beaujolais.

Dolcetto (dole-CHET-oh): A red wine grape grown all over the world, though its best representation is in Italy and is a great food wine with fairly high acidity and soft tannins, meant to be drunk young.

flight: A small (generally two- or three-ounce) sampling of multiple wines for side-by-side comparision. Flights are commonly organized by color, grape, region, or vintage.

fortified wine: Wine that has had neutral spirits added to it either during or after fermentation. The most common examples include Port, Madeira, Sherry, and Marsala, although there are hundreds of fortified wines made worldwide.

frizzante: Italian-derived term for a wine with very light bubbles.

Gamay (GAM-ae): The red grape of Beaujolais, also grown in other areas of France, Switzerland, and the U.S.

Gewürztraminer (geh-VURZ-trah-mee-ner): An incredibly fragrant white wine grape—as in rose petals and lychees—grown throughout the world, though the best versions generally come from Alsace and the northeastern part of Italy.

grape spirits: Grape wine that has been distilled until it is nearly pure alcohol, then watered down and used to fortify wines.

Grenache (gre-NOSH): Once the most planted red wine grape on earth, Grenache has now lost the marketing war to Cabernet Sauvignon and Merlot. In its four best locations (the Rhône, Priorat, South Australia, and Paso Robles), the grape is rich, fruity, and spicy. Because it often lacks palate-cleansing acidity and tannin, it is generally blended with other grapes capable of lending some structure, such as Syrah, Carignan, and Mourvèdre.

Grüner Veltliner (GROO-ner VELT-lee-ner): Principally grown in Austria, where it makes a peppery, fragrant white wine. The best versions deserve comparison with the world's greatest white wines.

Malbec (MAL-bek): A rich, full-bodied red wine made from grapes originally from Bordeaux, but now grown principally in Argentina.

Malvasia (mal-VAH-zee-uh): A white wine grape, most famously from Italy, with a beguiling floral aroma that is unforgettable.

Marsanne (MAR-san): This unctuous white wine grape is often blended with the more acidic Roussanne to give the final blend a nice combination of richness and structure.

Merlot (mer-LOW): Until the movie *Sideways* cast Merlot as a villain, it was one of the world's most popular grapes. The good news, for those who love the grape's velvety mouthfeel and dark fruit flavors, is that many Merlots are now bargains for the quality.

Mourvèdre (moor-VED-ruh): As a red wine, Mourvèdre can be tannic and high in alcohol, so Grenache and Cinsault are often blended in to soften it. It grows happily in France, Spain, Australia, and the U.S.

Müller-Thurgau (MULE-er TUR-gow): A varietal cross of Riesling and Madeleine Royale grapes, its major virtue is astronomical yields. Although it produces a few good wines, this grape more commonly shows up in brand-name wines such as Blue Nun or Liebfraumilch. It doesn't age well, and the acidity level seldom measures up to its sweetness.

Muscat (MUSS-cat): A wonderfully aromatic grape (smelling of paper whites and honey) used for white wines all over the world. Europeans have vinified the grape since Greek times. While the New World has had a later start, the Australians especially have created spectacular dessert wines. In Italian, known as Moscato.

Nebbiolo (neb-ee-OH-low): This grape is subject to early flowering before the last frost. In its youth, its tannins are tough but its aromas—roses, forest floor, smoke—are beguiling. As it ages (and it can age for decades), the tannins soften and the wine becomes more approachable.

négociant: A company that produces wines from grapes bought from various growers in an area.

neutral spirits: See "grape spirits."

New World wines: Wines from anywhere other than Europe.

Old World wines: Wines that come from Europe.

oxidized: Wines that are oxidized have been exposed to too much oxygen and will taste cooked and/or tired. The exceptions are the few wines that use oxidation purposely, such as sherry.

Pedro Ximénez (PAY-dro him-EN-ez): This white wine grape has the ability to generate a huge quantity of sugar. Its wines are used to sweeten cream sherries and to make dessert wines that are a small step removed from honey; aka "PX."

Pinot Gris / Pinot Grigio (PEE-noe GREE / PEE-noe GREE-jhee-oh): The two versions of this grape are capable of yielding fascinating white wine, ranging from the dense and heady ones of Alsace to the elegant and restrained wines of Colio. Watch Oregon, where vintners seem capable of making wines that carry the best of both worlds.

Pinot Noir (PEE-noe NWAR): One of the world's great grapes for reds, its best wines are indisputably from Burgundy, where the Pinots can possess an almost magical combination of delicacy and profundity, of cherries and perfume, strawberries and leather, and many more. Though without the complexity of those in the Old World, the dry reds produced in the U.S. and New Zealand (pay attention to the Central Otago area) are winning on fruitiness. Plan on seeing better and better wines from both areas.

Prädikatswein: The highest classification of German wines for recent vintages (since 2007).

puttonyo: A term, derived from the traditional Hungarian container employed to harvest the overripe grapes that make Aszú wines, the most famous of the renowned Tokaji wines. The number of puttonyos is code for the sweetness level and density of Tokaji Aszú wines. The range is from 3 to 6, and the higher the puttonyo level, the sweeter the wine. The greatest of the Tokaji wines—called Aszú-Eszencia—is even sweeter than Aszú.

Qualitätswein mit Prädikat: A term classifying the highest quality German wines; replaced by Prädikatswein in 2007.

Récoltant-manipulant (RM): In Champagne, this is a grape grower who makes and markets wine made from its own grapes. In the U.S., the wines are often called Grower Champagnes. The initials RM should be on the label only if the wine is a Récoltant-manipulant wine.

Riesling (REE-sling): The cool weather of Germany, Austria, and Alsace encourages the grape to retain its signature acidity. In hotter climes, the wine turns flabby and uninteresting. In the hands of a good winemaker, Riesling can make great wine at every sweetness level from bone-dry to dessert-in-a-bottle.

Ripasso: A process by which winemakers use the skins and lees left over after racking Amarone to give some additional character to the Valpolicella wines. The first and still one of the best was Masi's Campofiorin.

Roussanne (ROO-san): An acidic white grape often blended with the more unctuous Marsanne to give the final blend a nice combination of richness and structure.

Sangiovese (san-gee-oh-VAY-see): The most common grape in Toscana (Tuscany in English). All of the region's world-famous wines—Chianti, Brunello di Montalcino, and Vino Nobile di Montepulciano—are made from Sangiovese. Italians also grow the grape over most of the country.

Sauvignon Blanc (SAW-vin-yon blawnk): This grape grows well throughout the world. In the Old World, it does best in France and Italy, yielding well balanced, light, and elegant wines. The Old World's polar opposite in style is New Zealand, where the wine has a shocking amount of grapefruity acidity. In the Americas—particularly the Central Coast of California and the Casablanca Valley of Chile—the wine tends to have more tropical fruit aromas, a denser texture, and less acidity. Good examples also come from Australia and South Africa.

Sémillon (sem-e-YONE): Widely used as a blending grape with Sauvignon Blanc, this white wine grape is also the basis for Sauternes, the great dessert wines of Bordeaux. It's typically a low-acid grape that likes either cooler climates or to be combined with an acidic Sauvignon Blanc.

Spumante: The Italian term for wine with 3.5–6 atmospheres of pressure in the bottle from carbon dioxide, which is a similar level to that of Champagne or Cava.

Syrah / Shiraz (sih-RAH / shi-RAZZ): Same grape, two styles. The French Rhône style (called Syrah) is firm, with massive tannic grip, huge concentration, and aromas of blackberries, violets, and black pepper. The Australian version (called Shiraz) is a big mouthful of decadently fruity wine, all plums, berries, and caramel. Think of it as the Rhône's Debussy versus Australia's AC/DC.

tannin: A group of astringent and sometimes aggressively distasteful substances, also called polyphenols, that show up in red wine. They are a byproduct of the seeds, stems, and skins of the grapes used to make the wine, and sometimes the barrels used to age it.

taste-memory: Remembrances of aromas and flavors.

Tempranillo (tem-pra-NEE-yo): The primary grape of Spain's famed Rioja wine region. Tempranillo by itself can be light-colored, tannic, and acidic, so winemakers often blend in the robust Garnacha Tinta to give it more body.

terroir: A French term connoting the sum of all that is natural that affects a piece of land, including soil, climate, diurnal temperature shifts, and length of growing season.

Torrontés (tore-ohn-TACE): A grape widely grown in Argentina that yields wine with a floral fragrance, velvety mouthfeel, and delicious acidity.

Tokaji (TOKE-eye-ee): The name of wines produced in the Tokaj-Hegyalja region of Hungary.

umami: A taste akin to a savory broth. Some people regard it as a so-called fifth taste.

varietal: A grape variety like Merlot or Cabernet Sauvignon.

Viognier (vee-ohn-YAY): A peach- and apricot-scented grape originally from Condrieu in the northern part of France's Rhône Valley. There it makes an intense, steely wine with powerful aromas and startling acidity. In most of the United States, Viognier is grown in hot areas where farmers have to carefully manage the sugar in the grapes to prevent flabby and overly alcoholic wines. Besides California, both Texas and Virginia are producing top-notch Viognier.

Zinfandel (ZIN-fan-dell): America's grape. Often used to make sweet pink wine, its highest calling comes as a bone-dry big "burger and pizza" wine, full of peppery aromas and huge plum and dark berry flavors.

Acknowledgments

You wouldn't be holding this book in your hands were it not for the following people:

Emily—my sweet loving wife, center of my life for over thirty years—has read, analyzed, and offered opinions about the book. When I needed logistical help contacting wineries, she jumped in. And when I needed encouragement and help, she was always there. God bless her.

The team at Artisan, led by my publisher, Ann Bramson. They all demand the absolute best an author can offer, yet never leave you feeling alone. It was a team effort all the way, one for which I feel blessed.

Leslie Sbrocco, a wonderful wine author and Emmy-winning TV personality, who helped start me along the road to this project, and to the two greatest agents on earth, Lindsay Edgecombe and Danielle Svetcov.

To the people who got me started in wine writing, Emmet and Lisa Fox, and Virginia Wood, the food editor at the *Austin Chronicle* and a person I've learned so much from, both as a writer and reporter. Also, various editors who have given me the chance to reach a national audience, most especially Cathy Barber of the *Dallas Morning News*, Linda Murphy of the *San Francisco Chronicle*, and Lewis Fisher of Maverick Publishing. Also thanks to the various magazines I write for: *Wine & Spirits*, *Wines & Vines*, *Wine Enthusiast*, and others.

My mother and father, neither of whom drank wine. They didn't like it. They did like me, however, and filled me with the confidence to try anything.

Finally, thanks to all my family. It always helps to know you've got people who love you.

Index

Photo Credits

Photographs by John Anderson except for the following:

What's a doer to do?

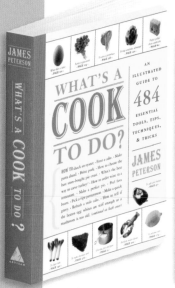
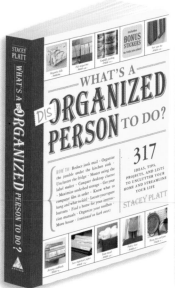